The Urgency of Indigenous Values

Haudenosaunee and Indigenous Worlds
Philip P. Arnold and Scott Manning Stevens, *Series Editors*

Syracuse University Press is pleased to announce the launch of a new series, Haudenosaunee and Indigenous Worlds, with the publication of *The Urgency of Indigenous Values*. The series expands the Press's historical emphasis on the "Iroquois" and Native American publications to better reflect current and diverse scholarship regarding oral tradition and de-colonial and Indigenous studies writ large, with a special emphasis on the Haudenosaunee.

The Urgency of Indigenous Values

Philip P. Arnold

Syracuse University Press

The generous assistance of the following is gratefully acknowledged:
The Department of Religion at Syracuse University

Copyright © 2023 by Syracuse University Press
Syracuse, New York 13244-5290

All Rights Reserved

First Edition 2023

23 24 25 26 27 28   6 5 4 3 2 1

For a listing of books published and distributed by Syracuse University Press, visit https://press.syr.edu.

ISBN: 978-0-8156-3815-5 (hardcover)
      978-0-8156-3808-7 (paperback)
      978-0-8156-5690-6 (e-book)

Library of Congress Cataloging-in-Publication Data

Names: Arnold, Philip P., 1957- author.
Title: The urgency of indigenous values / Philip P. Arnold.
Description: First edition. | Syracuse : Syracuse University Press, [2023] | Series: Haudenosaunee and indigenous worlds | Includes bibliographical references and index.
Identifiers: LCCN 2023006405 (print) | LCCN 2023006406 (ebook) | ISBN 9780815638155 (hardcover) | ISBN 9780815638087 (paperback) | ISBN 9780815656906 (ebook)
Subjects: LCSH: Indian philosophy. | Values. | Spirituality. | Iroquois Indians—Religion. | Indigenous peoples—Religion.
Classification: LCC E98.P5 A76 2023 (print) | LCC E98.P5 (ebook) | DDC 299.7—dc23/eng/20230425
LC record available at https://lccn.loc.gov/2023006405
LC ebook record available at https://lccn.loc.gov/2023006406

Dedicated to the life and work of three leading lights, CHARLES H. LONG, OREN LYONS, *and* JOHN MOHAWK: *men from different traditions who continually reveal new possible futures*

Contents

List of Illustrations *ix*

Acknowledgments *xi*

Introduction *1*

1. Collaborations in the Heartland of the Haudenosaunee
   Determining an Interpretive Location *12*
2. Indigenous Values *51*
3. Paying Attention *83*
4. Habitation *118*
5. Exchange *150*
6. Discovery and Indigeneity *182*

   Epilogue
   Value Change for Survival *221*

Bibliography *247*

Index *257*

Illustrations

1. Map of Haudenosaunee influence   16
2. Two Row Wampum belt   22
3. "The Eagle's View," IVI logo   46
4. Haudenosaunee Wooden Stick Festival logo   48
5. Mother Earth's Pandemic conference   49
6. Remembrance Wampum belt   237
7. *Gayaneñhsä·ʔgo·nah, The Great Law of Peace*, by Brandon Lazore   241
8. Poster for the conference "Religious Origins of White Supremacy" at Syracuse University   242

Acknowledgments

My deepest gratitude goes to the People of the Onondaga Nation: Clan Faithkeeper Oren Lyons (Turtle); Clanmother Audrey Shenandoah (Eel); Tadodaho Sid Hill and Betty (Gaeñ hia uh) Lyons (Snipe), president of the American Indian Law Alliance; Jake (Haiwhagai'i) Edwards (Eel) and Elsye Crouse (Hawk); Clanmother Virginia Abrams (Eel) and Clanmother Dorothy Webster (Eel); Clanmother Wendy Gonyea (Beaver); Clan Chief Irving Powless Jr. (Beaver); Sheri Waterman Hopper; Heath Hill; Denise Waterman; and Stephanie Waterman. Our gratitude extends to Mohawk Clan Chief Jake Swamp (Wolf), Seneca scholar John Mohawk (Turtle), Mohawk Knowledge Sharer Tom Porter (Bear), Oneida Clan Chief Robert Brown (Bear—our boys' Royane), Tuscarora scholar Rick Hill (Beaver), Mohawk Joyce (Tekahnawiiaks) King (Turtle), and Shawnee/Lenape Steve Newcomb, who have all been teachers and colleagues. I thank the extended Redhawks lacrosse community, especially Brian (Lab) Phillips (the beloved coach of our twin sons, Kroy and Clay, who guided them to adulthood playing this game); Ed Cathers; the Millers; the Bucktooths; the Lyons; and the Thompsons. Alf Jacques visited my class for decades, teaching me and my students about the spiritual dimensions of the "Creator's Game," and was the featured guest at our yearly Wooden Stick Festivals, held at Onondaga Lake. I am grateful for the artistry of Robert D'Alimonte (Beaver) and Murisa Printup (Turtle) at Tuscarora Woodworks, and Angela Ferguson, leader in the Onondaga Nation Farm Crew. Special gratitude goes to Yvonne Henhawk for displaying the severity with which Onondaga women guard their traditional knowledge, and for her later years cheering on our sons as Redhawk players. Layers of thank-yous to Jeanne Shenandoah for suggesting that our three-year-old sons try out for the Onondaga Redhawks, which profoundly impacted their lives and ours. Without lacrosse, our family would never have had the proper grounding to do this work.

Our Skä·noñh Center family is led by Sarah Shute and Tina Thomas and includes our Academic Collaborative: Robin Kimmerer, Shawn Wiemann, Betty Lyons, Sascha Scott, Scott Stevens, Sally Roesch Wagner, Darryl Caterine, Nell Champoux, Bea González, Deborah Holler, Joe Heath, Sandra Bigtree, Jeffrey Lambe, Valerie Luzadis, Rex Lyons, David McCallum, Bradley Powless, Holly Rine, Simone Thornton, Freida Jacques, Jack Manno, Emily Stokes-Rees, Wendy Gonyea, Rick Hill, and the support of Syracuse University Chancellor Kent Syverud and Dean Brian Konkol. So many continually bring the Skä·noñh Center to life.

Prior to our involvement with the Skä·noñh Center, my wife, Sandra Bigtree, and I were involved in founding Neighbors of the Onondaga Nation (NOON). We especially enjoyed working with Andy Mager in those early years, helping to organize the year-long Speaker Series in 2006 and 2010, at the Syracuse Stage. NOON has since become a stalwart of political and educational action in our region.

The History of Religions sangha was a loosely assembled group of academics that occasionally met with Charles H. Long and included a long list of people including myself, Davíd Carrasco, Jennifer Reid, Michio Araki, David Chidester, Graham Harvey, Inez' Talamantez, Rachel Harding, Charlie Winquist, Randal Cummings, Tracy Hucks, Yvonne Chireau, Vincent Wimbush, Robert Baum, and so many others who were involved with the American Academy of Religion (AAR) Arts of Interpretation group. Special acknowledgment to Lindsay Jones, whom we lost too soon. The Syracuse University Department of Religion has continually supported my work over three decades, for which I'm profoundly grateful.

Our work on the Doctrine of Christian Discovery (DoCD), with the American Indian Law Alliance (AILA) and Indigenous Values

Initiative (IVI), has been a formative force in the development of this book. Thanks to Tonya Gonnella Frichner and Betty Lyons, former and current directors of AILA, for their deep dedication to the UN Permanent Forum on Indigenous Issues, and for involving me and Sandy in this work. Betty Lyons's dedication to the Haudenosaunee is unsurpassed. Ever an inspiration and a delightful driving force, she takes on the work of a dozen people. Special thanks to Steve Newcomb, the intellectual innovator behind the DoCD movement; and to Tupac (Huehuecoyotl) Enrique Acosta and Eve Reyes-Aguirre of Tonatierra for their tireless work. We have been working with a number of great people on the DoCD including Sebastian Modrow and Gwendolen Cates. Through our not-for-profit IVI, we have worked with many dedicated volunteers including Gail Bundy, our founding board member, who worked tirelessly to help get us off the ground; Jake Edwards and Elsye Crouse, who offered us such valuable insight; Adam D. J. Brett, the sweetest techie genius and doyen of Religious Studies, who not only keeps us on course but also makes us all laugh; and many, many others.

Thanks to the hundreds of students at Syracuse University who have read and commented on parts of this book over the years. Thanks also to current and former graduate students Michael Chaness, Eglutė Trinkauskaite, Rob Ruehl, Ken Lokensgard, Alex Gonzalez, Christa Shusko, Abel Gómez, Mary Keller, Dillon Sampson, Sarah Nahar, Lisa Poirier, William Green, Dana Lloyd, and Adam D. J. Brett. Thanks to my editor, Colin Ainsworth.

In addition to those to whom I have dedicated this book, special thanks must go to three men who have been my mentors, colleagues, and friends over four decades: David Carrasco, who is my constant intellectual guide in the history of religions; John Mohawk, who was a giant of Haudenosaunee insight and scholarship; and Tom Porter, who is a leading light for the Haudenosaunee and the world. Thirty years ago, Mae and Mitchell Bigtree opened their home and hearts to our family, and we cherish Mae's beautiful baskets made of black ash and woven sweetgrass that our children helped her pick and clean each summer. With packed lunches of baloney sandwiches, it was uncanny the way in which Mitchell would drive and locate new fields of sweetgrass. It was our first introduction to the fact that that picking sweetgrass involved a spirit of gratitude.

Finally, all aspects of this work, now in its fourth decade, could not exist without my remarkable life partner, Sandra Bigtree. She is my closest friend and constant collaborator. Sandy has read multiple drafts of this book over the last twenty years. We are both incredibly proud of our sons, Clay and Kroy, who are remarkable young men and our constant inspiration.

The Urgency of Indigenous Values

Introduction

> Allow me to pose a question: When did the Earth's peril begin?
> And another: How can we escape this peril?

Since 1492, Indigenous Peoples have been trying to warn settler-colonial people that their values are leading to their self-destruction. Today, it seems that that caution is an inevitable fact. If we do not heed our Indigenous neighbors' urgent warning, the future existence of humanity will remain in peril.

For millennia, Indigenous Peoples have been oriented to living in proper relationship with the natural world. What emanates from this special relationship is a deep ecological knowledge that has produced bountiful varieties of food, regenerative ways of growing food and medicinal plants that have collectively transformed the world. It also fostered a way of living in peace, which grew stronger through the ages, until it was abruptly disrupted at first European contact. Today, we are in the midst of a crisis of values, and how we respond to this crisis will determine the prospects for not only our future but also the future of those who are yet to come.

It is to the hope of survival that this book is dedicated. I understand that the crisis we face involves opposing social, economic, cultural, and political realities. Values, I have learned, are the nexus of bridging those realities. Integrating Indigenous values into the way we relate to the Earth and to each other may help start the regenerative process toward a shared future.

There are thousands of Indigenous cultures all over the world, all of which have value systems appropriate to their locations. This book focuses primarily on the values of the Haudenosaunee, People of the Longhouse (Iroquois), with whom I have been working for over thirty years. This work recently culminated in the creation of the Skä·noñh—Great Law of Peace Center at Onondaga Lake in 2015, a place that is sacred because it is where the Great Law of Peace was founded over one thousand years ago, establishing the Haudenosaunee Confederacy. Through working with the Haudenosaunee, I have learned that when humans are in proper relationship with the natural world, they come to understand wellness, diversity, peace, and freedom through their engagement with the regenerative Earth.[1]

Categories Matter

These ideas can be hard to conceptualize. For me, the breakthrough came when I abandoned "religion" as a descriptive category related to Indigenous Peoples. As someone trained in the History of Religions, to abandon this category has been difficult, but it has also made it much easier to write this book.[2] Additionally, it has enabled me to critically engage religion and its history.

The original inhabitants have been called a variety of names: Native American, Indians, First Nations, Aborigine, Archaic, Indios, savages, heathens, and primitives, among numerous other categories and terms, and we will touch on the consequences of using some of them at different times throughout history. In the last few decades, however, the preferred category has become "Indigenous."[3] This word

---

1. See Tom Porter's remarkable book *And Grandma Said . . .* for an intimate portrait of the Great Law of Peace and how it works inside his family. In many presentations over the years, Tom has indicated that the Great Law of Peace is tens of thousands of years old.

2. Throughout this book I capitalize "History of Religions" to indicate the University of Chicago school.

3. The term "Indian," however inaccurate or offensive, is a fiduciary term that goes back to the original treaties that hold foreign governments—namely, the United States—responsible for upholding international agreements between Indian nations and colonial nations on Turtle Island.

is now the accepted global terminology for local peoples who have undergone the excesses of colonization and economic exploitation.

Indigenous Peoples have repeatedly told me that they have no concept or word for "religion." I've tried to write a book about Indigenous religions for over a decade, but it just didn't work. In spite of the fact that I am a historian of religions, "Indigenous religions" is simply not a viable category, for bringing these two words together actually forms an oxymoron: religion was used to systematically obliterate Indigenous cultures by attempting to destroy their special relationships with the natural world. If we are to survive together *on* this Earth, our notion of "religion" will have to undergo radical changes from that of being transcendent and exclusively superior to becoming more inclusive and realigning with Indigenous Peoples and their ancient values of living in proper relationships. These tensions, instead of leading to confusion, can bring us to an entirely new understanding of ourselves and possibly redefine religion.

Indigenous traditions value the Earth: they focus on aspects of life that engage with the ecosystems of their local environments. Shifting values from profit motives to regenerative engagement with the Earth requires a shift in the mythic and historical paradigms that haunt our colonial past.

"Values" is a category with layered meanings. It can indicate the ethical and moral structure of an individual or society, but it can also be used conversely, to structure the way in which one group takes control over another by reconstituting the natural reciprocal world into a commodified value system used to accumulate wealth. Both meanings are combined in the sociological category of "habitus," or the way a person or society perceives, reacts to, or interacts with the world.[4] In fact, there will be no improvement in human relationships with the natural world until our *values* change. Indigenous traditions are controversial because of the enormous gap between Indigenous and settler-colonial people's ideas of what constitutes the sacred.

---

4. Bourdieu, *Outline of a Theory of Practice*.

Why the White Guy?

It was the summer of 1983 in Boulder, Colorado. I had decided to pursue a PhD in the History of Religions because of the exciting collaborative work that Professor Davíd Carrasco was creating through his Mesoamerican archive. It was here that I was introduced to the work of Professor Charles H. Long, who helped to found the History of Religions at the University of Chicago. He was one of the most electrifying intellectuals in African and African American religions. Although I was excited by the prospect of such a career path, I was also deeply intimidated.

Professor Long was visiting for a Mesoamerican religions conference that I had helped organize as a newly appointed undergraduate assistant to Professor Carrasco's Mesoamerican Archive and Research Project. My fiancé, Sandy Bigtree, and I decided to invite Long and his wife, Alice, to a Sunday brunch at the beautiful Chautauqua Park to discuss my concerns and trepidation around going forward in this field. I chose this location because of the backdrop of those beautiful Flatirons, the mountains where I'd spent many years ice-climbing and learning about my deepest fears.

I asked Long, "How could a 'white guy' like me contribute to this discussion of colonialism and be taken seriously?"

Long replied, "If not you, then who else?"

I conveyed the difficulties of being a white guy and entering the area of Native American religions. Over the previous two years, I had become more and more invested in ancient Aztec ceremonial traditions around the rain deity Tlaloc, and I had been captivated by Long's presentation to the esteemed gathering of Mesoamericanists the day before our brunch. This scholarly grouping of archaeologists, anthropologists, archeoastronomers, and ethnologists from Mexico and the United States had been brought to Boulder to discuss recent excavations of the Templo Mayor in Mexico City, the central temple of the Aztec city Tenochtitlan.

Long's presentation focused on the colonial-interpretive dimensions of religion beginning at first contact carrying through to present-day journalists and scholars who heavy-handedly defined Indigenous Peoples as "heathens" and, therefore, subordinates. In Long's view, both the colonizer and the scholars who came after them were employed in different forms of the same enterprise—that is, to conquer and exploit the New World for their/our own ends and promote a settler-colonial worldview that perpetuated acts of conquest. Long argued, and I agreed, that colonizing attitudes still undergird our scholarly interpretations of Indigenous Peoples.[5]

My concern at Chautauqua was how a descendant of settler-colonial people (i.e., a white guy like me) could effectively contribute to Indigenous studies, given his criticism of scholarship. Long's response was that it could be effective because settler-colonial people are the source of the problem. In order for this area of study to move forward, it is critical to acknowledge that a settler-colonial mentality is still at the root of the problem itself. Indigenous Peoples cannot do this work all by themselves, without the collaboration of a wide variety of communities and worldviews that address these issues together and for their own reasons. Long said, "We can't simply declare that we are now in a post-colonial world! History of Religions requires us all to crawl back through colonialism and reassess together what it means to be human."

Since that day, I have come to understand from Charles Long, Davíd Carrasco, and others that this is essentially the work of the History of Religions: a collaborative interaction with others from a wide variety of interpretive locations for the purpose of forming new ways of knowing the world and understanding what it means to be human.

Over the last thirty years, my primary audience in teaching, writing, and community engagement has been communicating Indigenous

---

5. The term "Indigenous Peoples" will appear in this text in capitalized form and with the pluralized "Peoples." This is a reference to their status under the United Nations Declaration on the Rights of Indigenous Peoples that was passed on 13 September 2007. This is the first time that Indigenous Peoples gained status as human beings under international law and also acknowledges them as holding rights communally in distinction to the recognized rights of individuals.

values to non-Indigenous, settler-colonial people, perhaps more commonly referred to as "white people." Many of these people, like myself, are descendants of settler-colonial people who have little to no traditions of living in relationship with a living landscape, even after more than five hundred years. However, for a variety of personal and cultural reasons, there is constant and tremendous interest in knowing more about these Indigenous traditions. My classes enroll to capacity, sometimes exceeding 350 students. Simultaneously, Native American and Indigenous studies have experienced an exponential rise in the numbers of new faculty members who have come from Indigenous nations and communities. The changing demographic among faculty marks a critical element that defines the transformations currently going on in universities around the world. As a consequence, departments and programs in Native American and Indigenous studies have become more successful through these collaborations between different ethnic and racial groups.

The deep and intractable problems that face Indigenous Peoples around the world today directly emanate from the Age of Discovery. Discovery and conquest are extensions of the European imagination regarding the organization of the world through their antagonistic relationship to non-Christians, beginning with seventh-century Muslims. "Christendom"—a word we will return to later on—envisioned a new world order implemented through settler-colonialism. These fantastically fictitious values of what is today called "white supremacy" justified the theft and commodification of land, environmental devastation, language extermination, loss of ceremonial knowledge, forced conversion to religion, and economic exploitation. These effects exploded in 1492 and are felt to this day.[6]

---

6. The power of the European religious imagination and its role in the conquest of the New World, and its impact on Indigenous Peoples and the natural world, has been discussed extensively. See, for example, Todorov, *Conquest of America*; Cervantes, *Devil in the New World*; Cronon, *Changes in the Land*; Lyons and Mohawk, *Exiled in the Land of the Free*. For Vine Deloria Jr., in *God Is Red*, and John C. Mohawk, in *Utopian Legacies*, Christianity was used as a weapon against Indigenous Peoples around the world.

Problems of sexual violence, drug use, teenage suicide, and so forth do not originate within Indigenous communities. Rather, they are the lasting effects from the continued assaults of the settler-colonial mindset that devalue Indigenous Peoples and their lifeways, their traditions, and their lands. This book directly addresses non-Indigenous settler-colonial people and argues for the urgency of our understanding the depth, causes, and lethal power of these problems that may jeopardize our collective human survival on this planet. Long made this exact point all those years ago: that past and current issues regarding African Americans, Latinx Americans, and Native Americans in the United States were the result of a colonizing worldview forced upon them through various instruments of coercion and deceptive persuasion.

Why NOT "Indigenous *Religions*," or How the History of Religions Approach Can Be a Pathway to Understanding Indigenous Values

Most Indigenous languages don't have a word that directly translates as "religion." There is no activity that can be tagged explicitly as "religion" that is distinctive from the rest of community life. The category often expands to a "lifeway," "orientation," or "cosmology" that integrated every aspect of Indigenous life—political, economic, social, familial, and religious—but integrated into a whole.

Religion is problematic for many, and this is certainly true for the Haudenosaunee. Indigenous Peoples always return to the living values that direct human activity. What is and is not valued as central to all the social life is deemed valuable. Values determine how the material world is prioritized in relationships between human and nonhuman beings. Values also direct a system of exchange, the practice and deep respect of reciprocity that is one of the defining features to which some have feebly referred as "Indigenous religion."

In the academic study of religion, categories used to describe others determine the ways in which we engage or don't engage, define or misdefine, our subject. Conceptualizing one's subject as a possession prohibits any authentic exchange. Several constituencies that have been traditionally at odds with one another are either brought together or separated based on the use of categories that do not arise out of the lived patterns of the people being studied. Even though there are thousands of different examples of Indigenous traditions, this book is an effort to initiate a discussion of what they have in common with one another, and what they value as distinct from the world of settler-colonial people. Describing features of "Indigenous values" is a different sort of task than that of ethnographic description. Given the tremendous diversity of these traditions, not all Indigenous Peoples will recognize themselves in aspects of this volume. My goal is to attempt a dynamic approximation of a number of values deeply held and widely shared by the Indigenous Peoples and traditions with which I am most familiar.

My hope is to further conversation among readers and commentators. A related goal is to illuminate the issues and consequences that surround the category of "Indigenous values" within the discipline of the academic study of religion. I argue that, more than any other categories that can be imagined, Indigenous values challenge well-worn public and academic assumptions about the nature of religion as "faith" and "ideology." There are no clearer examples and resources for considering the religious dimensions of material existence than in an examination of Indigenous values. For example, sacred texts in these traditions are not as central as in other religious traditions and the general study of religion. Texts, therefore, are not an intrinsic focal point of the history of practices, ideas, or values of Indigenous Peoples. Indigenous values reveal that there are perspectives and orientations that permeate Indigenous cultural practices preceding the creation of religious texts. As a way of engaging the general and academic readers of this volume, I plan to do what follows.

In chapter 2, utilizing a variety of theorists of religion, I attempt to de-exoticize Indigenous traditions by emphasizing a range of human activities that connect the regenerative powers of the material exchanges between human and nonhuman beings. These activities are a basic element of Indigenous values, which I define in two ways: first, how human beings meaningfully inhabit the world; and, second, how habitation is fundamentally about exchange, specifically the exchange of gifts freely given between communities of human and nonhuman beings. Chapter 3 then attempts to characterize an Indigenous way of knowing a living world by focusing on "paying attention." Chapter 4 concentrates on relationships to land, and chapter 5 on the significance of exchange relationships, focusing on these attributes of Indigenous values in a way that can transform how we think about our categories and definitions of religion in general.

The historical phenomenon of cultural contact is crucial in trying to understand Indigenous values today. The collision of different worldviews, most especially between Christian Europeans and the rest of the world, is fundamental to the understanding of Indigenous values. As we well know, cultural contact has included acts of genocide against Indigenous Peoples, appropriations of land and culture, and systematic destruction of languages and ceremonial traditions.

With respect to Indigenous Peoples, the historical role that religion plays in colonization rarely concerned the highest attitudes of the human spirit. Rather, religion was experienced, more often than not, as the most aggressive force in the acquisition of power, wealth, and domination that has been foundational to civilization in the Americas and the world. This book seeks to understand Indigenous values as an interpretive tool to reveal a positive living resource within Indigenous communities, the distortion and demonization of Indigenous values and practices by a variety of settler people to destroy these traditions, and the colonizing aspects within the academic study of religion. This category necessarily involves its ability to describe Indigenous traditions while also accounting how it has been utilized by a variety of settler-colonial people to diminish and destroy these traditions. Bringing it into the urgency of our moment, value change for survival is the focus of the epilogue.

How the History of Religions Is a Pathway to Indigenous Values

My work is grounded by the Chicago school of the History of Religions, which is sometimes misunderstood to be the "comparative study of religion." Often the historian of religions attempts to self-critically engage religious traditions other than their own. The reasons for doing this work are personal, cultural, and academic, but the intended consequence is primarily to further the development of new knowledge in an effort to translate another tradition into one's own understanding, scholarship, or culture in the most powerful way possible.

Mine is not a confessional stance; I am not writing to assuaging my guilt for past cultural sins. Nor is my understanding of a History of Religions approach meant to promote a sense of self-hatred. Instead, following in the work of Mircea Eliade, Joseph Kitagawa, and Charles H. Long, the History of Religions shows us how to try and understand—or, at least, to be sympathetic toward—the multiple worldviews that are expressed through different human communities throughout history.[7] Indigenous Peoples and their traditions present us with a unique focus for the fact that their systems of knowledge are often at odds with scholarship. History of Religions methodology, however, creates a sympathetic space for intercultural understanding.

What is religion? Where does it come from? Is it human or divine? Historians of religion answer these fundamental questions in different ways, depending on their interests. In large part, however, our modern "civilized" worldview, the center of which has been the university, has been largely developed in opposition to Indigenous traditions, which are historically seen at odds with civilization. Therefore, an investigation and an articulation of the origins of the category of

---

7. Notable historians of religions who are colleagues and who work with Indigenous Peoples are Davíd Carrasco, David Chidester, Jacob Olupona, Jennifer Reid, Eglute Trinkauskaite, Mary Keller, Lisa Poirier, Lindsay Jones, Abel Gomez, and Dana Lloyd, among others.

"Indigenous" is also a critical investigation into the origins of the modern academy.

Modernity has largely positioned its development on some ill-conceived myths of its origins that have rigorously "othered" and demonized Indigenous Peoples, designating them as antithetical to civilization.[8] Foundational myths of the cultural superiority of civilization in opposition to Indigenous Peoples have been an ongoing part of university culture.[9] The stories of civilizational foundations in the Americas are partial, distorted, and epistemologically fragile because they don't acknowledge or genuinely appreciate the vital historical sharing and ongoing relationships between Indigenous Peoples and settler-colonial people. Ironically, since first contact, these relationships have more often than not facilitated the physical survival of the settler-colonial people. The "primitive-civilized" rhetoric has flown in the face of these relationships and created a fiction of the innate superiority of the Europeans.

The dominant mythologies of civilization are more fiction than myth—a distinction that will be addressed in this book—and it is now more urgent than ever that they be exposed. It is critical that the mythos of Modernity be reframed to include the important continued contributions of Indigenous Peoples. Shifting the dominating myths of the modern world toward Indigenous values moves us all toward a different way of relating to and valuing the world.

Much more is at stake today than our feelings of guilt about the past. A new level of commitment to the web of a living regenerative world must be encouraged, along with an acknowledgment of past practices of cultural aggression against Indigenous Peoples and their traditions and land. Reassessing the way Indigenous values are positioned within our world brings issues of material survival together with social and environmental justice. It is my intent to begin that work—or, possibly, continue it—with this book.

---

8. Francis Jennings's *The Invasion of America* was an early investigation in this regard.

9. See Long, *Significations*, chapter 6.

Collaborations in the Heartland of the Haudenosaunee

Determining an Interpretive Location

My home is Syracuse, New York. This provides an ideal location from which to reflect on the nature of Indigenous values. Syracuse, the site of Syracuse University, is located in Onondaga Nation territory, the "Central Fire" of the Haudenosaunee Confederacy—People of the Longhouse. Haudenosaunee territory stretches across upstate New York, but its influence could be felt to the north into Ontario, Quebec, and Nova Scotia, to the south into what is now Georgia, to the east into Massachusetts, and to the west into the Ohio River valley.

I have been visiting Syracuse since the early 1980s with my wife, Sandy Bigtree. Sandy is a citizen of the Mohawk Nation at Akwesasne (the eastern door of the Six Nations of the Haudenosaunee Confederacy), but she grew up in Syracuse. Our family moved there in 1996, when I took a job in the Department of Religion at Syracuse University as an American religions scholar. Returning to the heartland of the Haudenosaunee was a homecoming for Sandy and our twin sons. For me, this move fundamentally changed the way I teach and write about religion. My classes in Native American Religions and Indigenous Religions have been transformed simply by our geographic location.

Not only the home of Jim Boeheim's zone defense, Syracuse University is also a hub of college lacrosse. I developed a class, Religion and Sports, emphasizing that this game was first played over one thousand years ago at Onondaga Lake, less than five miles from campus. This Haudenosaunee game, Deyhontsigwa'ehs (Onondaga for "They Bump Hips"), was renamed "lacrosse" by Jesuit priests as a way to Christianize an ancient Medicine Game, by associating the stick with a bishop's crosier and the game with war. Deyhontsigwa'ehs is a critical part of Haudenosaunee cosmology, for the Creator Twins created all that provides life on Earth through the playing of the game. The Medicine Game is also called the "Creator's Game" (to be discussed in chapter 2).[1]

Our twin sons, Kroy and Clay, are citizens of the Oneida Nation of Wisconsin (member of the Haudenosaunee Confederacy) and have been playing competitive box lacrosse with the Onondaga Nation Redhawks since they were three years old. Today, they run a box lacrosse team called the Salt City Eels, and coach college lacrosse. The twins have shown me a whole new way of teaching Indigenous values through sports. This outlook has also resonated deeply with students, who are rarely encouraged to consider the significance of their physical location as a critical component of their intellectual development. Emphasis on classes, majors, team mascots, fraternities, syllabi, and even ideas tend to exclude the cultural geography of a school's location. Ironically, it is the academic study of religion that prioritizes "ideas" above "material life."

My work at Syracuse University has been living proof that Indigenous traditions fundamentally challenge the academic tendency to solely emphasize ideas because it requires that the scholar-student consider their physical locations as well. In anthropological terms, our academic "positionality" must also include the materiality of our lives and the cultural geography of our surroundings.

There are several personal and professional challenges to living in Onondaga Nation territory and advocating on their behalf. I feel fortunate to be working in this area. Our family has been defined by being here: due to colonial history, we had lost our clans. Even

---

1. See John Mohawk's extraordinary book *Iroquois Creation Story*.

though adopted into the Bear Clan at Oneida Nation territory in Wisconsin, Onondaga did not recognize their clans and prohibited them from participating in Longhouse ceremonies at the Onondaga Nation; being the Central Fire of the Confederacy, they remain most guarded. Our family is not bitter about our position, but, rather, much more attuned to the devastation wrought on Indigenous communities and traditions. This has heightened our respect for the traditional community, like the Onondaga Nation, for maintaining their traditions and for surviving outside cultural forces—such as Christian Indian boarding schools, missionization, and Bureau of Indian Affairs (BIA) governments—that have been dedicated to their eradication.

The undergraduate and graduate students who take my classes have been able to appreciate the pitfalls and possibilities of doing this kind of cross-cultural work, whether their primary area of interest is in postmodern theology, Buddhism, religion and popular culture, or Indigenous religions. Undergraduates, who are primarily non-native, see the potential benefit from this collaborative orientation. Their interests have helped me in the development of new courses in addition to Religion and Sports, such as Religious Dimensions of Whiteness, Religion and the Conquest of America, and Religion and American Consumerism. These cultural phenomena, I have found, are best explored collaboratively. These topics are often traumatic for both Haudenosaunee and non-native students, though in fundamentally different ways, but feedback indicates that students almost always benefit from these historical introspections.

Collaboration, then, is absolutely vital to the continuation of academic study. The following description of our work with the Haudenosaunee exemplifies a collaborative model of working between academic and Indigenous Peoples. Additionally, this illustrates how a "values approach" makes this kind of work more possible across Indigenous and settler-colonial worldviews. My intention here is to ground the more abstract theoretical discussions that will dominate subsequent chapters.

Amplifying and Extending Haudenosaunee Values

Figure 1 is an image of the Confederacy Belt, or "Hiawatha (Hayenhwátha') Belt," which was woven over one thousand years ago at Onondaga Lake with purple and white wampum beads (carved from quahog shells found along the Atlantic seaboard from Cape Cod to Long Island).[2] From left to right, the symbols represent the Seneca, Cayuga, Onondaga (symbolized by the Great Tree of Peace in the center), Oneida, and Mohawk Nations.[3] Underneath the Hiawatha Belt is a depiction of a Longhouse that extends across the northeastern United States with five fires, representative of the five original nations in the Confederacy.

The Hiawatha Belt was repatriated to the Haudenosaunee in the late 1980s from a museum of Anthropology at the State University of New York at Albany (SUNY). The return of this belt was the result of a protracted struggle between the Onondaga Nation, who are the wampum keepers, and the Iroquoianists, a group of non-Haudenosaunee academics who made careers out of controlling their historical narratives. This struggle, which had been ongoing for generations, illustrates the distinctive ways in which Indigenous and academic communities have historically had different interpretive locations and agendas and, hence, lack a collaborative understanding.

---

2. The name "Hiawatha" is the anglicized rendering of the Haudenosaunee name "Hayenhwátha'," who is a key person in the founding of the Great Law of Peace over one thousand years ago at Onondaga Lake. Unfortunately, due to Longfellow's poem "Hiawatha," that spelling is better recognized, even though Longfellow's fictitious character lived near Lake Superior, and the original Hayenhwátha' lived near Onondaga Lake. I will use "Hiawatha" because, even in Onondaga Nation territory today, we are surrounded by a boulevard, a lake, and a bar, all having used Longfellow's spelling.

3. The Tuscarora Nation became the sixth to join the Haudenosaunee in the 1720s, when they came north from South Carolina to escape the slave traders and aggressive appropriations of their lands by European settlers.

16   The Urgency of Indigenous Values

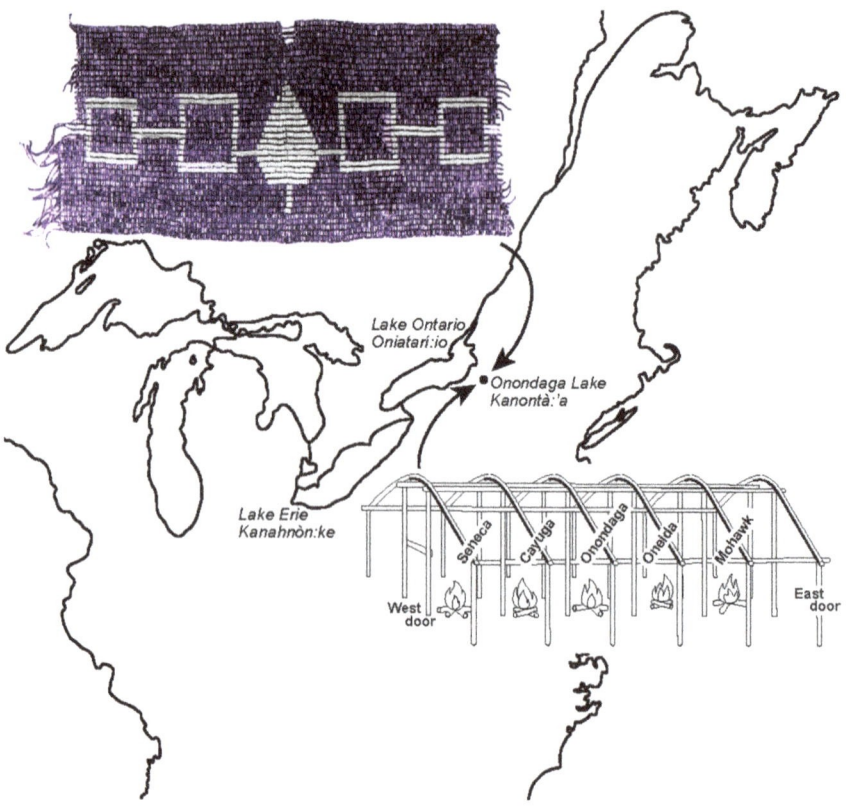

1. Map of Haudenosaunee influence. Hiawatha (Hayenhwátha') Wampum Belt represents the establishment of the Confederacy, with most recent archaeological data setting the date as August 18, 909 CE, at Onondaga Lake. The Haudenosaunee Longhouse shows the influential outreach of the Great Law of Peace: from Nova Scotia to the Mississippi River and from the Great Lakes into Cherokee Nation Territory. Created by Joseph Stoll, Syracuse University.

Since its return to the Onondaga Nation, the image of the Hiawatha Belt has been fashioned into a flag, which represents the Haudenosaunee's first union under the Great Law of Peace. We now find it prominently displayed by Haudenosaunee people as well as those honoring their contributions of peace, which have influenced the world.[4] This repatriation of the Hiawatha Belt has resulted in a culture renaissance of the Haudenosaunee and represents a victory of Indigenous Peoples over the colonizing orientations of the academy. It also illustrates why a collaborative methodology must emerge in future work with Indigenous Peoples. I argue that the scholar's work must move from objectification of the Indigenous "other" to a collaborative venture envisioning a shared viable future.

Working in Onondaga Nation Territory

Today, there are 574 "tribes" federally recognized by the United States, but only three still operate under their precolonial clan systems and they are all Haudenosaunee Nations: the Onondaga, (the capital of the Confederacy); the Tuscarora (which joined the Confederacy around 1720); and the Tonawanda Seneca. Grand Council still convenes at Onondaga; however, the United States officially recognizes only three of the six traditional governments. The other nations succumbed to pressure to reorganize under new tribal elective governments under the Bureau of Indian Affairs (BIA). These elective chiefs do not follow the Haudenosaunee Longhouse protocol of the Great Law of Peace.[5] In fact, every other nation territory, tribe, or "reservation" across all of Indian Country had to reorganize and accept these elective BIA governments. These chiefs are often Christian and do not share the same relationship with land as do

---

4. The Haudenosaunee flag is now being flown at Syracuse University and other universities across Haudenosaunee territory. This symbolizes a sea change in university-Haudenosaunee relations. See Greg Johnson's *Sacred Claims* for a helpful discussion of the ways that religious language is being used in repatriation efforts.

5. Dating the origins of the Haudenosaunee Confederacy is a matter of scholarly debate. Barbara Mann and Jerry L. Field cited 1142 CE in their article "A Sign in the Sky: Dating the League of the Haudenosaunee." More recent excavations, however, push this date back to August 18, 909 CE. See Rosen, *Corey Village and the Cayuga World*, 197. Some Haudenosaunee orators, like Tom Porter, set the date back ten thousand years.

traditional people. Elective chiefs have not historically participated in traditional ceremonies, nor have traditional people voted in BIA elections, for these elective systems are seen as a foreign threat to the precolonial representational form of democracy that defined their sovereign treaty status.[6] Longhouse people are matrilineal—that is, they are identified by their mother's clan.[7] It is the Clan Mother who chooses their clan's male "chief," or *Hoyane* (Onondaga for "Men of the Good Mind"), and they remain in office for life unless removed by the Clan Mother. The Haudenosaunee system of governance greatly impressed and inspired the eighteenth-century Founding Fathers of the United States and later inspired the suffragists who founded the Women's Rights Movement in 1848 at Seneca Falls, New York, where the first women's convention was held in Seneca Nation territory.

On March 11, 2005, the Onondaga Nation filed its historic Land Rights action in the US Federal Court.[8] It was based on a treaty created by President George Washington and known as the Canandaigua Treaty, Pickering Treaty, or George Washington Treaty, which was ratified by Congress on November 11, 1794. Legal scholars have referred to this historic agreement as the "mother of all Native American treaties."[9] This was the first nation to nation treaty

---

6. There has recently been a "disenrollment epidemic" among BIA established tribal governments that has exacerbated old divisions imposed in the past between "traditional" and "progressive" factions within each Indigenous nation: divisions established by colonial governments to purposely erode sovereignty, assimilate Indigenous Peoples, or effect their extermination. For example, see Galanda, "Tribal Nationhood."

7. "Longhouse" refers to the matrilineal clan system established by the Peacemaker over one thousand years ago at Onondaga Lake.

8. See the description of the Onondaga Nation Land Rights case on the Onondaga Nation website. *Onondaga Nation v. New York State*, Civil Action No. 05-CV-314, https://www.onondaganation.org/land-rights/ (accessed 26 December 2022).

9. Jemison and Schein, *Treaty of Canandaigua*. Vine Deloria Jr. referred to the Canandaigua Treaty as the "mother of all treaties" in his address "The Journey to Native American Sovereignty" at Syracuse University on 18 September 2003.

that established the United States and the Haudenosaunee as separate sovereign nations. The 2005 legal action was not the first; other Haudenosaunee nations had also previously filed land claims throughout upstate New York, including the Mohawk, Seneca, Cayuga, and Oneida.

Since the mid-1970s, stories about Indian land claims have come to dominate the media in upstate New York, often garnering intensely negative reactions among non-native residents. Nothing in American culture is more controversial than the contestation of land title. The Onondaga legal action, however, was unique, as it was based in the traditional values of the Longhouse tradition: peace, justice, and the environmental healing of land. In other words, this legal action was called a "Land *Rights* Action" and argued for the rights of the land, including its right to heal. It focused on respect and gratitude for Onondaga Lake, which is the site of the Indigenous roots of American democracy. This should hold special significance for all American citizens, but, unfortunately, the lake has been neglected and used as a chemical dump, making it the most chemically polluted lake in the United States.[10]

Although the Onondaga action is based in the same legal history as the actions of other Haudenosaunee nations, it is fundamentally different. Rather than a monetary settlement or a settlement that includes a casino deal with the state, the Onondaga Nation seeks to restore the integrity of the environment and to restore the land to its pristine state—hence their emphasis on "land rights" as opposed to "land claims."[11]

---

10. The symbolism of Onondaga Lake is a very powerful reminder of the two opposing ways in which the world is valued: through an indigenous reciprocity with the natural world, or a settler-colonial commodification of land.

11. The preamble of the legal action states these values clearly: "The Onondaga people wish to bring about a healing between themselves and all others who live in this region that has been the homeland of the Onondaga Nation since the dawn of time. The Nation and its people have a unique spiritual, cultural, and historic relationship with the land, which is embodied in *Gayanashagowa*, the Great

Inspired by the strong values of environmental healing exhibited by the Onondaga Nation, several non-Haudenosaunee people—including myself—have been motivated to promote the settlement of the Onondaga Land Rights Action. Sandy and I were originally involved in a grass-roots, community-based group called Neighbors of the Onondaga Nation (NOON), which emerged to inform local non-native people about the positive aspects of the Land Rights Action and its benefits for everyone. Institutions like the Syracuse Peace Council, SUNY–College of Environmental Science and Forestry, and Syracuse University, with the support of former chancellor Nancy Cantor, combined forces to hold two year-long educational series in 2006 and 2010 titled "Onondaga Land Rights and Our Common Future" that brought together environmental issues, global politics, social justice, and cultural identity. We determined it to be crucial to have Indigenous traditionalists or scholars share the stage with non-native academics in a collaborative format.

In my experience, these kinds of ongoing collaborations between natives and non-natives are very rare. They were made possible by all of the people in upstate New York who have had a long history of working tenaciously for ways that tilt toward justice and healing. With our family living and working in Onondaga Nation territory and seeing the nation's bold and principled stance on behalf of social justice and environmental healing, we are continuously inspired by this work. By merely living in Onondaga Nation territory, I find the way I think about teaching, academic work, and the discipline and definition of religion has changed completely. I am also fortunate to

---

Law of Peace. This relationship goes far beyond federal and state legal concepts of ownership, possession, or other legal rights. The Haudenosaunee are the land and consider the land, a relative. It is the responsibility of Nation's leaders to mindfully work toward healing the land, protecting it, and passing it on to future generations. The Onondaga Nation brings this action on behalf of its people, in the hope that it may hasten the process of reconciliation and bring lasting justice, peace, and respect among all who inhabit this area" (*Onondaga Nation v. New York State*, Civil Action No. 05-CV-314).

have trained as a historian of religions because it has provided me with the interpretive framework for dealing with these new methodological orientations.[12]

The Value of Cohabitation

Questioning how to best inhabit the world is critically important for all people living amid postcolonial cultural conundrums here in Central New York, and addressing these cultural conditions might potentially forge a path to our coexistence. In 1613, the Haudenosaunee and the Dutch struck an agreement for which a wampum belt was created. It is called the Two Row Wampum, or Guswentha (fig. 2). Tehanetorens (Ray Fadden), a noted educator, author, and activist, reiterates what I have often heard Haudenosaunee leaders discuss:

> These two rows will symbolize two paths or two vessels, traveling down the same river [of life] together. One, a birch bark canoe, will be for the Indian People, their laws, their customs, and their ways. The other, a ship, will be for the white people and their laws, their customs, and their ways. We shall each travel the river together, side by side, but in our own boat. Neither of us will make compulsory laws or interfere in the internal affairs of the other. Neither of us will try to steer the other's vessel.[13]

Since this agreement, however, European Americans have utilized cultural forces of missionization, mercantilism, and colonization, which violated the Two Row Wampum from the onset. To date, the Haudenosaunee have not broken the agreement. It is likely that Europeans were unable to appreciate this wampum from the very beginning.

---

12. For a History of Religions perspective on the mythic importance of "habitation," see Eliade, *Sacred and the Profane*, chapter 1.
13. Tehanetorens, *Wampum Belts of the Iroquois*, 73–74.

2. Two Row Wampum belt. A facsimile of the Two Row Wampum, or Guswentha, from a 1613 agreement between the Dutch and Haudenosaunee. Created by Anthony Gonyea, Onondaga Nation, for the Indigenous Values Initiative and displayed at the Skä·noñh— Great Law of Peace Center. Photo by author.

In 1968, a Dutch version of the agreement emphasized the exclusive rights of the Dutch to trade for beaver pelts with the Haudenosaunee. From the Haudenosaunee point of view, this was a cohabitation agreement with the itinerant Dutch traders of noninterference between two coequal residents of the land. The obvious contradiction is what "coequal resident" meant to the two parties of the agreement.

As the Haudenosaunee conceive it, a coequal residency on the earth is shared with nonhuman beings of the natural world. This was clearly outside the purview of the colonizer, who saw land as a resource held under his dominion. This notion of "dominion" carried over into intercultural relationships, reflecting that of a "father and son" as opposed to an Indigenous sense of "brothers" living side by side, moving parallel along the river of life.[14] The colonizer, conversely, would have to first respect the river as having its own intrinsic value. The overriding concern of the Haudenosaunee was how could two people live in peace with one another in one place if one had no regard for the place. The Two Row Wampum was an extension of the Great Law of Peace expressed in the Hiawatha Belt. Unfortunately, for whatever reason, this concept was completely lost on the colonizers.

I have increasingly come to think of the Two Row Wampum as more than a historical or political "document" from a particular period in time, but, rather, as an important methodological statement. It implies a limit to the human ability to know *others*.

We have been taught in university culture that, for the most part, everyone and everything is knowable. Although this is the legacy of the seventeenth-century Enlightenment project, this assumption about human knowledge violates the Two Row Wampum and inevitably leads to intercultural interference and ruination of the land. Peaceful cohabitation is less likely when one group of people has a

---

14. See Irving Powless Jr.'s *Who Are These People Anyway?*, which is full of remarkable stories told by one of the most influential communicators of the Onondaga Nation Council of Chiefs.

concept of unlimited access to knowledge.[15] Moreover, I have come to realize that it is impossible to completely know another culture: we know others only in a proximate and relational sense. The Two Row Wampum expresses a respect of differences between people. That knowledge has limits, and it is a fundamental tenet of establishing peaceful relationships. However, it is the unifying principle of being in proper relationship with the natural world that allows people to live peacefully beside one another with respect.

From Description to Collaboration

Over the last few generations, scholars of religion and others working in the descriptive task of the History of Religions have been vexed as to how to do their work. At least since Edward Said's work on Orientalism, questions about how the scholar of religion can adequately describe "the other" without interrupting or destroying them are among the most pressing methodological discussions in the academy. Likewise, in the History of Religions, methodological issues have become even deeper and more perplexing when dealing with the contentious nature of religion itself. One of the first things that Onondaga people tell my classes, for example, is that they have no word for or concept of "religion." Imposing external conceptual frameworks upon other cultures is often perceived as a presumptuous act that can lead to detrimental consequences. There is no denying how emotionally challenging this work can be, but doing the work is so much more important than getting waylaid by any personal hurt feelings. It is through collaboration that we must work to narrow the gap between mistranslation and miscommunication if we are to ever achieve an intercultural understanding.

A shift from an expert model of knowledge production to a collaborative model, which can better solve this methodological quandary, is exemplified in the Two Row Wampum. In my experience,

---

15. I will argue later that this is essentially a theological concept that derives from a colonial understanding of an otiosus deity.

rather than questioning what the Onondaga believe, or what ceremonies they perform—which will always be opaque to settler-colonial people—I ask, "What are the issues of most urgent *mutual* concern?" This approach requires me to interpret my own urgent questions (i.e., "What do I need to know to be more effective or useful in my work?") and then find answers through a collaborative process of discussion and action. No longer are the Haudenosaunee, the Aztec, or the Lakota my "informants," as they may have been in past academic endeavors. Instead, they are my collaborators in generating new ways of communicating solutions to urgent issues of mutual concern.

To some in the academy, this may sound like scholarship that fails in its academic responsibility to produce objective, unbiased knowledge. Work in anthropology and Indigenous studies, however, calls into question whether any unbiased knowledge can exist outside of the scholar's imagination. Likewise, as previously discussed, the fiction of writing facts about another religion most often leads to cultural practices that have devastating consequences for Indigenous Peoples. Instead, I now find that it is only in knowing through the process of collaboration that we are able to get to the root of the problems that face all of us today.

Originally the task of the scholar was to describe the traditions and ceremonial practices of small and distinct Indigenous communities. Never mind, for now, that these were missionaries, anthropologists, soldiers, lawyers, land speculators, and others who came with the express purpose of colonizing this country's original inhabitants. Up until the 1960s or so, scholarly activity was focused on accurately and truthfully describing the physical attributes of Indigenous communities. At the time, it was understood that, with the march toward civilization, these cultures would soon disappear along with the loss of an important chapter to the story of cultural diversity and the origins of human civilization. Through most of the twentieth century, this period was called "salvage anthropology."

In the late 1950s and 1960s, the veracity of these descriptions began to come under serious scrutiny. With an exponential rise in the number of good descriptive ethnographies, widely divergent interpretations of the same culture group began to emerge. These situations often led to fierce academic disagreements, but there are simple explanations for the divergent descriptions. Different scholars would rely on an array of "subjects" or "informants"—often those who had been culturally marginalized through colonization—to serve as experts in their research. More importantly, the scholars' own makeup (i.e., male or female, "insider" or "outsider") would determine what sort of ethnographic data would emerge. No longer could one assume that an ethnographic description was true, as in previous generations. Rather, it was understood to be an extension of the ethnographer's experience and cultural makeup. While we were told that the study of a particular group would be objective, the study was, in fact, more like a Rorschach test, telling us more about the ethnographer than the people they purported to be studying.

Over the last 150 years, the Western academy has learned that there is no privileged scholarly position from which to write about an ethnographic subject. There is no stable technique, either, for discerning the factuality or depths about another culture and reducing it to a written text: a book. The assumptions of the past make descriptive ethnographies deeply challenging. No amount of time spent in the field or degree of language ability will make a book about an Indigenous community any more credible or scientifically verifiable. Does this mean that ethnography is dead? Is writing about Indigenous Peoples worth the effort? And is writing about them worth the potential violence it could inflict upon them?

In a wide variety of styles, ranging from novels to political tracts, academics are coming to terms with the reality that there are limits to knowing about Indigenous Peoples. A finite human being cannot know the truth about another human community. As a result, the strategy has been to widen the scope of scholarly orientations. However, in the new writing strategies, there has been a shift in the task. No longer can we assume that writing *about* an Indigenous community is possible; there are too many intangible elements that have caused many to give up the descriptive task altogether. What has emerged instead is a new ethnographic style that is conversational. It is no longer considered responsible for ethnographers to write and talk *about* other groups. Writing is always a report about conversations *with* other people from the writer's interpretive location—a collaboration with the people they want to know and understand.[16] Generally, scholars who now write books on others are willing to take the responsibility of owning their work, by putting themselves in the narrative as a way of emphasizing the interactive nature of this knowledge. But what do people from radically different cultural contexts talk about? How does someone trained in the Western academic disciplines of the modern university talk with someone who inhabits an Indigenous tradition?

Historically, these conversationalists emerge from opposing cultural positions. As we will discuss, the old paradigms of civilized vs. savage or Christian vs. heathen do not serve us now as the dialogue model of ethnography—if it ever did. Undoubtedly, these mythic structures of the modern world will impinge on the conversation. If scholars of religion or culture are willing to devote themselves to the constant struggle toward understanding a radically different culture than their own, they have to conclude that the old paradigm did not work. Moreover, what are the keen interests and fascinations that entice people to become academics and write about Indigenous Peoples? How does one overcome one's cultural isolation to really appreciate Indigenous values over the static category of "Indigenous Religions"?

An intercultural conversation implies that one has questions that cannot be adequately answered in any other way. Traversing such a wide cultural divide, as the Two Row Wampum illustrates, is not an easy task under the best conditions. So, the first step in creating the context for an intercultural exchange is seeking clarity on the questions you want answered. Initially, this doesn't seem too hard; students often come to a subject on their own because they want answers. But scholarly training in the History of Religions,

16. For example, see Jackson's *Politics of Storytelling*.

comparative religion, and anthropology has sometimes not taken the development of the scholar's existential questions as seriously as scientifically defined ones.

In the study of religion, seeking answers to deep questions has sometimes been called "theology," which is often shunned in the social sciences. For some scholars of religion, the theological questions have to be kept completely separate from the descriptive enterprise. Yet I argue that developing one's own questions—urgent, burning questions—is what leads to a more successful intercultural conversation and, ironically, better descriptive work, even though the description is what occurs interculturally rather than as a feature solely created by an extraneous and hostile cultural position.

How does one ask a question in such a way that it can be heard and regarded by an Indigenous community? A question may be urgent for the ethnographer, but will it be as important for the Indigenous Peoples with whom he or she wants to converse? For example, exploring the nature of evil in the world might be an urgent question for a student of religion, but the same question might be of little relevance to Indigenous Peoples. I have found that "evil," or the "theodicy problem," assumes too much about the universal nature of grand, abstract theological concepts to be a conversation starter. I would never have initially asked the Onondaga people, for example, about the nature of evil. There has to be a basis here for an intercultural conversation.

Orienting a conversation around particular issues or empirical phenomena can lead to more fruitful discussions. For example, one might recast the question of evil to explore the fundamental nature of genocide, warfare, and strife in the modern world. Of course, this changes the nature of one's question, but it does so in a way that it is more likely to lead to future intercultural collaborative work. For the scholar, this requires a shift from what Charles Long has characterized as an "abstract universalism to an empirical universalism."[17]

---

17. See Long, "Matter and Spirit"; and "Mircea Eliade and the Imagination of Matter."

The scholar has to learn how to speak the language, and how to act appropriately by being respectful among the people with whom he or she is collaborating. The first consideration, involving the limits of knowledge, always raises the charge that scholarship is irrelevant if all understanding is relative and that there is no "truth." The argument goes something like this: if scholars do not strive for the truth, then there are no academic standards to be maintained. This book takes a different direction. If scholars are collaboratively working toward addressing their urgent issues of mutual concern, then the ethical and professional standards for scholarship will emerge to help foster that work. Rather than getting at the truth of the Haudenosaunee, for example, I am pursuing a collaborative enterprise, which means that I will take the time to understand their language, read background information and scholarship, get involved in creating community events and conferences, and take care to appreciate the limits of my location as a guest in their territory. Indeed, I am now more concerned and aware of my scholarly credibility, among both my Indigenous and academic colleagues, than I had been in graduate school. By the way, graduate school did not prepare me for this kind of work.

Today, there is an assumption among university administrators and faculty that extending scholarships and opportunities to Native Americans, for example, will serve as a benefit to everyone. Through higher education, native students will have more opportunities as teachers, school administrators, and environmental advisors to help revitalize their communities. The inclusion of Indigenous Peoples as collaborators will also fundamentally shift the nature of the university as a center for the production of knowledge. While coming to the university will undoubtedly benefit Indigenous Peoples, their worldviews will have a much more profound effect on the nature of the university. The collaborative model of scholarship could necessarily work to *Indigenize* the university itself, as reflected in the subject, style, and personnel of classes.

Graduate students of religion can be taught to collaborate well rather than be good at extracting information. Indigenous Peoples are well attuned to outsiders who want to extract their traditional knowledge. This sensitivity has developed over the course of five hundred years of devastating relationships with "civilized" people. Anthropological texts beginning with Columbus are littered with misinformation propagated by culturally arrogant ethnographers intentionally misguided by Indigenous Peoples, whose main motivation was to protect their traditions from prying eyes. Graduate students need to learn these lessons of past missteps; they have to appreciate the difficulties and cultural gaps so they can make honest and reliable connections. Moreover, students need the opportunity to develop their own urgent questions to help forge good relationships with Indigenous communities. This implies an exploration of oneself and others, as demonstrated in a number of excellent case studies where these are simultaneous pursuits.[18] This collaborative shift also implies that the graduate student no longer regards cultural conversation partners as informants, but as colleagues.

Thus, writing has a different status in the process of collaboration. Descriptions of Indigenous Peoples and cultures are *about* them. One can, for example, go into any major bookstore and find books *about* the Maori, the Navajo, or the Inca. In writing within a collaborative rubric, one would be reoriented toward issues of social justice, the environment, or other concerns. These works would be found in other sections of the bookstore and might actually be more descriptive, but all within the context of an exploration of *issues of urgent mutual concern.* Also, collaborations could be coauthored, have multiple authors, or be authored anonymously. A collaborative model means exploring one's own urgent questions with *respect* to others. It could be that a student does not need regular contact with Indigenous collaborators; in fact, this is most often the case. People are busy, and it is difficult and costly to travel long distances, but students-scholars still must work on their questions. They read, reflect, and write on the issues that are of deepest concern. Collaboration

---

18. One example is Raheja and Gold, *Listen to the Heron's Words.*

does not imply that there is always a censor for one's writing; only when one speaks about another tradition does one need direct contact. With most work, however, one is working within one's own creativity by reflecting on written materials and other resources to form as powerful and affective a piece of writing as possible. Collaboration is oriented around plying strategies of expression for widening the appeal of one's own work in the most powerful way possible. When dealing with urgent issues of mutual concern, strategizing for maximizing the effect of one's work is only natural. In the language of the Two Row Wampum, writing is a process of "polishing the chain— as expressed by the three white rows of beads between the two purple rows—between people of radically different cultural orientations.

I appreciate the irony of this single-authored book advocating for collaborative writing, but behind this work are the innumerable cross-cultural conversations and collaborations that brought it into being. Among the most prominent of these is the Skä·noñh—Great Law of Peace Center.

The Skä·noñh—Great Law of Peace Center

Our work at the Skä·noñh—Great Law of Peace Center illustrates a collaborative methodology based on a values approach garnered from the History of Religions. In fact, I don't think this center would exist without this methodology. In the years since it opened, the center has had an impact on the general understanding and appreciation of the Onondaga Nation and the Haudenosaunee in our region and at Syracuse University. What follows is a description of my involvement with the center and a description of what we have accomplished there.

In April 2012, a letter to the editor was published in the *Syracuse Post Standard* urging the Onondaga County Parks to reopen Sainte Marie among the Iroquois, which had gone bankrupt. This final plea was to preserve the memory of and honor the seventeenth-century Jesuit missionaries who had sacrificed so much in trying to force Christianity on the Onondaga. Their fortified mission, however, failed, and the Jesuits were coerced to leave twenty months after their arrival. Local residents had always referred to the historical site as the "French Fort." I immediately countered this letter with a response entitled "Replace Colonial Conquest Story to Begin Healing."[19] My letter contended that there was a much more important story that needed to be told at Onondaga Lake: the founding of the Great Law of Peace that brought five warring nations together, a peace that has lasted well over one thousand years. This message had influenced the Founding Fathers in the development of Western democracy, the women's rights movement, lacrosse, and regenerative agriculture, among other aspects of American culture. As a result, I was asked to direct the project that would repurpose the French Fort as the Skä·noñh—Great Law of Peace Center, which I agreed to do on a strictly volunteer basis. For me it was imperative that I receive no pay so as to keep the work free of controversy. Immediately, I formed an "academic collaborative" with my colleagues who were already working with the Haudenosaunee on other projects, which added institutional support that served to protect the Haudenosaunee message of peace and ensured that everything would be vetted through the Onondaga Nation because of the contentious history of this place.

In 1933, the Onondaga Historical Association (OHA, named for its location in Onondaga County) raised money to create a historical site commemorating the Jesuits' arrival in 1656. The opening event drew thousands of spectators who watched the reenactment of Hiawatha canoeing across Onondaga Lake in a white stone canoe. Upon completing the journey, Hiawatha ascended steps to greet Father Le Moyne, where Hiawatha exchanged six hundred square miles of the Lake and land for conversion into Christianity.[20]

---

19. Arnold, "Haudenosaunee History." This message has been amplified in Bigtree and Arnold, "Forming a 'More Perfect Union.'" See Debora Ryan's dissertation "A French Fort in the Salt City," and Ryan and Stokes-Rees, "A Tale of Two Missions."

20. "Hundreds of Baldwinsville people yesterday were mingled with the score of more of thousands gathered on the East shore of Onondaga Lake to see

Many components of this narrative were inaccurate. Hiawatha did not canoe across Onondaga Lake: it was the Peacemaker, and that happened over one thousand years earlier. Father Le Moyne arrived around 1653 and "discovered" the salt spring. Another group of Jesuits came in 1656 to establish the mission, but it failed, and they retreated in the dead of night in 1658. It was not until 1933 that OHA commissioned a nineteenth-century fort to be built, rather than an accurate seventeenth-century reproduction, so that they could better market a "cowboy and Indian"–themed tourist site. The historical narrative was taken solely from the "Jesuit Relations," which was almost entirely wrong from the point of view of the Onondaga Nation.

In 1971, OHA replaced the nineteenth-century fort with a more authentic seventeenth-century French fort. The triumphal Jesuit narrative remained the same, however, and there continued to be no real Onondaga Nation presence at the site. Urban Catholic Mohawks were often hired to dress in period clothing. By the 1990s, a new building was constructed near the fort to further expand the Jesuit narrative. It was renamed "Sainte Marie among the Iroquois."

It was during this time that my wife and I moved to Syracuse. Sandy, who grew up five miles north of the Onondaga Nation, had been away for fifteen years. We were thrilled to be raising our children in Haudenosaunee territory and to continue my work at the birthplace of the Great Law of Peace. Sandy was glad to be home but stunned that the French fort was now replaced with Sainte Marie among the Iroquois, knowing that that first encounter had been anything but amicable. Since 1656, no Catholic church has ever been built on Onondaga Nation territory. Nothing could be more

---

Hiawatha and Father Simon LeMoyne, and the colonists land from their canoes and claim the land of the Onondaga in the name of Jesus, while amplifying system of present day told of the pageantry, planes flew overhead, and newspaper photographers fluttered here and there to snap the latest view for the ever-waiting press" ("Marvin and Tappan Head Lysander-Van Buren").

satisfying than to be involved in repurposing what had been a Jesuit facility into the Skä·noñh—Great Law of Peace Center.

The success of this effort required that we converse with the Onondaga Nation leadership through a collaboration with educational institutions and community organizations in the greater Syracuse area. These included Syracuse University, the State University of New York College of Environmental Science and Forestry (SUNY-ESF), Le Moyne College (a Jesuit College), Empire State University, Onondaga Community College, the Matilda Joselyn Gage Foundation, and the Onondaga Historical Association. Planning also extended to a wide variety of other community groups and organizations including the Syracuse Center of Excellence, NOON, the Onondaga Environmental Institute (OEI), and the Onondaga Shoreline Heritage Restoration (OSHR).

The site is part of Onondaga Lake Park, which is owned by Onondaga County. The Onondaga Historical Association has a contract with Onondaga County to manage the site. While collaboration is necessary for this project, it is a very complicated and delicate process. By focusing on a values-driven approach, we have been able to navigate deeply held political divides. We are straddled between local governments and sovereign nations, public and private institutions, and Indigenous and settler-colonial orientations to the land. Although this venture is exciting, it is also challenging in that at every turn we are made aware of the deep cultural differences that exist. Nevertheless, collaboration is fundamental to Indigenous protocol, and keeping to the Great Law of Peace helps us acknowledge that each party needs to realize the tangible benefits of the Skä·noñh— Great Law of Peace Center.

The Narrative

The collaborative wanted to clearly amplify the voice of the Onondaga Nation. We decided early in the planning process that we did not want to achieve a balanced view of history but, rather, to present, for the first time, a strong Haudenosaunee perspective on their culture and history. One can read the Jesuit or historical accounts of the "Iroquois" in any library. To hear this history from the perspective of the Haudenosaunee leadership themselves is unique. Ironically, it is the high-tech environment of video screens and touch pads that allows for the Indigenous message of the Haudenosaunee to be communicated. Over thirty hours of interviews, mostly with leadership of the Onondaga Nation, have been edited down to six four- to six-minute video stations that are positioned throughout the center.

The six separate messages communicated at the Skä·noñh—Great Law of Peace Center are as follows:

1. Skä·noñh: Onondaga welcome greeting—"peace" and "wellness" only obtained through proper relationship with the natural world
2. Thanksgiving address: "Words That Come Before All Else"; "Bringing Minds Together"
3. Creation: Natural world prepares the Earth for human beings
4. Great Law of Peace:
    a. Peacemaker, Jikonsaseh, Hiawatha, Tadodaho
    b. Established at Onondaga Lake over one thousand years ago
5. European contact and genocide:
    a. Doctrine of Christian discovery, Jesuit-fortified mission
    b. Two Row Wampum, colonialism, Sullivan-Clinton Campaign, George Washington's Canandaigua Treaty Belt, Indian boarding schools
6. Haudenosaunee influences:
    a. Western democracy, women's rights movement, lacrosse, environment, regenerative agriculture, United Nations

Skä·noñh

The visitor enters the Skä·noñh Center and is welcomed with the greeting *Nya weñha Skä·noñh*, which means in Onondaga, "Thank you for being well." People who watch and listen to this welcome video learn that *Skä·noñh* is also the Onondaga word for "peace." As Clan Mother Freida Jacques says, "Peace, but in a deep way." Tadodaho Sid Hill explains, "Peace is only attained when human beings are in proper relationship with the natural world." This is the theme that unifies the values of the Haudenosaunee and is woven throughout the Skä·noñh Center. In this welcome exhibit, we introduce visitors to the Haudenosaunee. We do not use the derogatory term "Iroquois" because renaming was a colonizing tactic of assimilation used by the French Jesuits. Haudenosaunee is the ancient name that emanated from the natural world. The importance of maintaining language and ceremonies is fundamental to the survival of the Haudenosaunee. The videos in the center are designed for the non-Haudenosaunee visitor, but we have already found that people from different Indigenous communities also benefit from these lessons.

Thanksgiving Address, or "Words That Come Before All Else"

The second stop on the tour is dedicated to the Thanksgiving Address, or *Ganonhanyonh* (Words That Come Before All Else). This is an ancient protocol with eighteen separate elements that is given at the opening and at the closing of every Longhouse meeting. It is also recited at many other ceremonial events. It is not a prayer, but an address of gratitude, acknowledging all the living beings who maintain their duties and responsibilities for keeping the world alive. These beings are Human People, Mother Earth, Water, Fish, Plants, Food Plants, Medicine Herbs, Animals, Trees, Birds, Four Winds, Thunder Beings, Sun, Grandmother Moon, Stars, Enlightened Teachers, the Creator, and Closing Words. The recitation of the Thanksgiving Address can last for hours or minutes, depending on the context and the wishes of the orator. After each nation of beings is thanked, the refrain "Now our minds are one" is spoken. This unifies all intelligence of the natural world in a consensus. Clan Mother Freida Jacques says in the video, "Human beings are just a part of Life, they are not in charge of Life." It's pivotal to understand this as a core aspect of

Indigenous values. For many, these ideas are very big, and these big ideas are kept in big places, like in religion. For Indigenous Peoples, though, they are an inherited, and inherent, truth.

Creation

The Haudenosaunee story of creation is long and involved, usually taking a week or more to recite in Longhouse. At Skä·noñh, we have had to reduce this story to a four-minute video in order to keep the visitor's attention. We decided to focus on the basic values of the Haudenosaunee creation story, which recounts how a pregnant Sky Woman fell to Earth, which was submerged under water, and how beings of the natural world scrambled to prepare a safe place for her landing. Aquatic birds rose up and with joined outstretched wings were able to break her fall. Great Sea Turtle offered his back, where they gently placed her. Noticing that she had seeds in her clutched hands, others joined in to locate some mud, so that her seeds could be planted; various animals dove deep into the waters searching for it, but their attempts failed. It was finally a muskrat who was able to dive the deepest, and when he reappeared and released the small clump of mud from his claw, he gasped his final breath. With that bit of earth, Sky Woman began her first dance of gratitude, sweetly caressing the soil with her steps as she moved in the counterclockwise direction of Life. As she continued dancing upon Turtle's back, the soil began to grow, eventually expanding into Turtle Island. As Robin Kimmerer says in the video, the first interaction between humans and animals is one of care, which indicates that the Earth is alive and is feminine. As time went on, Sky Woman gave birth to First Woman, who thrived on the new Earth. One night she was impregnated by the West Wind, and she eventually gave birth to twin boys. The first was born the normal way, but after the second broke through her armpit, she died. From her head sprouted the Three Sisters—Corn, Beans, and Squash—and, from her heart, Sacred Tobacco. The twins were raised by Sky Woman, and, as they played the competitive game of Dehontsigwa'ehs, the Earth came to life. When the benign twin created the berries, the opposing twin placed thorns on it. The conflicts and competitions got so intense that the Creator eventually separated the twins into Day and Night, Sky and Earth, Life and Death. Through the game of Dehontsigwa'ehs, the Creator Twins created the world. Values of exchanges between human beings and the natural world are evidenced in this epic story of Creation. The notion of Skä·noñh is also the story's primary element.

The Great Law of Peace

The Great Law of Peace was founded at Onondaga Lake well over one thousand years ago. Today, the Haudenosaunee gather for ten days each year listening to the recitation of this story from respected traditional orators who, in their respective languages (Mohawk, Oneida, Onondaga, Cayuga, Seneca, and Tuscarora), deliver the Peacemaker's original instructions. Certain features of these stories are encoded within ancient wampum belts that everyone is encouraged to touch, for they bring the original instructions to life.

Long after the world was created, the Haudenosaunee lived peacefully upon Turtle Island, but, in time, they began ignoring their responsibilities and slipping from the Creator's original instructions. The people began to bicker and, soon, to argue, eventually escalating to full-blown warfare, when blood was shed across the land. The chaos was felt so far and wide that it eventually reached the Peacemaker, a Wyandot man of special powers, talents, and abilities, born to a virgin mother on the northern shore of Lake Ontario near the Bay of Quinte. One night, his grandmother was approached in a dream by a spirit being who said of her grandson, "He will be a messenger of the Creator and will bring peace and harmony to the people on Earth."

The Peacemaker was aware of all the bloodshed among the Five Nations, especially that coming from the most feared cannibal and powerful sorcerer of all, the Tadodaho. The Peacemaker soon embarked on his journey to restore Skä·noñh to bring peace to the warring nations. He carved a canoe from White Stone and crossed Lake Ontario, entering the lands of the Haudenosaunee, who, seeing his White Stone Canoe, realized that he had special powers, and heeded his instruction to return home to their people.

The Peacemaker next encountered a woman named Jikonsaseh, who demonstrated great love for her people. Because of her big heart, she would provide aid and comfort to warriors fighting on both sides by feeding and housing them, mending their clothes, and listening to their stories, but nourishing them, she was told, enabled them to return to their path of violence, perpetuating harm and grief. Instead, the Peacemaker told Jikonsaseh to take a specified number of women into the woods, where they were to follow his instructions. They would each be approached by a single animal, bird, or fish, and this would identify their clan family. In reestablishing the clan system, the necessary realignment was made with the natural world. Because Jikonsaseh was first to accept his message of Skä·noñh, the Peacemaker declared that women would carry clanship and bear the responsibility for protecting their clan lineage. Additional instructions followed: Clan Mothers would name all children within their specified clan; Clan Mothers would choose their Clan Hoyane, "Men of the Good Mind," and they would have the authority to remove him from office; and they would determine the ceremonial cycles. The "Hoyane" title is nonhierarchical—the opposite of "chief." They are chosen according to their ability to use Skä·noñh, to bring minds together into agreement. They are extraordinarily adept at this skill, and it is for that reason they are chosen. Good-mindedness, or Skä·noñh, facilitates equity among human and nonhuman beings in the natural world. After meeting Jikonsaseh, the Peacemaker then traveled to spread the message of peace to all the newly established Hoyane of the Five Nations and their clan families.

Traveling from village to village, the Peacemaker next encountered Hayenhwátha' (Hiawatha), a gifted orator of peace who had lost his voice due to deep grief over the death of his seven beloved daughters. Unable to function in a normal human way, he wandered aimlessly throughout the territory. When he arrived south of Onondaga at Tully Lake, he gave a command to the birds and witnessed the waterfowl rise up from the water with such force that they carried the water with them. As he walked along the lake bottom, he picked up the small shells of freshwater clams and placed them in his deerskin pouch. After he had passed across the lake, the waterfowl returned to the water. On the shore he began making strings of shells, which was the first use of wampum. He said, "If I found or met anyone burdened with grief as I am, I would use these shell strings to console them. I would lift the words of condolence with these strands of beads, and these beads would become words with which I would address them." Unfortunately, however, Hayenhwátha' was unable to resolve his own grief.

Hayenhwátha' then met the Peacemaker, who took his bag of wampum shells and fashioned wampum strings that would relate to his body. The Peacemaker removed the lump from his throat so he could speak, then wiped the tears from his eyes so he could see, and, finally, brushed away the dust of death from his ears so he could hear. With the wampum strings and the Peacemaker's words, Hayenhwátha's grief was finally lifted. This ceremony uplifted the mind, spirit, and body of the grieving Hayenhwátha', making him once again a fully functioning human being. This condolence wampum ceremony became the way in which all visitors were to be greeted by the Haudenosaunee. The recognition of grief was seen as not only fundamental in helping to clear hearts and minds but also vital to restoring Skä·noñh.

It was determined by the Peacemaker that the condolence ceremony would be used to raise all Hoyane, and, to this day, wampum is central to condoling new Hoyane and raising them into their life office. Wampum is also woven into all treaty belts, as a reminder that broken agreements quickly return all those involved to a state of warfare. Wampum is also used to address grief when one has lost a loved one.

The Peacemaker, Hayenhwátha', and Jikonsaseh then brought all Five Nations under this Great Law of Peace, so that, together, they could approach the dreaded Tadodaho. Without Tadodaho joining this peace, it would fail. The Peacemaker explained that one nation alone is like one arrow: it can be easily broken. However, if you take five arrows, bundled together with the sinew of a deer, they will not break. Likewise, when Five Nations bring minds together as one through Skä·noñh, they, too, not only become impervious to breaking, but grow stronger from attracting others to join under the protection of the Great Tree of Peace. All living beings connected to, and through, one another—these are values of the Haudenosaunee.

The Peacemaker, with forty-nine Hoyane, used the power of their good minds to transform Tadodaho's thinking from sorcery and death to the protection of peace. United, they were able to comb the snakes from Tadodaho's hair and straighten his twisted body. Using their combined strength, the Peacemaker and Hayenhwátha' restored Tadodaho's humanity. Once a grotesque body of death, the new Tadodaho stood erect like a tall tree. He would be the only Hoyane chosen by the men, and his title would be without a clan so that he could represent all clans. Deer antlers were placed upon his headdress to represent his new status as the defender of the Great Law of Peace. The Peacemaker negotiated an important role for Tadodaho in the newly established confederacy: he would have the authority to call the Grand Council together, which would meet in his territory at Onondaga, and he would also be responsible for ensuring that all the Hoyane would keep the good mind and maintain Skä·noñh. This decisive moment completed the circle of unity through the transformation of one of the most heinous minds in the land.

The lesson for all of us is that, no matter how dysfunctional a society can be, there is a way back to peace. Through the Peacemaker's instructions, Jikonsaseh helped reconnect the women to Mother Earth and establish the clan system; Hayenhwátha' was relieved of his grief through wampum; and, by bringing *all* minds together, they were able to bring Tadodaho to humanity. This peace is so powerful, it has been successfully maintained for thousands of years, and it was this governmental structure that inspired the Founding Fathers of the United States.

Contributing to this union, a game of Dehontsigwa'ehs was played among the Five Nations at Onondaga Lake. Together they planted the Great Tree of Peace (Skaęhetsi'kona), which would represent the clan system of the Haudenosaunee Confederacy in having reestablished Skä·noñh. The Tree of Peace serves as a metaphor for the way peace can grow if it is nurtured. Like a tall tree, peace can provide protection and comfort. And, like a pine tree, peace spreads its branches to create a place where we can gather and renew ourselves. Like the White Pine, peace also creates large white roots (*tsyoktehækęæta'kona*) that rise out of the ground so that people can trace their journey to the source. If anyone truly desires peace, they can follow the sacred white roots to the capital of the Confederacy here at Onondaga, where they can learn of the words of the Peacemaker, whose message is that we all can nurture the Tree of Peace.

The Peacemaker had the warriors uproot a great white pine, which left below a gaping hole. The fifty Hoyane and warriors threw their weapons of war beneath the Great Tree, where they were swept away by an underground stream, at which time the tree was raised again. This is the origin of the phrase "Bury the hatchet." The Peacemaker said that the Hoyane will be standing on the Earth like trees, deeply rooted in the land, with strong trunks, all the same height (being equal) in front of their people, to protect them, with the influential power of the Good Mind. Atop the tree perches an eagle, because of his clear far-reaching vision to protect the peace.

European Contact and Genocide

Initial cultural exchanges led to an immediate clash of values. The Haudenosaunee world was turned upside down by the invasion of European colonists, who came to exploit the land and subdue Indigenous Peoples. For the first time in thousands of years, radical ideas of conquest and ownership invaded and upset the natural state of Skä·noñh.

The concept of "land ownership" was inconceivable to Indigenous Peoples because it was the vital landscape from which their identity emanated. The question is not "Who is the rightful owner of a certain land?" but "How could anyone believe they have the authority to own land—to own your mother?"

From first contact, Indigenous Peoples in the Americas questioned what kinds of people would exploit the Earth that sustains them, or choose to live under the domination of men, governments, or gods. What kind of society abuses women and children? What kind of society pollutes water and desecrates the land? Who are these people that never bathe? The Haudenosaunee raise Hoyane who are most gifted in the art of persuasion so they can bring minds together under the Great Law of Peace and flourish. These abilities were developed beyond anything European colonizers or intellectuals of the time had even begun to comprehend. There were no discussions or even concepts of "equity" or "freedom" that included women, let alone the prospect that the landscape could be part of that equation.

Instead, Europeans arrived using Christianity to justify their right of conquest and the subjugation of Indigenous Peoples living on land they considered terra nullius (empty lands), or there for the taking, to create a new world order. This resulted in catastrophic cultural, spiritual, environmental, and political consequences and profound turmoil, including the loss of untold millions of human lives through warfare and disease, as well as most of their homelands.

What happened in 1656 between the Onondaga and the Jesuits at the site of the mission of Sainte Marie de Gannentaa is a microcosm of the larger story. We are left with only two sources of opposing information by which we try to understand this past: the accounts given of seventeenth-century Jesuits who traveled here and left in 1658, or the oral history of the condolence wampum belts of the Onondaga. By looking back to the first encounters, we can examine the lingering impacts of these events.

In addition to friendships there were wars and land thefts. Also discussed are treaties and their violations, Indian boarding schools, and other challenges to the survival of the Haudenosaunee.

Continuance and Contributions

Remarkably, the Onondaga Nation survived the tidal waves of colonization and, to this day, continue to live within their original homelands. Their council fire still burns, and the Great Law of Peace still continues to inspire the decisions of the Hoyane, Clan Mothers, and Faithkeepers.

Most US citizens are unaware of how profoundly their culture has been shaped by the Haudenosaunee or what took place at Onondaga Lake. Many of the best and most admired attributes of American society have their roots among the Haudenosaunee, among whom early colonists saw freedom and liberty at work. It was a practical model of how a society could respect the rights of all living beings, with everyone working toward the common good. Ideas such as popular initiatives, town meetings, caucuses, women's rights, and representative government were being practiced here long before the American Revolution. The colonial leaders took great inspiration from the Haudenosaunee Great Law of Peace, observing how their influence extended throughout the northeast. They studied Haudenosaunee political protocols and employed them for many generations in making peace treaties with many other Native nations.

The Haudenosaunee inspired the Founding Fathers of Western democracy and the Founding Mothers of the women's rights movement. Settlers and contemporary agriculturalists have long recognized the importance of regenerative multicrop agricultural practices (which simultaneously produced more topsoil). Their foodways and medicines have transformed the world, just as scientists continue to be inspired by traditional ecological knowledge and practices today.

Indigenous Values Initiative (IVI)

It is my deeply held belief that it is our job as educators, and as human beings, to contribute to this continuance as well. This is how we maintain and promote Indigenous values within our society.

With the opening in November 2015 of the Skä·noñh—Great Law of Peace Center, we decided it was necessary to create a new nonprofit organization to continue to promote Haudenosaunee values. This same year, we had grieved the loss of Tonya Gonnella Frichner, who had founded the American Indian Law Alliance

(AILA), a nongovernmental organization (NGO) that advocates for Haudenosaunee and Indigenous Peoples' rights and responsibilities to the Earth at the UN. Before Tonya's passing, she transferred AILA's leadership to Betty Lyons, Snipe Clan and Citizen of the Onondaga Nation.[21] Tonya, who was Lyons's "auntie," had been training Betty for this work long before her illness. Also in 2015, the IVI became AILA's fiscal sponsor so we could work in a supportive role to Lyons and AILA and help organize events around the UN Permanent Forum on Indigenous Issues.[22] This event brings in thousands of Indigenous Peoples from around the world who often lack the status to speak on the UN floor.

Lyons and AILA have been an effective conduit in lending a voice to these silenced Indigenous nations. Sometimes these travelers are murdered, vanish, or face imprisonment when they return home because they come to the UN to expose how multinational corporations continue to pollute and destroy their homelands as they exploit their resources. IVI and AILA work together on a number of other events, always educating the wider public on the traditions and challenges facing Indigenous Peoples.[23]

21. To see more about Tonya and Betty, see the American Indian Law Alliance website, https://aila.ngo/about/ (accessed 27 December 2022).
22. The work at the UN on behalf of Indigenous Peoples is largely done through the Economic and Social Council (ECOSOC). The United States and other "First World" member states have withdrawn their support of ECOSOC, leaving it in an underfunded and relatively powerless position. Nevertheless, it remains committed to putting forward reports from the UN Permanent Forum on Indigenous Issues. See https://www.un.org/development/desa/indigenouspeoples (accessed 27 December 2022).
23. The Indigenous Values Initiative logo "The Eagle's View" depicts the tree that represents the Great Law of Peace of the Haudenosaunee (Iroquois) Confederacy of Five Nations: Mohawk, Oneida, Onondaga, Cayuga, and Seneca (Tuscarora joined in the eighteenth century). This union is reflected in the five needle clusters on the White Pine, which was planted over 1,000 years ago by the Peacemaker at Onondaga Lake. Planted on Turtle's back (Earth), this Great Tree of Peace influenced Western democracy, women's rights, Deyhontsigwa'ehs (lacrosse), and sustainable agriculture. Its White Roots continue to grow in four directions today.

3. "The Eagle's View." Indigenous Values Initiative (IVI). Logo design by Sandra Bigtree.

IVI, which was incorporated in 2014, has focused on three areas. First, the message of the Haudenosaunee must be maintained at the Skä·noñh—Great Law of Peace Center and educate predominantly non-native people that these tenets underlie their American identity, thus renarrating their foundational myths. The Great Peace thrived for over one thousand years and came to transform the world through their values, which are oriented to the Earth. IVI connects scholars, activists, and others with the Haudenosaunee to present and challenge new ways of thinking. Faculty, students, and staff at a variety of educational institutions can work through IVI as a resource for curriculum development.

Collaborations in the Heartland   47

Second, beginning in 2013, IVI sponsored a series of Haudenosaunee Wooden Stick Festivals at Onondaga Lake, the Onondaga Nation, and Syracuse University. This was to bring attention to the origin of Dehontsigwa'eh's, or lacrosse, as a game of peace that was played during the founding of the Great Law of Peace and helped to establish reciprocity in our relationships with the Earth. Figure 4 is our logo from 2017, the year of our most ambitious event, when a festival at the Onondaga Nation was held simultaneously with the Lacrosse All-Stars North American Invitational, an international box lacrosse tournament. This culminated with a scrimmage at the Syracuse University Carrier Dome between the Haudenosaunee Nationals, Israel's National team and Syracuse University's men's lacrosse team. This has proven a very powerful way of communicating the values of the Haudenosaunee through a game that is greatly loved and admired all over the world.[24] The game is also played in the Sky World and was played as the world was created long ago.

Third, since 2014, IVI has hosted regular conferences on the Doctrine of Christian Discovery (DOCD, described in more detail in chapter 6). Figure 5 is the flyer for the co-sponsored event "Mother Earth's Pandemic: The Doctrine of Discovery." In August 2020, IVI, AILA, and Syracuse University brought together an international array of speakers comprised of Indigenous Peoples and their allies in a conference that drew over six hundred attendees.[25] Since the conference, the talks have been viewed over 10,000 times, and the Doctrine of Discovery website has been visited over 250,000 times per month. The artwork *Broken Treaties* was created in 2014 by Brandon Lazore of the Onondaga Nation. The Haudenosaunee man with wampum belts draped over his arms is wearing a gas mask as

---

24. See "Deyhontsigwa'ehs: The Creator's Game, Lacrosse Weekend 2022," accessed 27 December 2022, https://indigenousvalues.org/laxweekend21/.

25. "Mother Earth's Pandemic" was transformative in our ongoing series of events on the Doctrine of Christian Discovery. For more, see our online description at https://indigenousvalues.org/mother-earths-pandemic/ (accessed 27 December 2022).

48   The Urgency of Indigenous Values

4. Haudenosaunee Wooden Stick Festival logo, digitized from the work of Tracy Thomas.

he stands in front of the stark representation of a dollar bill with the American flag as a backdrop. The image is prophetic of what happens when promises are broken. This perspective stems from past relationships that show the disjunction between a Haudenosaunee system of values and those of a settler-colonial system of values. This image captures the message in this book.

With the establishment of IVI, the collaborative work between Indigenous Peoples is better assured in our region of the world and beyond. We are most concerned with furthering the story of the Skä·noñh—Great Law of Peace Center as the new narrative that is transforming the way people of all ages think about their past,

Collaborations in the Heartland   49

5. Mother Earth's Pandemic: The Doctrine of Discovery was an international conference hosted virtually by IVI and AILA in August 2020. This image is based on Brandon Lazore's print *Broken Treaties* (2014) and brings together many of the things around the Doctrine of Christian Discovery.

present, and future. It is work like this that must be done all over the world to truly further and reestablish Indigenous values.

Conclusions

"History" based exclusively in the writings of non–Native American "experts" has silenced authentic Indigenous voices. Therefore, the work of the Skä·noñh Center has focused on presenting the Great

Law of Peace as told by the Haudenosaunee themselves, as an ancient yet vital reality today.

We promote the Haudenosaunee understanding of Skä·noñh from its time of origin at Onondaga Lake through the ages of discovery and conquest, from the founding of the United States to the present. It cannot be understated that the ancient protocol of the Longhouse tradition, or the Great Law of Peace, has been continuously practiced by the Onondaga Nation in this place for over one thousand years. The nature of this collaboration is historic and unprecedented in our area. The result of the activities of the organizations and institutions coordinated by allied supporters over the last several years has resulted in a real desire for non-native people wanting to know more. I, personally, as a scholar, a person, and a descendent of settler-colonial people, have found this to be tremendously inspiring. Descendants of settler-colonial people—we "white people"—are coming to understand that knowing about the values of the Haudenosaunee and other Indigenous Peoples is critical for our shared future survival. This project *exemplifies and grounds* the orientation of this book. Quite simply, there is *an urgency* in understanding and appreciating Indigenous values, not just as a cultural form of the past but as a living tradition of the present and a way to realize the possibility of a viable future.

The Skä·noñh—Great Law of Peace Center is both the culmination of a collaborative methodology rooted in the History of Religions as well as a material manifestation of what collaboration can create. It demonstrates an educational advocacy and an appreciation of both Haudenosaunee values and Indigenous values. In this way, it seeks to authentically represent their voices and address their concerns about the past, present, and future. It is to the continuation of this work that I dedicate this book.

2

Indigenous Values

> Religion is solely the creation of the scholar's study. Religion has no independent existence apart from the academy. For this reason, the student of religion, and most particularly the historian of religion, must be relentlessly self-conscious. Indeed, this self-consciousness constitutes his primary expertise, his foremost object of study.
> —Jonathan Z. Smith, *Imagining Religion: From Babylon to Jonestown*

Smith's statement that religion is a construct of the academy best illustrates how conceptually problematic "Indigenous religions" is as a valid category. It also helps bring to light the long history of conflicts and aggressive interpretive moves by scholars of religion that have wreaked havoc upon the people to whom the category has been applied. "Indigenous religions" is a descriptive term that reflects back a disturbing history to academic culture. While Smith's call for a "relentless self-consciousness" is a requirement for studying any religion, I will argue that this is particularly important as we make the shift from "religion" to "values" when describing Indigenous traditions. In essence, this is where the work starts.

Many people are shedding older categorical phrases like "primitive," "native," "aboriginal," "archaic," "tribal," "savage," and the like. Adopting "Indigenous" and "Indigeneity" is descriptive of these same groups of peoples. Simultaneously, this describes a certain mode of religiousness that locates the sacred *in the world*. This is in contrast to "global" religions, which tend to locate the sacred *outside of* or *beyond the world*. Many of these terms that enjoyed acceptance in the past are outmoded and pejorative now. In general, controversies over the use of these terms have more to do with the degree to which they were used instrumentally by colonial forces to subjugate and control Indigenous Peoples. The terms did not emerge from within the communities themselves.[1]

Indigenous Peoples are, of course, found on every continent around the world. Their existence pre-dates the colonial nation-states that took control of their territories and today retain the power to legitimate their existence at the UN. There are Indigenous Peoples who are still practicing their ancient traditions while remaining in close proximity to these nation-states throughout Africa, the Americas, Australia, Asia, Polynesia, Europe, and the rest of the world.

The term "Indigenous" was first used by a delegation of Native American leaders from across the United States on their trip to the UN in Geneva, Switzerland, in 1977. Before leaving, they decided that it would be necessary to present themselves before the international community as peoples being uniquely connected to their place of origin, yet sharing in the same orientations to the Earth that defined their uniqueness. The account of this historical trip can be found in the book *Basic Call to Consciousness*.[2] Since first introducing "Indigenous" to the UN, the term has now come to represent Indigenous Peoples around the world.

Deploying the category of "Indigenous" or "Indigeneity" clearly expresses a value system that is oriented to the Earth, with a wide-ranging and diversified cross-cultural field of similarly held values. The term can be considered global in scope because you can find these traditions all over the world. Indigenous traditions do not

---

1. My first job out of graduate school was at the University of Missouri, Columbia, as titled faculty in "tribal religions." I couldn't have articulated it fully then, but the title really bothered me. I managed to have it permanently changed to Indigenous Religions.

2. Oren Lyons, a Faithkeeper at the Onondaga Nation and the designated speaker on the 1977 trip to Geneva, related this story to me about the importance of the term "Indigenous" when working at the UN.

adhere to a single institutional or creedal structure. Traditions are made up of radically diverse people, places, languages, and ceremonial traditions where a way of life is derived from and defined by a place, or home. Indigenous Peoples have adopted this category as being descriptive of what they regard as critical to their sense of "being in" the world, "being in" their own laws and values and tied to their original instructions.[3]

"Indigeneity," therefore, defines an orientation to the world that radically contrasts with those of the world's "great" or "global" religions, like Christianity, Islam, and Buddhism. "Indigeneity" implies a unified system of values, not a unified religion, which is fundamentally distinct from, yet has the ability to "speak" to, the global religions. Thus, Indigeneity helps to clarify the opposing value systems operating between Indigenous and global traditions that emanate from these radically different orientations to the Earth.

Indigeneity is *descriptive of a particular type of religiousness*, not a particular religion. Diversity of traditions is implicit because Indigenous Peoples inhabit different landscapes: the land diversifies the people, which explains why these traditions never became institutionalized as a nationalistic state practice. Unlike the tendency within global religions such as Christianity, there is no aspiration for a single unifying theme, deity, or community of practitioners. Global religions tend to resort to uniformity of belief and practice, which can lead to religious intolerance, fundamentalisms, strife, and conflict. Instead, Indigenous Peoples are united through their orientation to the sacred manifestations in the land, or that being intrinsic to the material world. The unifying characteristics that join "great" religious traditions together, however, come through their orientations

---

3. Work at the UN since 1977 has included efforts for Indigenous Peoples to be recognized as human beings with community rights, not just individual rights. The plural "s" in Indigenous Peoples has been an international effort over the last several decades to change the old designation of "populations," which is also used to define herds of reindeer, to peoples. Where appropriate, this text will utilize the plural.

to their faith-based beliefs systems as written in creedal texts, or that which is extrinsic from the material world.

Today, approximately five hundred million people around the world describe themselves as "Indigenous." They have all suffered the consequence of this collision of worldviews and value systems. Colonialism subjected Indigenous Peoples to religions other than their own through aggressive efforts such as the forced implementation of boarding schools and missions around the world. Until a generation ago, these were funded and jointly run by governmental organizations and Christian denominations in an effort to assimilate and evangelize the man and kill the Indian. Sadly, if there was resistance, the latter became all too real.

This book also responds to the increasing popularity of the category of "Indigenous" and "Indigeneity" and explores why it has become so significant. It has been taken up by a number of different constituencies and is, per Smith's statement, a recent creation that has now taken on a life of its own, well outside of Smith's scholarly study. It is essential, even urgent, that the implications of this categorical shift be acknowledged and assessed. What are the consequences of this move in the academic study of religion for our understanding of the general phenomenon of religion? What are the consequences for our understanding of people who have embraced this category, or aspects of this category, as their own? What are the accompanying shifts in theories of religion and methods for studying religion? I argue that the concept of "Indigenous" profoundly transforms the religious landscape. After seriously entertaining this category, I argue that we can no longer think about "religion" the same way.

This book also provides an overview of the problems and possibilities of the category in several excellent specific studies. Books on Native American, aboriginal, First Nations of Canada, and African traditions, to name a few, are available to illuminate the specific attributes. This book is to be used as a companion to those texts to help orient readers to the wider theoretical issues in religion while learning more about themselves through this collision of worldviews. At a minimum, I would like this book to help descendants of settler-colonial people appreciate why they should care about the Indigenous.

The Problem with "Religion"

For Indigenous Peoples, the concept of "religion" itself has often been associated with the culturally intrusive practices of colonialists and conquerors. Religion has most often been utilized as a means to destroy societies through missionization, evangelization, and conversion. It has been used to justify a host of destructive cultural forces including forced assimilation, destruction of languages, relocations, destruction of land, pollution of water and air, education, and to justify the "natural inferiority" of Indigenous Peoples. In contrast, Christianity and other global religions understand the sacred to be separate from other material dimensions of life. Religion is not in itself a discrete area of human activity; this makes little sense in an Indigenous worldview. There is no aspect of a given life that is held distinct from the rest that could ever be accurately described as "religious."

Yet Indigenous Peoples readily acknowledge the sacred and spiritual dimensions of a living world. Their traditions assume the ongoing interaction between human beings and all other types of beings, including spiritual beings. Ceremonies are created and performed in order to interact with other beings within and associated with animals, plants, earth, stars, wind, rain, thunder, lightning, rocks, ancestors, and other nonhuman beings. For these reasons, many Indigenous Peoples prefer to think of their traditions as *spirituality* rather than *religion*.

It is challenging to find an adequate term in English that approaches this Indigenous sensibility. This problem of language continually limits our collective academic enterprise. Academic concepts have hindered intercultural understanding and have generally degraded these traditions. Part of the Protestant Christian legacy of the academy is our tendency to think of knowledge as all-encompassing and limitless. The Christian God is believed to be omniscient, or all-seeing and all-knowing. Indigenous religions, however, assume that all human understandings and interpretations are limited. All of our knowledge is contingent on some other living being outside of ourselves and therefore necessarily collaborative.

Because of the difficulties with the term "religion," allow me to submit that the term "values" is the best descriptive category that we have, as academics, to discuss Indigenous Peoples and their traditions. "Values" implies a real-world assessment of a relationship between the world and a human community. What a culture values can be completely materialistic, as in an object's transactional value—in an exchange system—or it can refer to deeply held moral frameworks as a culture's value system. Because "values" traverses both practical and moral frameworks, it expresses fairly well an Indigenous sensibility.

"Values" also implies a religiousness that can be apart from an institutional framework. "Indigenous values" resonates closer with what is referred to as "religion" while also challenging it. To explore the consequences of Indigenous values, we will return to some earlier insights from previous generations of scholars of religion regarding these traditions. In the end, it will be important for us to reconceptualize the nature of religion so that it can include Indigenous traditions. Ultimately, to understand the future of religion, we must understand the past as "values."

The Possibilities of "Religion"

The ambiguity of the term "religion" can be liberating, too. The central organizing principle of my department at Syracuse University, as is true for many other departments, is not the certainty of religion, but the question "What is religion?"

Although my colleagues and I all teach about religion (e.g., Judaism, Christianity, Islam, Buddhism, Hinduism, Indigenous religions), we conceptualize "religion" very differently from one another. We could never agree on a single definition of the concept itself, and my department is not unique. There is a tremendous diversity of opinion in all departments of religion regarding its essential characteristics. To some degree, this diversity of opinion can be accounted for by the diversity of places and contexts where religion is taught. Seminaries, secular universities, technical colleges, and the like all develop their classes, programs, and departments of religions very differently from one another.

The debates about how "religion" is to be defined have been ongoing for generations. If one were to assemble the most used and agreed upon definitions of religion over the last 150 years from all the leading intellectual giants, one would find that there is virtually no agreement. Some cynics may define religion as a diseased mental state—a kind of psychosis—while others have seen it as a resource for ultimate, all-encompassing truths. Some have theorized religion as being the social glue that holds people and communities together, while others view it as the solitary pursuit of a questing individual. Some have thought of religion as primarily a feature of human experience, particularly the experience of death, while others have tended to see it as a duty or cultural responsibility in which the person participates in ceremonies as a way of perpetuating their tradition of maintaining balance in an interacting cosmos. Some see religion as oppressive while others see it as a force that liberates the oppressed. None of these interpretations are any more right or wrong than the last. The point here is that religion can be all of these things simultaneously. It is contentious ground because of its ambiguous nature.

However, the understanding that religion is ambiguous, while readily acknowledged within the academic study of religion, tends not to be shared in the wider culture. In fact, just the opposite seems to hold true in the media. Religion is seen as a "thing," and its meaning is understood to be readily apparent. Most often in the United States, religion for many of us is not ambiguous at all, but a defining reality, even a thing or object that exists independent of human imaginings. Most people have an institutional concept of religion, as being embodied by a set of beliefs, rules, and rituals of a particular church, temple, mosque, or synagogue. Others have a superstitious or faith-based notion of religion, thinking of it as internal to the human heart or mind. Ironically, religion is most often regarded as deeply individualistic, which is often at odds with its cultural and social function. In any case, the sense of religion within mainstream culture is virtually always definite. It should be obvious to anyone, then, that the *phenomenon of religion* most often expresses its contentious and ambiguous nature rather than any level of certainty. Most often religion, for the religious, is a cipher, an uncertainty, a mystery at the center of human existence that cannot be unraveled or deciphered. The certainty in what defines "religion" has much to do with the imposition of order and control over a phenomenon that is always revealing itself in a great diversity of ways. Religion, in spite of generally popular belief, is always getting out of its conceptual box.

A contemporary example of this tension between religious occurrences and certainty would be the countless Marian apparitions—miraculous appearances of Mary, the Mother of Jesus Christ—that have appeared to Christians all over the world. This is a good example of the relationship between popular religion and how it can be made "official" by the church.

For our purposes, let's think of Marian apparitions as occurrences of the sacred, appearing to a particular people at a particular place and time, that are essentially chaotic religious mysteries, or ciphers, that emerge before they are ordered and controlled by the Catholic Church. This phenomenon is analogous to the relationship of Indigeneity to religion and exemplifies the ambiguity of "religion" in the academy. Is a Marian apparition a sure sign of religion? Mass psychosis? Hysteria? An externalization of trauma? Something else entirely? My intention here is to defamiliarize the familiar image of Mary, the Mother of Jesus—so we can understand how religious phenomena are generated through the difficulty of describing and defining them. How one understands a Marian apparition also weighs heavily on one's interpretive location.

Images of Mary have regularly appeared to people in a number of different contexts over centuries. Their varieties are too numerous to list, but it should be noted that they involve people of diverse economic positions, genders, ages, ethnicities, language families, geographical locations, and qualities of health. Mary appears in a variety of environments and media, including caves, hills, buildings, statues, icons and paintings, windows, clothing, trees, rocks, springs, and grease spots; oil, tears, blood, and other fluids are often associated with her as well. She appears with messages and often heals people that see and interact with her.

Catholics primarily witness and celebrate apparitions of Mary; these devotees are usually Christian, but not always. In spite of people generally associating them with Catholicism, very few Marian apparitions that have been viewed over the centuries have been officially recognized by the Catholic Church. While news of a new apparition spreads quickly among lay Catholics, it can actually take several years, decades, or even centuries for the Church to investigate and sanction the apparition. In other words, it takes some time for the institution of the Church to catch up to the phenomenon.

Our interest here is not the question of the apparitions' veracity, or how they express the truth of the Christian message, but the notion of when they can be considered actual religious events, or an official part of a religion. Does a religious occurrence start with the phenomenon (i.e., the appearance of Mary by those who have the ability to see and speak with her)? Or does its religious status begin with its institutional recognition by the Catholic Church? One could argue both ways, but I will emphasize the former as the orientation to religion that is most analogous to what has been called "Indigenous traditions."

As with Marian apparitions, religion results from the ambiguous appearance of a sacred reality to a group of people at a particular place and time. It is completely chaotic and seemingly random. The ongoing creative fountainhead of institutional religion is the chaotic "manifestation of the sacred" that may or may not be originally understood to be connected with religion. That said, *certainty*, with respect to religion, expresses the imposition of order onto the phenomenon, in this case by the institutional acceptance and sanctioning of a Marian apparition by the Catholic Church. For our purposes, this process can be seen as the movement of the Indigenous traditions orientation co-opted by a global religious theology.

The particularity of religion drops out of this movement. The more popular a religious phenomenon, the more ambiguous it is, and the less it is controlled by human culture or an institutional hierarchy. This is reflective of an Indigenous sensibility. If one were to catalog the varieties of Marian apparitions just within the United States—weeping statues, windows of buildings, salt stains on highways, potato chips, even on the rear end of a dog, to name just a few (just google it!)—they would seem to be completely random. The example of Marian apparitions illustrates how an Indigenous traditions sensibility is a source of religious inspiration and innovation throughout all religions, not just "tribal" or "primitive" societies.

Global religions, therefore, rely on Indigenous creativity and innovation to renew themselves. The strength of the category "Indigenous traditions" is that it can be utilized to see dimensions of all religions. Among the most religious people throughout human history are those who are sensitive to the *phenomena*, attuned and devoted to the appearances of the sacred that come as new messages from their local landscapes. In this sense, religious phenomena are the vital essence of all religious understandings. This, I would argue, characterizes an Indigenous traditions orientation.

The previous discussion of Marian apparitions is an example of the "hierophany," a "manifestation of the sacred," according to Mircea Eliade, the scholar who popularized the use of this phrase. For Eliade, all religions have their origin in and are founded by a hierophany. The hierophany, then, is the creative center of religious life.[4]

Two senses of the hierophany will be important throughout this book. The first is that the appearance of the sacred always takes place in the *material world;* the sacred *manifests* in the world. This is what noted historians of religions Charles H. Long and Davíd

---

4. See Eliade, *Myth of the Eternal Return.*

Carrasco refer to as the "*materiality* of religion" (emphasis added).[5] Although religion often deals with fundamental *spiritual realities*, these are not at odds with the material realities of the hierophany. There is a fundamental connection between spiritual and material life. Second, the hierophany itself is always associated with a founding point of origin: a place or land, a time, and a people. As with the Marian apparitions, it is through the hierophany that religion comes into being in a particular place. In spite of the fact that religions may evolve and move from their places of origin, there is an enormous prestige associated with where and how they came into existence. As we will discuss later, this is a very important aspect of Christianity, which historically has set itself as in vehement opposition to Indigenous Peoples and their traditions.

The sense of religion as connected with its founding is particularly important for Indigenous Peoples. The connection to a point of origin is, however, an essential part of virtually all religions. This is one reason why Indigenous Peoples and their traditions have been consistently referred to as "primitive," "archaic," and the like. While these are now understood to be pejorative terms, the intention of using these categories, according to thinkers like Tylor and Eliade, was to associate these people with the foundation of religion. To put it bluntly, the original meaning of these categories has been lost due to political and economic pressures using the characterization of Indigenous Peoples as an obstacle to the progression of an oppressive capitalistic system. These terms, at their most positive, connect specific groups of people with the original, founding character of the world's religions. The nature of the hierophany, like the phenomenon of the Marian apparition, is a physical appearance of a spiritual reality. By its nature, the hierophany is impossible to create, control, or subdue by human effort; it cannot be fully known, understood, or expressed by any single person, group of people, or tradition.

---

5. See Carrasco, *Imagination of Matter*.

Indigeneity requires us to radically reconceive the very nature of religion. For many scholars, religion is at the center of all human societies, and, by rethinking its nature, our understanding of what ultimately orients us to the world will shift. Thinking about Indigenous values, which are associated with the foundational aspects of religion, requires us to reorient ourselves to the essential character of human existence.

Indigenous, Indigeneity, Indigenousness, Indigenize

"Indigenous" is an adjective defined as "native; originating in and typical of a region or country; natural or inborn; and pertaining to plants, animals or *inhabitants*" (emphasis mine). Indigenousness, Indigeneity, or being Indigenous refers to a life being lived in a place. The emphasis here is on one's meaningful connection to the land. By extension, the religious worldviews of Indigenous Peoples refer to successful ways that human beings can meaningfully inhabit a place. As terms, "Indigeneity" and "Indigenousness" are less used but are necessary to describe an Indigenous relationship with the natural world. Indigeneity both defines characteristics of the relationship between specific groups of people to the world they inhabit, and it also describes a universally empirical human mode of being in the world. It calls attention to an attribute of all human communities that informs behavior, that connects human beings with each other and the nonhuman living world upon which humanity depends. Human survival, very literally, depends on fostering proper relationships with the living world. The terms "Indigeneity" and "Indigenousness" describe groups who self-consciously fashion their societies on their dynamic relationships with cohabitants such as animals, plants and other living beings.

Historically, academics have shared a lively interest in Indigenous Peoples, often viewing them as closer to the origins of religion and, therefore, foundational to civilization. Unfortunately, the same motivating factors that have led to captivation with Indigenous Peoples have simultaneously led to scholarly revulsion. Scholars of religion have imagined that, when observing the behaviors of ceremonies of sacrifice, for example, they were peering into the past and the essential origins of their own religion of the ancient Near East. The relationship between "primitive religions" and the "Semites" was a fascination of the renowned nineteenth-century Old Testament scholar W. Robertson Smith.[6] According to Robertson Smith, the importance of sacrifice exhibited an inability to distinguish between the actual living and nonliving among both primitives and ancient people; it was their inability to understand the difference between the living and dead worlds (instead of understanding that the entire world was alive) that measured their level of civilization. Sacrifice could be used to characterize these people and their traditions as demonic, backward, and uncivilized. Theories of the origins of religion were often used to justify domination, slavery, forced conversion, oppression, and, most importantly, the taking of Indigenous lands. Perhaps counterintuitively, for the colonizer it also indicated a simultaneous fascination and disgust with their own Christian origins: the religious measurement assigned for all things civilized. "Primitive religions" expressed an ambiguous relationship between religion and the self-perception of academic society.

In their most positive meaning, terms like "primitive," as used by scholars such as E. B. Tylor, indicated that Indigenous societies exhibit what is "primary" to human culture.[7] Thus, the category of "primitive religions" reveals that, while investigators of religion thought they were witnessing activities of primitive "others," they were also active in witnessing what they deemed to be essential and original in *themselves*. When they theorized the nature of primitive religions in the nineteenth century, they were simultaneously theorizing their own religious origins and thus the foundations of their understanding of civilization. It is critical to note that the fault lines of civilization fell on the determination of what was deemed to be

---

6. Smith, *Religion of the Semites*.
7. Tylor, *Religion in Primitive Culture*.

living and dead between the animated and the inert. This was how a given group prioritized which living beings mattered more and which living beings mattered less in determining whether or not they were civilized or not—in other words, how a hierarchy of living beings was expressed in a given groups' worldview.

"Indigenous," "Indigenousness," and "Indigeneity" are primarily about being connected to a place. While some human communities celebrate this as a meaningful connection and others do not, it is important to remember that a material need for survival connects everyone to their physical world. All human activities, ranging from ceremonial events to mundane tasks, take place somewhere, in some geographical location. We all have our places that mark us as people, like a hometown, neighborhood, region of the world, or country of origin. In the next section, I offer some suggestions of ways to think about the value of places, with the intention of de-exoticizing Indigenous traditions.

Where Are You From?

Everyone is from someplace. Asking someone, "Where are you from?" usually means, "Where were you born," or, "Where did you grow up?" In the globalized context, these are often different questions. Many people would not have a single answer to these questions. In any event, the questions imply a value judgment: "What place do you regard as most valuable to your sense of yourself?" They do, however, help strangers grasp the identity of a stranger. One could answer them in a variety of ways, depending on the context of the person who is asking, but the answer is value laden: both the question and the answer express an Indigenous value, or a sense of belonging to a place.

Indigenous values are completely oriented around the extended family. As opposed to the nuclear family, the extended family connects individual persons to far-ranging networks of mothers and fathers, siblings, cousins, aunts and uncles, grandparents, clans (patrilineal and matrilineal), moieties, and nations of the living and the dead.

Articulating where one is from determines to whom one is related. Ceremonial life for Indigenous Peoples often revolves around concerns for the continued health and well-being of the extended family, which is not limited to a human family but includes all nonhuman beings inhabiting the natural world. This view is often expressed in clan activities, ritual responsibilities, and healing ceremonies. For example, the Lakota saying *Mitakoyasin* ("All my relations," or "We are all related") highlights the nature of expansive understanding of the extended nonhuman family.[8]

Determining where one is from includes a whole host of relationships. For example, one's place of birth can mean one's citizenship, country of origin, affiliation with a nation-state, or international status. It can also determine one's language, culture, style of dress, or taste in food. A place of birth connects an individual to a lineage, a situation, and a landscape of relationships that include human history, as well as the flora and fauna of a place that has constituted one's life. A place of birth could be accidental and seen as incidental to the life of one's parents, but that does not preclude one from having a place of origin. Legally, even, it is imperative that one have an origin in some place. So, what does a place of origin mean?

Even though one's place of origin—or hometown—can only be determined by a single individual, it necessarily includes a host of others who are involved with that individual life. Birth itself is something that necessarily involves others. Indeed, the people involved in birth are both living and dead, current family members and ancestors. The tally of all the human beings involved in the birthing process is a monumental task.

In this context, perhaps it's not a mistake that we say a birth "*takes place.*" One is born somewhere, which that event grounds as a meaningful place. A place of birth is never an abstract or insignificant space. The conditions of one's birth requires the interaction and coordination of people, places, and things. Answering the question

---

8. See Brown, *Sacred Pipe*.

"Where are you from?" is associated with one's Indigenousness, Indigeneity, or the way one values a place of origin, however that may be conceived, within a nexus of human relationships. Therefore, "Where are you from?" implies another question: "Where are your people from?"

It is not necessarily a causative relationship, but there is a relationship between places, ethnicities, and cultures. The proximity of one's place, however that is understood, in relation to culturally significant events, exerts an influence on the individual throughout their life. As noted, the language in which one thinks connects them to a place and determines their relationship with the world.

This is empirically true, but also an important point in our consideration of the religious significance of "Indigenousness." Place is simultaneously mundane, obvious, pragmatic, empirical, *and* profound, essential, and sacred. This highlights an important point about Indigenous values: they deal with aspects of life that are most obvious, mundane, and practical but in a manner that is also profoundly *religious* in the phenomenal meaning of that term.

Material life is made possible only through a dense and complex set of relationships inclusive of all life forms, human and nonhuman, living and dead. Determining where one is from is a way of beginning to enter into those relationships in a manner that is authentic to the uniqueness of an individual's existence.

What Do You Eat?

There is nothing more culturally loaded than the meaning of food. As we know from a quick look at the religions of the world, food is of enormous concern, deeply connected to religion and religious practices. The vegetarianism of Hindus and Buddhists, kosher for Jews, and fish on Fridays for Catholics, to name just a few examples, are all associated with moral and ethical considerations that connect human beings with their understanding of the sacred.

Food is of the utmost importance because it is a direct link between human life, community, and the world. It is a simple fact of existence that everything living eats. In the case of human consumption, communities decide, usually over the course of a long period of time, what is and what is not food, and the diversity of things that human beings regard as food is staggering. It is often a source of real disagreement and incredulity in intercultural contexts; thus, food is a fruitful place to begin intercultural conversations.

Pragmatic concerns regarding the acquisition of food include a wide variety of variables over which human beings exercise very little—if any—actual control. The phenomenon of food requires the correct combination of elements, beings, and forces to result in something adequate for human consumption. As is often noted by anthropologists, there is a big difference between "hunter-gatherer" and "agriculturally" based groups. Their distinctive food gathering techniques say much about their cultural priorities. For example, while hunter-gatherer communities often have to migrate over great distances, agricultural groups are often sedentary. Most groups, however, have divided the activity of acquiring food into gathering at one time of the year and growing crops at another.

There are profound differences in the ways people relate to places depending on the acquisition of food. Throughout human history, food has been the focal point for most ceremonial activity, particularly when dedicated to those sacred beings that are intimately involved in the life-giving forces needed to grow and care for food—the spirit of food itself. The entire physical and spiritual cosmos is intimately involved in creating food. Material elements of water and minerals, for example, are the basis of life-giving forces. Living beings of all types—insects, reptiles, mammals, flora—are involved in its growth and regeneration.

Food, then, is a primary focal point of sacred stories and ceremonial activities for Indigenous Peoples and the basis of Indigenous values. Food is a source of reflection, conversation, and divination for the purpose of acquiring knowledge. The knowledge of how to grow or acquire food is attained through a number of different avenues that include all of those beings involved in its production including human (living and dead), floral, faunal, climatological, and spiritual.

For Indigenous Peoples, food requires that human beings become conversant with living beings of all types, so there is a high value placed on individuals who can communicate with other beings. Learning the languages of plants, animals, the weather, and the Earth is an arduous process that can often take an enormous toll. Human exchanges with nonhuman beings frequently take place between people of a particular lineage or those who have the right training, or from someone who has survived a traumatic illness or near-death experience. Messages with spiritual beings can be exchanged through dreams, or inspired by creative acts of dance, song, and art as a means to restore balance to an impending threat or danger encroaching upon a community.[9] These messages pertain to the most vitally important act of growing food: the community's survival.

During that time when the body is asleep, the spirit wanders and interacts with other spiritual beings. At these times, there is an easier interaction and communication with a nonhuman world. Often Indigenous Peoples understand that certain dreams can result in pragmatic knowledge. This knowledge is necessary for interacting with a world that is not within the orbit of human control, but is nevertheless a world upon which human life is dependent; it allows Indigenous Peoples to develop *technologies* and *strategies* for interacting with food that extends into a web of interactions with all living beings. In this sense, "technology" is more a literal translation from the Greek *techne*, which is tied to the activity of knowledge, especially with reference to practical knowledge of material culture. Technology can include those sacred objects used in ceremonies that have been acquired through dreams because they are used for the perpetuation of material life. A significant dimension of all religion is the innovation, development, and utilization of new technologies

---

9. Literature on Indigenous Peoples' knowledge system nearly completely focuses the human and nonhuman relationships on the training and recognition of healers, leaders, and ceremonialists.

in this sense of the term.[10] For Bronislaw Malinowski, who did his work among the Melanesian people of New Guinea in 1915–18, food was the primary focus of their ceremonial and religious lives. The languages used in their gardens defined who they were as people because it connected them with the larger cosmos through the growing of food.[11]

In the next chapter, we will discuss food as an aspect of Indigenous values in much greater depth. For now, it is important to see that the value Indigenous Peoples place on the spiritual dimensions of food holds that human beings are just a single element in the perpetuation of the cosmos and, by necessity, no greater or lesser than any other being that participates in these processes.

From an Indigenous perspective, *Creation* is always ongoing. This, too, is a dimension of food. Creation is a central, orienting feature of the religions of the world. Often, as in the global "religions of the book," creation is associated with the beginning of the world, at some time in the distant past. Indigenous stories of Creation are often situated at the beginnings of the world, but those stories are told and retold endlessly as vital indicators and lessons about how the world works, about how human beings should regard a living cosmos, and what they should consider the essential or spiritual nature of reality. These moral lessons are not ideological, requiring a creed or doctrinal statement, as in global religions, but are essentially empirical. Stories (or "myths," as we will discuss in chapter 4) illuminate the ways in which human beings have successfully interacted with spiritual beings of the past and thus how they can interact with those beings in the present and future. Sacred stories constitute practical knowledge in that they guide the listener to interact in respectful and

---

10. Mircea Eliade refers to this dimension of religion as *homo faber*, the human propensity to create their world. For Eliade, this is an essential component of human beings, which he describes as *homo religiosus*, or as being "hard-wired" as religious. See *Forge and the Crucible*.

11. Malinowski, *Coral Gardens and Their Magic*.

appropriate ways with those forces that feed and perpetuate their communities. Stories are not seen as created by human beings, but as provided to people through dreams or other means. Food is complicated and of profound significance in all contexts, particularly among Indigenous Peoples.

Communicating with beings involved with food and its production also requires knowledge of places. In this sense, communicating with spiritual beings is more literally "Indigenous." The Earth is the foundational reality and, from an Indigenous perspective, there is no greater urgency than to communicate with it, which is conceived of in a wide variety of ways but always as a living being. Geographical features are often associated with features of the body of the Earth. Specific sacred places are where the living spirt of the Earth can most readily interact with human beings; of particular importance are caves, rocks, cliffs, mountain peaks, and springs. These places are the sites where significant ceremonies of gratitude, gift exchanges, sacrifices, and the like take place. These events may be initiated by an individual or a group, but they are always performed for the regeneration of the entire human community through the Earth.

Even though the living Earth is a focal point, a great many other beings are involved in the regeneration and acquisition of food. A wide variety of spiritual beings need to be addressed at specific locations across the landscape, at places that have been determined over millennia as best suited to this purpose.[12] At these places, a host of beings are actively engaged for the purposes of sustaining the human community. Most often, Indigenous practitioners will perceive the deep connection between specific places, spiritual beings, and certain ceremonial practices as indistinguishable from one another; in other words, relationships with spiritual beings are inseparable from sacred places themselves. Separating Indigenous Peoples from their places (i.e., from the places that they *inhabit*, in a religious sense, as opposed to the places that they *own*, in a modern sense) has had

---

12. For example, see Basso, *Wisdom Sits in Places*.

traumatic consequences, particularly during the European Age of Discovery, which is associated with conquest and colonialism.

In order for human beings to eat and thus perpetuate their material lives, some other being must die. Killing and eating are directly linked, which is often why food and morality are directly linked in most religions. Regardless of whether it is meat, grain, or vegetable, the fundamental material reality of human existence is that our lives are predicated on the death of some other life. Vegetarianism does not solve this material conundrum, because plants also contain spirit. For Indigenous Peoples, this is a central point of their ceremonial lives. Human beings have a debt to those whose lives have been taken for their sustenance. The *materiality* of food requires a religious response.[13] The ritual payment of debt often takes the form of sacrifice—human, animal, or vegetable—as well as expressions of gratitude. The ceremonies used to satisfy this debt are often specific to a place, a temple, or a ceremonial precinct. Of great importance are the attempts to attain information after the ceremony to see if the gift actually satisfied the debt. Communications are very subtle and have to be "read," sometimes by special diviners, which must then be publicly verified.

Indigenous Peoples are understood in this book as fundamentally pragmatic and empirical. Their ceremonies track those elements and living beings responsible for human sustainability, and they are remarkably attuned to the underlying conditions of their survival. Addressing the conditions of continual creation and re-creation is the basis of human life. There is no more clear a marker of cultural identity than food. All cultures are oriented around the phenomenon of food. The values of Indigenous Peoples highlight the

---

13. By *materiality*, historians of religion, like Charles H. Long, have meant the way material life in all of its appearances (including food) is essentially a religious orientation. Human beings cannot perceive the world just as it is in itself but must develop interpretive tools for understanding the world as essentially religious, mythic, and ceremonial. See Carrasco, *Imagination of Matter*.

importance of food as a spiritual reality that exists in the nexus of living relationships.

What Are You Wearing?

Indigenous Peoples are often easily identified by what they wear. The materials that go into the manufacture of clothing and other adornments of the body associate the person wearing these items with their homeland and their history. Animal and plant materials that go into the clothing are grown from their territory. The symbols woven into the cloth or skins physically connect them to the natural world. Mythic stories and ceremonial practices are articulated in these adornments. With the right knowledge one can determine where an Indigenous person is from just by looking closely at what they are wearing. Culture is embedded in their clothing and helps them maintain proper relationship with the land.

Weaving cloth from the wool of animals raised by their families, or using fibers from plants that have been gathered in their homelands, physically connects Indigenous Peoples to their places of origin. Their identities are intimately associated with all of the lives that have gone into the manufacture of their clothing, making them keenly aware of the cycles of life and death. In this way, the Indigenous value of clothing is very similar to that of food.

Western culture often associates what we wear with our social place, our commitments to different communities, our human identity. This is not something that we are always aware of in daily life. The kind of fabrics or jewelry worn can indicate our social status, nationality, religion, among many other aspects of our lives. The symbols encoded in clothing often strongly reflect our passions. Insignia and designer labels can speak volumes about our commitments, our origins, and our aspirations. Wearing sports clothes to support one's favorite team, for instance, connects you with or disconnects you from other sports fans. These choices are not just simply about covering the body but about expressing to others who you are, where you are from, and with whom you are affiliated.

Indigenous Peoples often utilize elaborate masks, headdresses, clothing, and other adornments to mark moments on the calendar year or a person's life. Likewise, there are special ceremonial events or rites of passage in all of our lives that are also marked by special bodily adornments, such as birth, marriage, and death. Clothing, again, not only affords protection from the elements but also expresses our connection to the material world. With clothing, we amplify our relationship to the world around us. We embody our symbolic story. What we wear associates us with our identities.

Identities are also marked on our skin—for instance, in permanent forms such as tattoos. These embellishments to the body have their origins in Indigenous traditions. The distinction between Indigenous and Modern understandings of clothing and bodily adornments, however, is that they connect Indigenous Peoples with long spiritual regenerative traditions rather than serve as predominantly individualistic expressions.

Where Did It Happen?

Human life is made significant through a series of moments, events, or experiences that bridge the physical maturing process of the body with social and cosmological processes. Care for the human body is achieved by establishing proper relationships to other bodies. The example of food carries through to a number of other ceremonial processes that exemplify a concern with the maintenance of the body. Life pathways in which every human being grows and progresses are ceremonially marked.

Birth, puberty, adolescence, marriage, and death are the key moments in a human being's life. They are marked by ceremonial events in virtually all religions and generally referred to as "rites of passage" to emphasize the ways that these events create, in an *individual*, an experiential connection between their lives and the lives of the rest of their community. This constitutes the *materiality* of one's own body with other bodies: they represent an opportunity to connect the physical and spiritual, the individual and the social, and the material with outward experience to promote an inward cultural awareness.

To the general phenomenon of rites of passage, we must add some more specific religious elements that connect with Indigenous values. Although academics tend to emphasize the social and cultural dimensions of these ceremonial moments, Indigenous Peoples express these events as *sacred*. In other words, the reasons for performing rites of passage are not primarily social, but spiritual—not just to connect human beings more deeply to other human beings, but to nonhuman spiritual beings as well. As in the case of birth, or the question of "where one is from," rites of passage are not primarily about connecting with living human beings but with a host of other types of beings.

Birth is not a phenomenon confined to human existence. As we saw above in the case of food, birth is a process that requires a widely diverse group of beings to coordinate their energies in such a way that new life can come into being. Yet to characterize birth as a fundamentally social event misses the profoundly sacred *religious* sensibility at work in these ceremonies. A successful birth is a celebration of new life, of a renewed connection with a cosmos of living beings beyond the human community. The appearance of a baby is analogous to growing food, in that living beings have to be actively in relationship with one another so that a new human life can be produced. The birth event includes the active presence of departed family members, or ancestors, who also help in coordinating efforts to produce new life.

In Indigenous traditions, human birth is directly connected with the regeneration of life in food, the movement of the seasons, the tidal flow, the shifting of celestial bodies (e.g., the sun, moon, stars, planets). The *materiality* of human life, most particularly in birth, requires that ceremonies marking this event address as many of these cosmological beings as is known and is possible.

Various stages in the processes of a human birth indicate the deep and abiding connection that people share with the rest of the cosmos. The nine-month gestation period, the uterine development of the infant in water, the fetus taking its food through an umbilical cord: these are just a few realities that are ceremonially highlighted and organized by Indigenous Peoples.

Material attributes of the birthing process demonstrate that the child who emerges in the human community is the result of an intersection of energetic forces that are fostered by the activities of beings which are largely not human. Everything that appears in material form is a result of the coordinated efforts of a large number of beings. Ceremonies that celebrate a birth brings not only the child into a new set of social relationships but also the human community into a renewed connection with the cosmos through birth.

Following from the question "Where are you from?" is the question "Where were you born?" As noted in the discussion of "home," births *take place*, and these events create meaningful places.[14] Ceremonies dedicated to a child and commemorating a birth often happen in powerfully significant places. These activities align the life of the child with the lives upon which human lives are contingent.

Again, this is not a sentimental but a practical activity. Birth is an event that fosters the interdependence of the human community with other communities of living beings. Birthplaces are powerful sites because they are where the interdependence that makes human life possible is realized. In effect, these are places of hierophanies where a sacred world *manifests* itself.

Rather than celebrating romantic love between two people, in the marriage ceremony Indigenous traditions tend to emphasize the joining of families and lineages. A successful marriage is based on interpersonal attraction, to be sure, but, more than that, it is about bringing two families together. Ceremonially, the delicate balance

---

14. Thanks to Jonathan Z. Smith for this term, which expands on this idea of place as a human activity. Ceremonial activities have to *take place* in that they form an abstract space into a meaningful place. See *To Take Place*. In a graduate seminar with Professor Smith, I was introduced to a cross-cultural, comparative study of marriage ceremonies that forever transformed my thinking about the History of Religions.

between the family and the marriage couple is dealt with in a number of ways, including how the ceremonial space is arranged, how different constituencies participate in the wedding, and who is responsible for paying for or supplying the wedding guests with food.

Marriage is good for the future prosperity of any group of people, but particularly so for Indigenous communities that rely on the perpetuation of their traditions through joining people and families together, in at least two ways. First, marriage brings together individuals in a community sanctioned through ceremony. For Indigenous Peoples, the wedding is a ceremonial occasion that concerns the entire community, not just particular families. Combining the lives of two people creates the conditions for a viable future.

Second, the marriage ceremony emphasizes the possibility of children, often as the wedding's most pronounced symbolic element. Children bring together families, clans, moieties, communities, countries, and enemies, like nothing else can. They are the most potent expression of a viable future. The child is a social and physical intersection of energies that are produced by a wide diversity of beings. The wedding ceremony symbolizes the hope of children in wedding attire, in dance, in food, in music. Indigenous wedding ceremonies highlight an awareness of bringing children into the world as an act of responsibility to the continuity of their community, rather than as an act of romantic love between the couple. Marriage, then, is much more of a community than an individual event.

▲ ▲ ▲

Death is perhaps the most traumatic event a human being has to face in any culture. From an Indigenous perspective, death is the dissolution of the body and the return of a spirit. This implies that the elements that go into making up the living body must go back to their points of origin after death—it is the reverse process of birth. The physical body begins the dissolution process at death. Elements of the human body recombine with the Earth, plants, animals, and other human beings. As the body disintegrates, it becomes nourishment for a whole host of other beings. Bodily disintegration serves as a signal for the dispersal of the soul or souls that are part of the physical body.[15] Just as the physical body begins a journey to become part of other bodies through decomposition, after death the soul begins a journey to join other souls. That said, these processes of bodily disintegration must happen in the right way in order to help the departed spirit.

For Indigenous Peoples, the funeral is primarily about directing the body and soul of the dead to the right places so that the dearly departed can have good fortune. The treatment of the corpse, prayers given, songs sung, tears wept, dances performed, food eaten are always primarily for the spirit of the deceased, not for the grieving. Funerals also have to be timed to specific parts of the day. These occasions happen at specific locations, with the body placed so as to maximize the benefit of the ceremony for the dead person. Indigenous Peoples have developed a tremendous variety of ways to conduct funerals.[16]

As previously mentioned, funerals are held largely for the benefit of the deceased rather than the living and focus on the maintenance of the soul as it becomes loosened from the body. Aspects of the funeral can direct the soul to a new home from which to enjoy the life after death. Usually, these ceremonies express a modest notion of reincarnation—at least the idea that, if the conditions are right, the departed person may be returned to the community in another form. This kind of concern for the dead, however, is not just sentimental but also material. There is no firm ideological division expressed between the soul and the body. Dealing with death is an expression

---

15. A creative interpretation of the Indigenous traditions of South America can be found in historian of religions Lawrence E. Sullivan's "Terminology," in *Icanchu's Drum*, 467–614. Moreover, the style of Professor Sullivan's book has served as an inspiration for this section.

16. The wide spectrum of funerals has been a topic, in and of itself, of anthropological study. Often ceremonies about death more clearly reflect the character of a society than any other single ceremony that is performed. See Metcalf and Huntington, *Celebrations of Death*.

of affection for the entirety of the ancestors who, as we have seen, play an active role in the lives of the living. Caring for the deceased in the funeral is for everyone's benefit. Making sure that the dead are not confused or lost is of great concern for the entire community who assemble for the funeral. Future connections with spiritual beings by means of connecting with the ancestors can be either positively or negatively affected by the status of those who have passed away.

Though the funeral is for the dead, it also serves a purpose for the living. Although not of primary concern, dealing with the grief of the living is still of great importance. If grief over the sudden loss of a loved one were allowed to fester then the consequences could well be catastrophic. Death throws a veil of grief over the living that needs to be dealt with so that the community will be able to survive. In effect, grief separates people from all living beings; a person adversely affected can be isolated, depressed, and unresponsive to the loving embrace of a community. If left unchecked, grief can grow into anger, depression, and frustration that could negatively impact the family, clan, and the nation.

Unchecked grief can also affect relationships that extend beyond the human community to the entire cosmic balance. Various strategies—such as songs, weeping, food, dancing, and condolences—are employed both during and after the funeral to help those most closely affected find a way out of their grief. It is important to acknowledge that these practices are not done primarily out of a sense of sympathy, but primarily for reasons that have to do with the material survival of the group.

For Indigenous Peoples, sickness can serve as a sign that human beings are not correctly oriented to the cosmos. When properly related to other living beings, the human body is healthy. This means that the interrelationships between people and a living cosmos are as they should be. A sick body indicates that some violation has occurred that has to be reckoned with. Sickness is a sign that those beings that are responsible for keeping the body working by supplying it with food, water, sun, and all the things necessary for life, have not been given their due—that their debt has not been satisfied. While it might be a single person who becomes sick, curing them requires the attention of the entire community, because sickness is a sign indicating the general health of the cosmos. Sickness isn't the individual's problem: it's everybody's problem. Oftentimes, the cure is effected through making an appeal to an offended spiritual being—such as an ancestor or an animal—or by utilizing herbal medicines. Frequently, expressions of gratitude and songs will accompany the use of medicines to more fully address a spiritual presence responsible for the health of the group. Curing ceremonies require an enormous commitment from the entire human community and are everyone's concern.

Where They Play Games

Sports are not usually associated with Indigenous values—or with religions in general—but I have included them here because they form another way to characterize the uniqueness of these traditions. Sports are much more than entertainment, because they often reflect cosmological principles; playing them can influence or celebrate features of the cosmos. In Indigenous traditions, games promote healing and peace between groups, foster fertility (both in human beings or in agriculture), and map the movement of celestial bodies.[17]

Most modern sporting events have origins rooted in Indigenous ceremonial activity, with the Olympics as the most obvious example. Every four years, the warring city-states of ancient Greece would halt their bloody ways to test each other on athletic fields. The most frequent reason cited was to please the gods of Olympus. One could ask, "Why would a sporting contest please the gods?" In contrast to our current understanding of sports and entertainment, an Indigenous perspective would emphasize the sacrificial elements of the

---

17. This is the translation of the name of the sporting arena Tsha'Hoñ'noñ-yeñ'dakwa' on the Onondaga Nation Territory near Syracuse, New York. This beautiful facility is full of symbolism pertaining to the Haudenosaunee. It is dedicated to promoting their Indigenous game Deyhontsigwa'ehs ("They bump hips"), or lacrosse. It highlights the centrality of sports as an extension of their community and their understanding of the cosmos.

sporting contest. Young men (and, in some cases, women) would willingly submit their bodily energies in the sporting event for the benefit of the Creator and the spectators. From this perspective, sports serve as a form of self-sacrifice where the participant gives up some of his or her own life in the service of a larger living world.

Numerous sporting traditions have their origins in Indigenous traditions, including hockey, soccer, lacrosse, and even golf. These sports connect the community to the land in specific ways. The fields where these sports were played were often places of significance with particular orientations to human communities or celestial bodies. Games have likewise served a sacred purpose in bringing together different groups into a united community. It is perhaps intrinsic to human beings to be competitive with each other; Indigenous Peoples understand this aspect of human creativity in such a way that it unites different constituencies of the community through the interchange of talents—expressed as athletic gifts—that are focused on the game.[18]

There is a cosmological principle of renewal and regeneration intrinsic to playing games. Analogous to the yin and yang of Taoist philosophy, most Indigenous traditions conceive of the underlying structure of the cosmos as composed of antagonistic forces: contracting and expanding, or ascending and descending. These forces are expressed in a variety of oppositions in stories of Creation, of which stories of sexuality, sky and earth, twins, warfare, and sacrifice often form the basis. Oppositions have been often noted by theorists as essential to religion and mythology, but less often these are connected with the phenomenon of sports.[19] Sporting events activate these

---

18. On the ways in which sports are understood to be intimately associated with religion, see, for example, Cousineau, *Olympic Odyssey*; Miller, *Gods and Games*; Higgs, *God in the Stadium*; Vennum, *American Indian Lacrosse*; and Zogry, *Anetso*. See also Arnold, *Gift of Sports*.

19. This brings to mind the work of the noted scholar of mythology Claude Lévi-Strauss, whose concept of "structuralism" emphasized the oppositions as intrinsic to all mythic thinking. For an example of this way of thinking about myth, see *Mythologies*—a remarkable demonstration of the creativity of his methodology.

cosmological principles of oppositions and utilize them for the purpose of maintaining and regenerating the community. Sporting events are seen as good for growing crops, healing people from ailments, encouraging the emotional state of the family and community, and fostering the physical health of the body. In short, and perhaps in contrast to popular opinion, sports promote peace. The popularity of sports in the modern world echoes their significance in Indigenous ceremonial events that exchange energies between elements of the cosmos.

Conclusions

Consistent antagonism between scholarly and Indigenous communities indicates their widely divergent worldviews. It is, therefore, no small feat to attempt to bridge the gap between the intellectual traditions of the West and Indigenous values.

In this chapter, it has been my intention to present Indigeneity as an obvious, even mundane, aspect of human life. In spite of a vast diversity, I would argue that there is a universally human basis for Indigenousness. Unlike most of the world's religions, Indigenous Peoples are not oriented by doctrinal creed or a sacred text, but, rather, the premise that universal features be exemplified as material existence. The History of Religions has explored this aspect of religion, but the category of "Indigenous" enables us to articulate it in a new and productive way.

Over several generations, many scholars of religion have asserted that the idea of what we now call "Indigenous" should be a foundational feature of all religions. These religions have been articulated as being primary (i.e., primitive) and archetypal (i.e., archaic) and the like. Unlike more inherently negative categories that have demonized Indigenous Peoples as contrary to religion—such as "heathen," "pagan," and "savage"—over the last 150 years these traditions have been seen as fundamental to a modern academic understanding of religion.

In short, the most meaningful dimensions of all human life are Indigenous. Assertions of identity are most often associated with one's cultural location, place of birth, language, community, and ritual marks, all of which resonate with Indigenous practices. Rather than thinking of Indigenous values as remote from or opposed to modern life, this book seeks to utilize ways to think of life and religion differently.

▲ ▲ ▲

It is important to remember that, in the past, Indigenous Peoples and their traditions were considered detrimental to civilization, where their only value pertained to their representing the bottom of human social evolution. However, in spite of fervent efforts to exterminate them, Indigenous Peoples persist today and are even flourishing in many places around the world.

Moreover, Indigenous traditions are not stuck in the past. They are dynamic, changing, and responsive to the constantly changing status of global culture. In fact, they are currently organizing themselves around issues of urgent mutual concern. Today, more than ever before, Indigenous Peoples are organizing themselves to assert their values as an alternative to global economic forces. Their emphasis is on the subtle spiritual dimensions of material life rather than on the ever-transforming human environment of global consumption.

Indigenous Peoples exist in a cosmos of living relationships that are undergoing continuous reformulation, regeneration, and renewal. If there is any hint of resistance to change in these religions, it is to the incursions of an intrusive human-centered worldview that insists on the hierarchical status of human beings over and above each other and all other living beings. Such a view would be contrary to the proper balance that has to be acknowledged within each living cosmos. These are not so much assertions as they are facts within Indigenous traditions, intrinsic to living life today, as they were lived yesterday, and as they will be lived in the future.

3

Paying Attention

When I was very young and being disruptive my parents would often sternly command, "*Pay attention!*" Reflecting on this now as a parent, I think they were communicating to me that misbehavior was not who I was, but rather the result of my being oblivious to my surroundings: I was acting disrespectfully to myself and those in the world around me and thus behaving in a dangerous manner. I have come to understand that this was wise advice and an important attribute of surviving in a complex world.

The phrase "Pay attention" has stayed with me throughout my life, and I now find myself saying it to my own kids—even as they grow into adults—in the hope that it will empower them to more ably relate with the world.

▲ ▲ ▲

I am intentionally using the term "world" throughout this book to mean how human beings engage in the complexity of life. In many ways, this term stands in for "worldview," which combines cultural, material, social, psychological, and other dimensions of life in which all human beings are engaged. More than "worldview," though, the term "world" is used intentionally to be inclusive of all material phenomena, internal and external, upon which human life depends.

"Paying attention" is a commonsense orientation to the world that also expresses an Indigenous sensibility (i.e., the importance of appreciating the meaning and significance of one's location). It is an important attribute of Indigenous knowledge and a strategy by which human beings who are successful in their adaptations to the world can find their place or their home, or plant roots to flourish.[1]

To pay attention requires a strategy for dealing with a wide array of phenomena in the world so that survival can be better assured. It is a method of discernment, a hermeneutic, that adjudicates between good and bad, useful and detrimental, viable and deadly. For our purposes, paying attention is an activity meant to discern an appropriate interpretive location—where we are coming from—for promoting an understanding of the workings of life. This is not mysterious nor mystical but an obvious and material process that everyone must negotiate, and that is of pragmatic concern for all human beings.

Paying attention is also an activity that focuses on how relationships with the world can support and sustain a human reciprocal existence. For the scholar of Indigenous values, these questions are important in discerning one's cultural biases and essential prejudices. One's relationship with and orientation to the world is the method by which new knowledge can be generated.

For more than thirty years, I have been involved with Indigenous Peoples, both personally and professionally. After having been trained in the academy how best to study other people's religions, it has become clear that an "extractive" or "expert" model of knowledge is both unwittingly violent and ultimately limited. Moreover, this mode of research does not reflect the actual activity of interpretation, which is always collaborative and conversational. As discussed in chapter 1, new knowledge about traditions—particularly Indigenous oral traditions, where there are few sacred texts (written

---

1. Originally, I had wanted to title this book "Paying Attention" because I felt it was so central to an Indigenous way of thinking. I conceived of this project as a "self-help" book that would challenge the Western idea of the self; after all, there seems to be such a huge market in self-help books today, and perhaps this book would be helpful in introducing another sense of the self. But it became clear that the modern notion of the self is too bound up with consumer capitalism, and that such a book might engender hostility, something that neither Indigenous Peoples nor I would find productive.

in the Western sense of a "text"), and where previous models of academic researchers are viewed with suspicion—are giving way to new methodological models of collaboration. Promoting specific kinds of collaborative relationships is made possible only by paying attention to the details. Collaborative methods have proven much more effective in helping non-Indigenous Peoples and descendants of settler-colonial people to understand and appreciate Indigenous values.

As a methodology, paying attention is useful for Indigenous Peoples and non-Indigenous scholars alike. Even though it is a survival strategy, it is also involved in human processes of interpretation. Though they bring different cultural foreknowledge to the case, Indigenous Peoples or historians of religion are both interested in developing empirical knowledge that meaningfully orients them to their worlds. However, there are critical differences.[2]

As a historian of religions, I continually ask, "What is knowledge production for? How is it useful?" These critical questions highlight the differences between the intellectual labor of Indigenous and academic thinkers. All knowledge begins in an essential prejudice, or what some have called a "bias," that informs the ways that knowledge is produced by paying attention.[3] We all have a point of view. According to phenomenologists, this is an essential feature of being human, but scholars have been trained to think that the kind of knowledge that is generated in the university is objective. This mistaken assumption has had profound and tragic consequences for Indigenous Peoples. This begs the question, then, as to whether any academic study of Indigenous Peoples may in fact be a continuation of human cruelty.

---

2. A classic study of the processes of hermeneutics (the philosophical dimensions and art of interpretation) is Gadamer, *Truth and Method*. It is the work upon which much of this section of interpretation is based.

3. This has been an ongoing topic in the philosophy of religion. Merleau-Ponty's discussion of this issue is of particular importance; see *Phenomenology of Perception*.

To illustrate some of these points: I recently had a short conversation at the home of a highly respected speaker on the Onondaga Nation. It was early spring, during maple syrup season. We spoke about the ash trees near his home, which were dying from an invasion of the ash borer insect that is moving north because of the mild winters. We agreed that this was due to climate change, but he added that his maple trees were dying from the top down. For the Haudenosaunee, the maple is the "leader of the trees," and its condition indicates the general health of our environment. Maple trees dying from the top down is part of a prophecy going back over two hundred years to Handsome Lake called the "Gaiwiyo" or "Good Message"; he was pointing out the physical evidence of this prophetic tradition. These material observations address the urgent issues facing all human beings: where our worlds intersect in the forest. I was aware of the prophecies, and, initially, I didn't ask him anything about this knowledge, but it all emerged from a conversation about our surrounding forest. The spiritual legacy was confirmed by the material world. I was paying attention, and so was he, and so was Handsome Lake all those years ago.

A wide range of knowledge is required to live. Paying attention combines foreknowledge—or those strategies that are learned—and the material context that requires our interpretation. Together, they become the source of new insights for methods and strategies in understanding the world. Aspects of one's ability to pay attention (i.e., the what, who, why, and how to which one pays attention) are derived from cultural training as well as the material context.

Paying attention is also the entry to every "religious" and "values" orientation understood by humans. It describes a process by which distinctive human communities have come to their own understandings of the sacred, combining the pragmatic with the profound, the local with the cosmological, and the personal with the universal in a way that connects human communities to the ways of the world. What starts off as a survival strategy often develops into a profound orientation to our existence. Paying attention is a human mode of being aware that a sacred reality can express itself in anything at any moment of our experience. This is a widely shared perspective among Indigenous Peoples throughout the world.

Religion and World Domination

I have noticed a reticence in our public media to discuss religion's role in world domination. From the point of view of Indigenous values, however, there is no cultural phenomenon more central for the engine of assorted traumas around the world than religion. This is precisely why the academic study of religion—and, I argue, the History of Religions in particular—is of such critical importance.

The "West" as a material-cultural-mythic aggressor vis-à-vis the "rest" begins with the category of the "primitive." For Charles Long, the slash between primitive/civilized was determinative of our modern existence.[4] In that slash could be perceived the intense and sustained intimacy, fascination, and wonder between Christian and non-Christian, as well as an impulse for terror, hatred, fear, and dread.[5]

The category of the "primitive" has exerted an ambiguous, albeit foundational, presence in the West's understanding of religion. For example, Sir Edward Burnett Tylor, an anthropologist of the nineteenth century who worked in a museum at Oxford University during the height of the British Empire, literally wrote the book on "primitive religion." His job was to organize and physically pigeon-hole materials into boxes that flowed from the colonies into the center of the British Empire, upon which, (in)famously, "the sun never set."

Never before had academics seen such a tremendous variety of sacred objects. Materials extracted from their home communities were transformed into museum artifacts and objects of the colonization. Objectifying and organizing what had been considered living beings proved to be a daunting task of decipherment that would

---

4. Long, "Primitive/Civilized," in *Significations*, chapter 6.
5. Otto, "Mysterium Tremendum," in *Idea of the Holy*, 13–24.

result in the reinterpretation and reimagining of "religion" for the primitive and the civilized alike.

A consequence of this cacophony of cultural paraphernalia and Tylor's powerful scholarly imagination can be described as an existential dilemma in the dramatic creation of "Western civilization." The simple fact of such tremendous cultural diversity resulted in an identity crisis for English colonizers, as exemplified by the number and variety of cultural objects coming into the center of the British Empire. This identity conflict expressed itself most profoundly in the colonizers' attempts to reconceptualize and universalize the origins of religion (i.e., to include all of human societies throughout all of history). Doing so ultimately emphasized the inherent superiority of Christianity—particularly the Protestant Christianity of the British Empire of the West.

"Animism," the theory of the deficiency of primitive ways of thinking, was Tylor's solution.[6] In so-called primitive societies, animism innovates what eventually was to become "religion." While it serves as a justification for British colonial expansion, ironically it also created an inverted priority of the primitive over the civilized. Primitive animism was foundational to civilized Christian empires.

Today, a "new animism" developed by Graham Harvey, among others, is emerging that further prioritizes Indigenous Peoples' insights into a living Earth comprised of relationships with nonhuman persons that forms the basis of human existence. This is a place Tylor would never have imagined his theory of animism going: to be used toward critiquing civilization altogether.[7]

---

6. See Chidester, "Animism," in *Religion: Material Dynamics*, chapter 1. This text discusses how E. B. Tylor built an entire definition of religion on a social evolutionary scale from primitive to civilized based on the Zulu of South Africa and their understanding of the spiritual significance of a sneeze.

7. See Harvey, *Animism*. Along with Miguel Astor-Aguilera, Harvey edited the volume *Rethinking Relations and Animism*, which contains articles by a range of theorists including Marshall Sahlins, Nurit Bird-David, Amy Whitehead, Kenneth H. Loensgard, and Fabio R. Gygi.

Expansionist cultures of Europe created an intellectual tradition that placed human beings at the center of the world and assumed that humans have the ability (and responsibility) to know the universal truths of all things. Entire academic disciplines were created to deal with the workload that resulted in this assumption of universal knowledge. This cultural response to global expansion came to be known as the Enlightenment of the seventeenth century. From our perspective, however, it was the fifteenth- and sixteenth-century Age of Discovery that created the preconditions for this intellectual revolution (to be discussed further in chapter 6).

Central to all of these epochs was the question "What is religion?" The remarkable thing was that, from the central vantage point of the British Empire, knowledge of the universal was *possible*. The superiority of Europe's worldviews and its colonial imperial apparatus was assumed to be the natural extension of Christendom and the Age of Discovery. In order for Tylor to succeed, his work required him to interrogate what, in his mind, was essential and foundational for all human beings: a desire to answer universal questions. The imperial thrust of the British Empire thus resulted in an academic turn toward a hierarchically imagined universality in a secular orientation moving from "primitive" to "civilized." Ironically, the more colonialism pushed Europeans into direct, intimate, and ongoing cultural contact with "primitive," non-Christian people with radically different traditions than themselves, the more fraught the question of European origins became.[8]

The traumatic 1519 encounter between the conquistador Hernán Cortés and Moctezuma Xocoyotzin reverberated throughout Christendom. Writing of his experience as a foot soldier in Cortés's army, Bernal Díaz del Castillo captures the awe and splendor of the Aztec city of Tenochtitlan.[9] He describes a paradise, reminiscent of tales

8. For an examination of colonialism in India, see Nandy, *Intimate Enemy*.
9. A Nahuatl word meaning "prickly pear cactus growing among rocks" and referring to the original hierophany, or "manifestation of the sacred," where an eagle was seen with a serpent in its beak sitting on a cactus growing out from a

told in his native Spain, teeming with life and remarkable architecture in the middle of an inland sea: "I stood looking at it and thought that never in the world would there be discovered other lands such as these, for at that time there was no Peru, nor any thought of it. Of these wonders that I then beheld today all is overthrown and lost, nothing left standing."[10] Two short years after the encounter, the entire city was destroyed. Paradise was found and then destroyed.

In spite of the devastation, Tenochtitlan continued to exert a powerful influence on the Christian theological imagination for future generations. Indigenous orators questioned why Christians would accept the dominion of an almighty God who came to inhabit the human form of Jesus Christ who failed to persuade everyone to follow him. Sixteenth-century theologians proposed questions such as "How could Jesus Christ, the savior of all human beings, not have visited great populations of people across the waters, such as the Aztecs? How was it that inhabitants of the New World had never received the Christian message?"

These theological questions have vexed settler-colonial Europeans from the fifteenth-century Vatican to the Church of the Latter-Day Saints. Thomas, the doubting apostle, was thought to have sailed to the New World because pre-Aztec inhabitants of Tolan spoke of their mythic Quetzalcoatl, the great priest/ruler who was the model of authority for the Aztec.[11] According to the myth, Quetzalcoatl was disgraced and banished to the east over the sea, only to return as the conqueror Cortés. Upon learning of the story of Quetzalcoatl, Cortés quickly fashioned himself as the returning king. This mythic

---

rock in the middle of a lake. The current Mexican flag captures this founding event of the Aztec capital city. A recent version of *The History of the Conquest of New Spain* was edited by Davíd Carrasco, including passages excluded in other English versions and insights from interpretive articles.

10. Carrasco, *History of the Conquest of New Spain*, 157.

11. Carrasco, *Quetzalcoatl and the Irony of Empire*; Todorov, *Conquest of America*.

framing reportedly confused and disarmed Moctezuma, the last leader of Tenochtitlan, and hastened the fall of the city.

Cortés's ruse had the desired effect. This encounter between Spanish conquistadors and Aztec nobility fired the developing European theological imagination around the meaning of the "New World." The fall of the Aztec was due to deceit and superior weaponry as demonstrated by Christendom's monarchs and their tactics of theological control. This is perhaps most eloquently expressed by the Italian diplomat Niccolò Machiavelli in his book *The Prince*, which was published in 1532, soon after initial contact and the fall of Tenochtitlan ushering forth the conquest of the New World. Controlling the narrative is perhaps the most important element of colonialism.

▲ ▲ ▲

The question remains: Can any single academic, from his or her own cultural location, ever completely know and understand "others," given the centuries-long contrast of worldviews? Shouldn't the conditions of conquest, colonialism, and domination, particularly in their religious formulations, throw suspicion on this collaborative methodology? These questions were accompanied by pragmatic concerns regarding how "best" a civilized and enlightened Christian country could efficiently dominate the entire world. For what reason and to what end?

Following Charles Long, the discipline of History of Religions grew out of these interpretive conundrums; it calls into question the nature of religion. Is religion primarily a theological justification for conquest or the spiritual realities that anthropologists tell us are universal in all human societies? The cultural contact research by Asad, Masuzawa, Long, and Chidester interrogates the possibility of what we call today "religious diversity."[12] If religion is a universal

---

12. See Asad, *Genealogies of Religion*; Masuzawas, *Invention of World Religions*; Chidester, *Savage Systems*; and Long, "African American Religion in the United States," in *Ellipsis*, chapter 16.

feature of all human communities, as early interpreters of religion maintained, then who are we to define it with respect to contact with Indigenous Peoples? E. B. Tylor seems to think that religion cannot simply be equated with Christianity, but that view runs counter to the European narrative of civilization.

Cultural interactions with Indigenous Peoples around the world have been driven by a religious imperialism, which they define as Christendom, or the Kingdom of Christianity. Our modern existence has been defined, in large part, by this imperialism. Among social justice issues related to the transatlantic slave trade, land theft, genocide, ecocide, and other traumas, this focus on conquest and colonialism has led to an existential environmental crisis for all of us.

Tylor developed animism from the assumption that primitive people could not distinguish between dreams and reality.[13] Tylor's insight was to appeal to a common human denominator in defining religion as a social evolutionary phenomenon. This broke with previous assertions of religion as Christendom. For him, the origins of religions are to be found in the universal phenomenon of death.[14] Specifically, Tylor believed that it was dreaming of the dead, where the living were informed in a nocturnal state how to perform a ceremony, that bridged the living and dead communities. For Tylor, even though the phenomenon of death is universal to all living things, the way death is organized and understood is radically diverse. There is something basic, something primary, something *primitive*, about death that makes it intrinsic to the origin of religion.

---

13. Tylor had used a British anthropologist's observations of the Zulu of South Africa, specifically their interpretations of sneezing, to substantiate British colonial authority and cultural superiority. See Chidester, "Animism," in *Religion: Material Dynamics*, 23–29.

14. In 1871 Tylor wrote his influential book *Religion in Primitive Culture*, which was a very early attempt by an "armchair anthropologist" (meaning someone who did not venture out too far into the "field") while looking at the material record of a wide variety of human cultures to theorize the origins of religion.

The universal phenomenon of spiritualism was Tylor's contribution to the study of religion. According to him, in primitive societies, human beings cannot distinguish between the waking world and the dreams of the dead. Thus, the origin of religion is the consequence of a confusion between the spiritual and "real" worlds among primitive people, which was rationalized through Christianity. Tylor's conviction was that, with civilization, human beings would overcome the need for spirituality and religion, thus becoming fully enlightened people who could soberly know the truth of the world. In the interests of defending the empire, however, Tylor wasn't paying attention, but, rather, whitewashing his own cultural constitution and prejudices.

In addition to Mircea Eliade, the History of Religions has a direct lineage to the work of James George Frazier (*The Golden Bough*), William James (*Varieties of Religious Experience*), Rudolf Otto (*The Idea of the Holy*), Gerardus van der Leeuw (*Religion in Essence and Manifestation*), and Joachim Wach (*Sociology of Religion*). They all theorize that the ceremonial lives of "savage," "primitive," and/or "archaic" people are their primary data for the development of civilization.[15] According to these scholars, primitive people and societies manifested the most basic and fundamental religious orientations. For many of these theorists, archaic and "primitive" people represented a past that was frozen in time. By traveling to anywhere in the colonized world, one could be seen as going back to the origins of the human race, right or wrong. In spite of their being contemporaries of these theorists, therefore, previous generations of scholars of religions have tended to characterize "primitives" as examples of religion's origins who are relegated to the ancient human past. Even though these scholars project primitives into the past, they also insist

---

15. For Eliade, the "archaic" are prioritized in a distinctive way. This term is descriptive of a people who concern themselves with the fundamental, *archetypal* meanings embedded in human consciousness. As distinguished from Jung's "archaic," however, Eliade is much more interested in how archetypal structures are involved in material life and then revealed in human religious activity.

that knowing them is fundamental for understanding all religion; what is primary about religion is perceived in primitive society. A tremendous fascination with primitives, or those whom we now call "Indigenous Peoples," made these societies influential in our understanding of modernity. The irony of these theories of religion is that they tended to base their interpretations of the contemporary world based on the colonized other—ultimately, "paying attention," but short-changing themselves in their own process.

The Other Other

There is a relationship between the "empirical other" of the Indigenous Peoples under colonial control and the "Holy Other" that has been seen as the originating event of religion. For Eliade, hierophanies are the ways that the Other world of power, or the Holy Other, reveals itself. There is a keen sense that these manifestations are of ultimate practical importance because human life is contingent upon this sacred world and predicated on a larger material reality. Eliade coined the term "hierophany" to characterize the appearance of a sacred reality in the material world.[16] Otto, alternatively, articulated the founding event of religion as an awareness of the Holy Other. In German usage, the term was used to denote an ultimate and absolute power that was opaque to direct human comprehension.[17] In spite of its remoteness from rationality, religion was understood by Otto as being wholly contingent on the Holy Other.

According to early historians of religions, the experience of the Holy Other undergirds the structure of the whole of material existence. This means that religion is not the result of human agency; rather, that humans come to understand their agency to be derived, in part, from the power manifesting in nature, places, and other human beings. The hope of these early historians of religions was

---

16. Eliade, *Myth of the Eternal Return*; Eliade, *Patterns in Comparative Religion*.
17. Otto, *Idea of the Holy*.

that, through studying the ritual and mythic expressions found in religious traditions, it would be possible to understand the fundamental characteristics of the Holy Other in archaic forms across its wide variety of cultural expressions.

In my own experience, the category of "hierophany" works in a descriptive sense when discussing the status of the sacred with Indigenous Peoples today. An example is the regard with which the Haudenosaunee hold Onondaga Lake, near my home in Syracuse, New York. The traditional values that undergird the Haudenosaunee tradition of the Great Law of Peace, also referred to as "Longhouse tradition," were delivered over one thousand years ago by the Peacemaker.[18] For these historical reasons, Onondaga Lake is understood to be a sacred place, but for millennia the lake has also been a place of healing, with a tremendous variety of springs, medicinal plants, and animals.[19] Beginning with French Jesuits discovering salt springs in the sixteenth century through the heavy industrialization of salt that continued through the twentieth century, the ecology of Onondaga Lake was destroyed. However, during this entire time, the Haudenosaunee continued to regard it as a site of the hierophany, both historically and materially.

Recent attempts to clean up the lake have been contentious, marked by unending disagreements between governmental-corporate interests and environmental-Haudenosaunee concerns. Ceremonies are performed there today, most often in private, to acknowledge with gratitude the hierophany that occurred and to reignite that moment when human beings interact with sacred beings: the Earth's waters, fish, birds, animals, medicine plants, and all other nonhuman beings that comprise the material world. A few years ago, eagles returned

---

18. This is a rough translation that is often discussed. Some have suggested it be called "the Great Binding Peace," for there is no Haudenosaunee concept of "law."

19. On the Onondaga Nation website, this is discussed as "History, Birth of a Nation." See https://www.onondaganation.org/history (accessed 29 December 2022).

to the lake to nest, which was taken as a message that human and nonhuman interaction can regenerate the lake.

While historians of religions of the past have apprehended the hierophany by examining the traditions of primitive people around the world, this was essentially an extension and justification for colonialism. Most academics claim to know that the true nature of religion was based largely on the study of Indigenous Peoples. Early historians of religions conflated the empirical other of primitive people and the Holy Other of religion, both of which undergirded material life: the primitive as the resource for the engine of empire, and the "Holy Other" as the foundation of civilization and Christendom.

The Search for Religion's Origins and Modernity

Colonialism brought Europeans into an intimate and contentious cultural contact with empirical others labeled "primitive." The result was the creation of modernity, which, for our purposes, spans from 1492 to the present.[20] There is a direct correlation between the imperialism of the West and the History of Religions' formulation of the mystery and fascination of the Holy Other as the founding hierophany of religion.[21] It is the fiction of the transparency of empirical others—variously expressed as "heathens," "savages," "primitives," and the like—that Western historians of religions can peer in to their worlds unimpeded, thus establishing the character of scholarly knowledge.

---

20. Several will disagree with this assessment of the beginning of modernity; I am most interested, however, in its mythic or fictive underpinnings. I am not talking about modernity as an aesthetic or intellectual movement, but as a phase of cultural development that was initiated with the shock of world domination and colonialism. Moreover, I am interested in the ways in which modernity has been mythologized in our current cultural context. Most US citizens, for example, will readily understand the significance of 1492 as the point of origin for the New World.

21. See Masuzawa, *Invention of World Religions*. Masuzawa's concern is in how the History of Religions is implicated in the imperialism and world domination of the West over other religious traditions.

While they are rendered as being positive (i.e., the noble savage) or as being negative (i.e., the wild savage), the empirical other, Indigenous Peoples, have been excluded from the cultural exchanges that created modern civilization. Indigenous Peoples are often discussed, examined, and sympathized with, but rarely acknowledged or understood as having any influence in what constitutes the material and intellectual basis for the development of modernity. Likewise, Indigenous Peoples have been seen as fundamentally religious, but their hierophanies have not gained the same status as the gods of global religions. According to Long, Indigenous Peoples have instead been *signified*, meaning that they have been predetermined by Western intellectuals as transparent and peripheral to modernity.

Herein lies the conundrum, the central entanglement of this work: Indigenous traditions are put on a pedestal, or a place of privilege, *and* simultaneously despised as backward examples of the uncivilized. In both contexts, "primitives" have been conceived of as the raw materials, or natural resources, to be consumed in the advancement of Western civilization and religion.[22] This social evolution from primitive to civilized was established by early academics, anthropologists, and historians of religions. Although it was an assumption, it came to define our current understandings of Indigenous traditions. Categories such as "primitive," "savage," and "archaic" are foreign concepts to Indigenous Peoples because their society is not hierarchically structured. The Haudenosaunee organize their society around the clan relationship to land. Clan leaders are chosen according to their abilities of persuasion, ultimately bringing minds together in gratitude to the natural world. "Indigencity" is different on all counts, and this profound contrast can present a new model for thinking about the future of religion.

22. It is significant that Indigenous Peoples are consistently categorized as paired with the *natural world* as opposed to the *human world*. Most collections of Native American artifacts in North America, for example, are housed in museums of natural history and not in museums of art and culture.

History of Religions and the Challenges of Modernity

As discussed, this book follows from the Chicago school, founded on the work of Joseph Kitagawa, Charles Long, and Mircea Eliade. History of Religions, as such, is a child of the Enlightenment. The comparative study of religion became a legitimate aspect of the development of the secular university at a time when European powers were coming into intimate contact with Indigenous Peoples all over the world. The development of modernity is of dramatic significance for the origins of religion; therefore, a discussion of the origins of religion is not one of the "beginning of time," but, rather, the "beginning of intercultural contact and modernity," which was when these questions became urgent. As we will explore, the ideas of world religions and primitive religions became necessary as a critical point in the development of the West.

Religion takes on an important and ambiguous role in cultural contact, with consequences for what we are seeing in our contemporary world. The *materiality* of modernity, characterized as global capitalism, came out of the catastrophic encounters between Western expansionism and Indigenous Peoples. During the colonial era of discovery, imperial Europeans, who wanted to move into lands not traditionally their own, came into persistent opposition with Indigenous Peoples, who wanted to stay connected with their places of origin. Religion was used to articulate the deepest reasons why it was best for the life of the group to maintain either imperial or Indigenous ways of valuing the world.

European imperialist expansion, which has negatively impacted Indigenous Peoples all over the world, has caused profound trauma. Colonialists used religion as a tool in three very specific, interrelated, and pointed ways. First, in order to effectively colonize other people, they framed Christianity as a "utopian" belief (derived from the Greek, meaning "no place"). Thus, religious orientations were considered movable and centered around individual salvation through an engagement with an institution or a sacred text; this Euro-Christian worldview stood in marked contrast with an Indigenous worldview of being oriented to a material place. Second, the Christian religion was exclusively posited to a particular group of people, who subjugated and colonized various non-Christian Indigenous Peoples (predominantly of color) from around the world into slavery and working classes, whom they utilized to successfully establish the imperial colonial enterprise. Transatlantic chattel slavery, for example, was originally organized as a Christian appropriation of non-Christian or heathen lands, resources, and human bodies. Third, religion was conceptualized as hierarchical in order to justify the existence and perpetual status of a class of semidivine human beings, such as popes, cardinals, kings, queens, and aristocrats. In colonial outposts, an underclass of people were created from the inbreeding of European and Indigenous women that usually involved rape. These populations were to serve the upper classes in sustaining the great chain of being. This religious orientation emphasized the "natural" hierarchies of male over female, human over animal, civilized over primitive, and established the conquest of good over evil. Human fascination with the physical power and mastery of war technology was the logical consequence of hierarchical domination. Colonial powers used these three religious strategies to assure the colony's success and substantiate the superiority of civilization.

In actuality, however, the *materiality* of the colonial situation—the survival and success of the colony—was wholly dependent on Indigenous Peoples. Tobacco, sugar, corn, tomatoes, potatoes, furs, and spices, along with new concepts of "equity," "freedom," and "peace" that included women and the natural world, had all been enjoyed for thousands of years before first contact.

Much of the topsoil had been depleted in Europe, and the world was already experiencing famine. Through traditional practices of regenerative agriculture, a plethora of Indigenous foods would transform diets all over the world. This traditional ecological knowledge had been acquired over thousands of years through a direct engagement with the natural world that was based in ritual ceremonies of gratitude. With the arrival of Christianity, a new framework of domination was imposed over the Earth and its peoples. New mercantile interests required the colonization of Indigenous knowledge and the commodification of Indigenous plants, foods, and land while methodically stripping away their sacramental relationship with the Earth. So, while the *ideology* of colonialism and modernity has devalued Indigenous Peoples as "primitive," "savage," "pagan," and "heathen," Europeans elevated and posited their religions as "civilized," while, in actuality, the traditions of Indigenous Peoples were foundational to the actual materiality of colonialism and modernity.

Colonial interests appropriated Indigenous Peoples' intimate knowledge of their lands, increasing the monetary wealth necessary in fulfilling the Euro-Christian religious vision of world domination. This rapid accumulation of wealth was treated as further proof that the colonial religious pursuit was blessed by God. At first contact, however, colonists had to learn about foods, medicines, clothing, building materials, animals, hunting, and governmental and social organization in order to survive. This crucial knowledge came from the very Indigenous Peoples who had been characterized by the Church as inferior. In spite of these views of Indigenous Peoples, Europeans were completely dependent on them. There is a profound disconnection between how Europeans expressed religious superiority and at the same time were completely materially reliant on those whom they oppressed.

Because of these religious claims of superiority, the West has largely remained ignorant of the degree to which it has been Indigenously constituted. There is a strange combination of intimacy and domination in colonial culture. In spite of a rhetoric of cultural purity and superiority, Europeans very often had children with Indigenous Peoples from the Americas and Africa—an assimilation tactic used to breed slaves or create cultural infiltrators. As a result, colonists and their descendants were related to entire groups of people whom they professed to own as slaves and despise. Yet, at the same time, they were also learning about plants, animals, and other aspects of Indigenous knowledge. Clearly the colonial situation disallowed the colonists to pay attention to what really mattered.

Recent scholarship has demonstrated how those ancient ideas and practices constitute much of the contemporary culture and thought we enjoy today—a baseline for the civilizations we identify with.[23] Indigenous influences have gone unrecognized by past academics, even though material and bodily aspects of global culture are propped up by a staggering cultural diversity due to the aggressive interactions between European and Indigenous Peoples initiated by the Age of Discovery.

This disjunction between Western *ideology* (what people think and believe) and *materiality* (how people are physically constituted and sustained) reveals the profound ambiguity at the center of modern religious understandings. This ambiguity concerns, for example, the exclusivity, purity, and truth of the global religions, which have given rise to fundamentalisms that are primarily generated around interactions between colonizing forces and Indigenous Peoples.

The primary religious referent of the History of Religions for negotiating the contact with empirical others has been with regard to the sacred. In sharp contrast to other areas of the academy, this discipline does not attempt to reduce the phenomenon of religion to a quantifiable and controllable set of data, but instead lets the phenomenon of religion speak for itself.

For Eliade, the primary concern of the historian of religions is with the "cipher" of religion that, by its nature, cannot be deciphered.[24] This recognition of religion's undecipherable nature leads to at least two theories within the History of Religions. First, the

---

23. One of the most exciting areas of collaborative research going on today in Indigenous studies is in the area of Indigenous food sovereignty. My colleagues Robin Kimmerer, Kyle Whyte, Mariaelena Huambachano, Chie Sakakibara, and Jane Mt. Pleasant, and community activists like LaDuke and Angela Ferguson are working to relearn Indigenous farming techniques. Among the knowledge regained is how these practices and foods transformed the world at colonial contact.

24. Eliade, *History of Religions*, 1:1–8.

perspective of the insider in describing religious phenomena and approximating its power and significance cannot reduce the sacred to something entirely of human construction. Adequate descriptions of other religions require that *the sacred be treated as a decipherable, active, vital presence within a cultural context and is irreducible to other discernible phenomena.* This acknowledges a respectful distance between the historian of religions who is attempting to describe a religion and an adherent. Second, the contact situation and the globalized condition of modernity involves a host of human communities that, when described most powerfully, provide an intervention into Western hegemony.

Religion is almost totally indecipherable and ambiguous, particularly in those thoroughly modern nation-states that have defined themselves as embracing the "freedom of/from religion," as in the United States, where these religions have developed as a response to colonialism. Historians of religions posit that the ambiguity of the sacred has promoted religious revitalization; this quality allows for a myriad of interpretations that address ever-changing cultural conditions. There is a direct relationship between the irreducibility of the sacred and a religion's ability to generate new conceptions of human life and community. In essence, modernity is inherently an ambiguous phenomenon, and therefore a religious conundrum. The issue of certainty, as it pertains to the clarity of the sacred, has been central to those cultures and individuals promoting the Imperialist agenda of world domination.

The significance of place and the position held by religion determining human cultural expressions is what attracts the historian of religions. Historically, the categorization of religion as an abstract object of study hindered any real understanding of our human identity in relationship to the natural world, making that relationship irrelevant. The detrimental effects left upon humanity and the Earth trace back to the creation of the empirical other: the central feature of religious academic discourse. However, simultaneously, contact with the Holy Other (with a capital "O") has been conceived as awe inspiring by its engagement with absolute power or the manifestation of the sacred in the Earth (i.e., the hierophany). This conundrum of being and *not* being in the world inspired the founding of the History of Religions, where the two "others," empirical and Holy, have been brought together to exemplify the ambiguity of religion and modernity as a point of reference for generating new understandings of distinctive human cultural expression.

Colonization, Materiality, and Movement

A defining feature of modernity has been mobility: the *freedom of movement*. The consequences of moving freely into territories not traditionally their own were radically disruptive and destructive to Indigenous Peoples' lives, traditions, and practices—according to the Geneva Convention, a cultural genocide.[25] Therefore, freedom of movement for European people meant the loss of freedom for Indigenous Peoples, who were forced from their homelands, where their experience of freedom resulted from living in proper relationship with a regenerative Earth. Cultural contact between European immigrants and Indigenous Peoples has resulted in opposing materialities where distinctive religious worldviews have collided in traumatic conflict.

Paradoxically, colonization requires the disruption of meaningful places and makes the History of Religions possible and necessary. Although the devastation of Indigenous Peoples' places have had a

---

25. According to the Geneva Convention on the Prevention and Punishment of the Crime of Genocide, Article 2 (ratified 9 December 1948), any of the following acts committed with the intent to destroy, in whole or in part, a national, ethnical, racial or religious group, as such:

(a) Killing members of the group;

(b) Causing serious bodily or mental harm to members of the group;

(c) Deliberately inflicting on the group conditions of life calculated to bring about its physical destruction in whole or in part;

(d) Imposing measures intended to prevent births within the group;

(e) Forcibly transferring children of the group to another group.

long, sad history in the European and Mediterranean worlds, these practices become particularly acute during the fifteenth century, or what became the modern era. Central to the imperial and colonial projects of Europeans in developing their New World Order was first determining occupied lands as terra nullius (or "empty lands") by the Vatican. Colonization required religious concepts that would justify leaving one's home and seizing another's, with the theft by God.

Modernity epitomizes this shift in the human material orientation from *locative* to *utopian*.[26] Allow me to submit "utopian" as an example of the conceptual tool of colonization, where a positive value is expressed as an idealized understanding of the perfect place, heaven, or a promised land. These particular concepts emphasized the ultimate significance of "placelessness" and its use to give new meaning to the word "freedom" in justifying land theft.

Conversely, among the Haudenosaunee, freedom comes from establishing a proper relationship with the land and connecting to the regenerative life force of creation. Because of the genocide perpetrated on them by discoverers, colonists, and merchants, Indigenous Peoples were forced to radically transform their traditional practices in order to maintain their *locative* orientations, whether they remained in their traditional landscapes or were forced out of them.[27]

The very structure of modernity, then, has been generated by a powerful fiction where human freedom is associated with belonging nowhere and everywhere simultaneously. In the modern context, human identities are largely ideological constructions (i.e., what one thinks and asserts with their mind) rather than a bodily or material

---

26. This distinction comes from Jonathan Z. Smith's *To Take Place*. Smith develops this model in order to conceptualize ancient Near Eastern religious orientations, but it is equally applicable to the New World context, with some emendations. See Arnold, *Eating Landscape*.

27. I am asserting that the religious practices of Africans who were enslaved and sent to North America, for example, are better understood as "Indigenous religions" than as Christian. See Long, *Significations*; and Olupona, *Beyond Primitivism*.

association with a particular landscape. People's lives are ultimately determined intellectually through books, institutions, or a myriad of media modalities, all of which are removed from an immediate living reality. Creative religious impulses of the modern era are rigorously signified by abstract and displaced utopian concepts like the Bible, Heaven, or Hell.

Indigeneity requires us to gauge the entire spectrum of cultural devastations within the colonial encounter from the perspective of the colonized and colonizer. What was lost? What remained? What was transformed? What were the cultural mechanisms that allowed for devastation or survival? Answers to these questions are different for the colonized and colonizer, but are possible focal points for comparative, collaborative, and future work with Indigenous Peoples through the History of Religions.

"Religion" expresses the consequences of world domination through the ages of discovery and colonialism. Indigeneity helps us to better define the devastation levied on both: not only those who colonized and conquered but also those who were invaded and ravaged. Indigeneity calculates the loss on both sides of settler-colonialism. This approach completes a hermeneutical circle, or a return to the self—whether Indigenous or settler-colonial—in light of our relationships with each other. It attempts to regain a critical interpretive location within the context of modernity from the point of view of the History of Religions.

History of Religions and Materiality

The origins of religion lay in the communications that human beings receive from the material world. The History of Religions describes other traditional practices through the transformative regenerative power of these communications and exchanges. Whether or not a scholar subscribes to a religion, the most potent way to describe one is to write about the hierophany and the Holy Other as an intimate reality that exists in the world. Some might say that it is best to write from the perspective of the insider so as to understand the evocative power of their tradition.[28] Whether one is inside or outside of a tradition, the opposing orientations make it extremely difficult in communicating, cross-culturally, the religion's message, or even the urgent need to heed the warning. It is descriptively significant to make comprehensible how the world speaks to human beings within a religious tradition and how the adherents respond, so as to make an intervention into our current religious understandings.

This work has proven to be particularly challenging for those of us writing about Indigenous Peoples, who exemplify a keen sense of attunement to these messages from the world. In other words, this religious sensibility is sensitive to these messages due to Indigenous Peoples' cultural emphasis on continuously and assiduously "paying attention."

The interpretive strategies of Indigenous Peoples that appear in the History of Religions align in their pursuit to articulate the materiality of religion, or the meaning of material life, but, as previously

28. There is a wide divergence of opinion on this point, and some would maintain that it would be irresponsible scholarship to take the point of view of the religious adherent. They would argue that it is more valuable to be an outsider and critic of the religions one studies. But I stand by my assertion that most historians of religions attempt to write from the perspective of the insider for four reasons. First, the history of the History of Religions has emphasized the importance of "getting inside" the adherent of a religion. As discussed, this more powerfully approximates why a given religion can exert so much influence in a human community. Second, it would be very hard in today's academic climate to be a critic of a given tradition, where the scholar is not necessarily on the outside, nor the informant on the inside. One has to adjudicate the subtlety of criticizing those people whom one is intending to write about. In the case of studying Indigenous values, the critical stance is best located outside of this relationship, as we will discuss. Third—and following from Smith's point about the scholar pursuing their choices—it wouldn't make much sense to me, as a scholar of religion, to completely violate my fascination with a given religious phenomena. It would be unsatisfying to simply be a critic of something that I was neither a part of nor would even choose to be involved in. Why bother? Fourth, to be a universal critic of the category of "religion" would put its institutional value and survival in jeopardy. If one chooses to be a scholar of religion, then isn't it worth defending as a discrete area of investigation within the academy?

mentioned, Indigenous Peoples are anathema to the culture of the university. At best, they have been used as resources for reflecting on general human progress toward civilization. Writing and teaching within the History of Religions is a way of short-circuiting the divisive effects of negatively appropriating Indigenous Peoples within the academy. In its recent past, after Eliade, the discipline was dominated by the quest for understanding the sacred in all of its manifestations and has become an encyclopedic enterprise inspired by assumptions fueled by the possibility of such knowledge. Such a far-reaching understanding of the sacred now seems unreasonable and unattainable because there is universal affirmation of the cultural embeddedness of our understandings, which make any universalization of this work indefensible.

According to Eliade, material elements such as water, stones, mountains, and trees have always been the primary referents for religious creativity and activity throughout the world. These features of material life are important as methodological points of reference.[29] For historians of religions today they serve as obvious points for interhuman/intercultural contact. The key feature of the relationship between human beings and the material world is that the meaning of a single material referent—say, a particular plot of land in Jerusalem—can have a completely different meaning for different groups of people because of the different worldviews that connect to specific attributes of the material world. The disjunctions between the scholar and the religious adherent (if they are not one and the same) can be accounted for by grounding one's issues and topics materially.

The History of Religions has developed the methodological tools to discuss contact, if it is rooted in a phenomenology (i.e., in the cultural appearances of material life). This can be extended to the phenomenon of intercultural contact with respect to material life.

We can no longer assume that Indigenous traditions are outside the institutions of the West. Though the "white males" of the past don't continue to fully make up the present academy, that way of

---

29. See Eliade, *Patterns in Comparative Religion*.

thinking is ingrained in university culture, no matter who is doing the academic work. The intellectual values of university culture are still at odds with Indigenous cultures, in spite of the growing diversity of faculty. The university has come a long way in transforming itself into a multicultural, multiethnic, multiracial, gender-balanced center of learning, but there is still great value placed on thinking about "the other" as distinct from "ourselves." From its inception, the History of Religions has been populated by those who have been deemed other to the Western university, including not only those who are atheist, Jewish, Christian, Muslim, Hindu, and Buddhist, but also Africans, African Americans, Europeans, European Americans, Asians, Asian Americans, Chicanos, Latinx, Native Americans, and ongoing permutations of these and other categorical distinctions. In the History of Religions, those who have been other to the Western academy have found a home.

Methodologies of the History of Religions have been constructed in such a way as to give as authentic a voice as possible to others moving into, but not yet constituted by, the academy. Others proximate to but excluded from the creation of modernity can actively participate in the vitality of the discipline by engaging in methodological discussions through their orientations to their material worlds. It is no longer simply the case that the scholar of religion passes judgment about "other" religions, but, rather, becomes actively engaged in a more subtle and risky venture of exploring how the other has been materially involved in creating all aspects of our shared existence. "Paying attention" has taken on new meaning for me. It is now about listening to how best to transform our institutions of knowledge production and dissemination; it is to transform our involvement in understanding this delicate work with regard to the study of religions as ancient value systems.

History of Religions, Diversity, and the Future of the University

Today, a struggle is perceived to be going on for the heart and soul of the university. Various strategies have been adopted to include other underrepresented groups. Some scholars have lamented that this contributes to a loss of the central organizing principle of the Western intellectual tradition, based in the Western canon; others maintain that this politics of domination has been justified and instigated by the university, so the inclusion of those once peripheral to its development can now be an important catalyst for corrective measures. The History of Religions, I would argue, is in a position to contribute important insights to these debates.

First, the West was never constructed out of its own whole cloth, but arose from the complex material situations that grew out of world-dominating enterprises. Empirical others have always been in close proximity to European expansion; therefore, there is no Western civilization that is self-sufficient and separate from those that suffered its oppression. Intellectual moves to defend the scholarly community of the university (or the modern nation-state, for that matter) have always been developed with reference to what was perceived as a dangerous other, either in its midst or just outside its walls. The more proximate the other, the more dangerous the other was perceived to be. It is the universities' push toward defining their work with clarity that, ironically, obfuscates the cultural realities of intercultural contact.

Second, and more importantly, if there is to be a future for the university, it must find ways to collaborate across all sorts of cultural, gendered, racial, and ethnic lines—however arbitrary the history of the development of those lines may be. The History of Religions has developed (and continues to develop) interpretive strategies for interrogating the meanings of the modern world by engaging human creativity at its deepest level; by design, it seriously navigates the worlds of marginalized people. Indigeneity moves academics and students out of conceptual boxes in order to confront the material world as a mystery. The future of the university will require that it enable its intellectual activity from outside of our disciplines to an exploration of radical material diversity.

The pressure exerted by an approximation of other meaningful orientations to material life (or other *materialities*) generates a critical position within the university. It is not simply an authentic reduplication of another's voice, but a rigorous amplification of that voice toward an audience to which scholarship can be redirected. In the final analysis, the empirical other cannot be completely relegated to a scholar's interpretation. They cannot just be a dimension of oneself whose existence is simply an extension of the writer's imaginative labors, as has been the case in the past with respect to primitive religions. Rather, the other works on, and with, the historian of religions, sometimes by exerting enormous pressure to be known and, in so doing, to transform. While this may happen in large measure within the imaginative and creative confines of the scholar's work, it nonetheless unmasks the intimate other as a critical voice to unleash new possibilities for understanding the world.

The materiality of our present situation is a mythic historical construction of the past, which was constituted out of sustained cultural contact between a wide variety of others who have been deemed as "heathen," "savage," "primitive," and the like. Yet all people who have been brought into intimate contact since the Age of Discovery have created the present world. From a History of Religions perspective, the material world is not so much a factual reality as a mythic one that requires constant critical creative engagement. For example, this concept of constant engagement was central to the way the Haudenosaunee made alliances. When they advised the Founding Fathers in Philadelphia on how to form a more perfect union, the Haudenosaunee used the analogy of the "Covenant Chain," which represented the new alliance between colonists and the Haudenosaunee: the chain was silver, which indicated that the metal needed incessant polishing to keep the alliance bright. The Haudenosaunee had first introduced this concept to the Dutch in 1613 with the Two Row Wampum–Covenant Chain Treaty Belt, which at that time established the first nation-to-nation alliance with the colonists of living in friendship forever on this land, without interfering with each other or damaging the shared environment. It was then brought into discussions with the Founding Fathers as a way to live in peace with the land.

Collaborative Methodologies and the Future of Religion

"Paying attention" is presented here as a strategy of Indigenous Peoples for understanding the sacred realities that reside in their places. For them, the material world is not an assemblage of lifeless matter made useful only by human intervention. Instead, the world is understood as the source of all life upon which human life is completely dependent. When the world reveals itself, Indigenous Peoples *pay attention* to those signals because they know that human survival depends on this larger living reality that continuously reveals itself. Modern people consider human life the primary living reality, but Indigenous Peoples consider the *world* the primary living reality to which they give the greatest amount of attention. Messages come from the living world, and, by heeding these messages through ceremonial engagement with the Earth, these people have been able to survive in their home places for millennia. Paying attention, in its Indigenous context, is a viable *religious* strategy that determines human survival.

Past methods for studying Indigenous Peoples have objectified them as the earliest forms of religiousness. Rather than being considered active participants in the current world, they have been seen as a member of the past, as examples of a prereligious, or "primitive," religious society.[30] In colonial, industrial, or consumerist contexts, Indigenous Peoples are seen as the cultural raw materials for civilization and are therefore organized and made useful through the process of objectification—namely, scholarly study and writing. As the modern world develops, however, we are faced with larger and larger more intractable problems that were addressed by Indigenous Peoples long ago. As we have seen, Indigenous Peoples have been active in the development of the modern world in spite of rigorous attempts

---

30. Johannes Fabian discusses this need to attain coevalness (i.e., the working assumption that we all inhabit the world at the same time) between the researcher and the society under study so that there can be a real intercultural exchange between people. See his *Time and the Other*.

by academics to dismiss or ignore them. Articulating the place of Indigenous Peoples as responsive to problems facing modernity—for instance, racism, environmental devastation, gender inequality, or denial of the nature of the sacred—goes a great way toward highlighting the nature of the problem.

Because of the contentious intimacy between Indigenous and settler-colonial people, numerous attempts have been made recently to create new sorts of collaborations in universities. There are several methodological consequences to this move toward collaboration, a move I will characterize here as an urgently needed corrective to the past practices of objectification and appropriation. Minimally, collaboration can be characterized as "talking with" rather than "talking about" Indigenous Peoples. This begs several questions, all of which amount to a fundamental shift in the way academics have conceptualized their work. What follows is a discussion on how to more effectively work in this area, given its contentious history.

How Do We Know Each Other?

Intercultural communication always involves speaking in or around some other language. Whether the conversation is in English or an Indigenous language, something is always lost in the translation. People on either side of the conversation will only be able to understand what makes sense to them. While this may seem like an obvious point, it is important to highlight because, in the recent past, academics have written about interactions with Indigenous Peoples as if they comprehended the totality of their experience.

University culture has tended to objectify others by means of a magical sleight of hand that is an active element in the creation of books. The authorial third-person voice transforms the difficulties of intercultural communication into data, which translates into ethnographic fact. This may be seen as an extension of the Protestant understanding of God as all-knowing and all-powerful, where the scholar substitutes their own presence for that of the divine. In the development of the modern world, this notion of God expresses authority and power. The contemporary university has exchanged the role of the Protestant God with that of the "expert." Thus, all "authorities" assume the role of an all-knowing agent in their third-person writing strategies.

Acknowledgment of collaborative techniques, such as joint authorship and first-person narratives, have all tended to emphasize the approximate, subjective ways of knowing, which stand in stark contrast with totalizing, objective knowledge.

What Do We Talk About?

For the religious studies researcher, simply talking about oneself or one's own cultural location is not an adequate way to generate an intercultural or interreligious dialogue. When dealing with people who speak different languages, or who speak from radically different worldviews, it is most often constructive to talk about things that are shared: a common denominator that can frame the interaction.

In other words—and perhaps counterintuitively to some—conversations about abstract theological concepts are not very interesting or helpful in working with Indigenous Peoples. Although the nature of God (or the sacred) may be the researcher's ultimate question, it is rarely useful in starting a conversation.

Instead, religious conversations most often revolve around specific attributes of material life that are shared. Again, this may seem obvious—for instance, like beginning a conversation about the weather—but studies about Indigenous Peoples have tended to move to what is regarded as the most profound aspects of these traditions without taking stock of the methodological consequences of such a move. The material consequences and conditions of this conversation must be held accountable. Indigenous Peoples have unique ways of expressing themselves on which scholarly work should shed light. They require attention to the materiality (i.e., paying attention) of their situation at all times, instead of blindly interpreting conversations regarding sacred texts or abstracted ceremonial observations. Useful conversations about Indigenous Peoples reflect on trees, rocks, water, plants, animals, sun, moon, stars, and the like, which are reminiscent of Eliade's "morphologies of the sacred."[31]

From start to finish, Indigenous traditions are concerned with materialities. So, in a sense, collaborations with Indigenous Peoples about religion are primarily concerned with the obvious: the attributes of our world that are shared and of mutual concern. This last consideration shifts the collaborative methodology in a radically different but necessary direction.

So, What Are the Urgent Issues of Mutual Concern?

As Jonathan Z. Smith has argued, the primary task of the scholar of the History of Religions is discerning the questions one wants to ask. What is deemed valuable, important or not, or what is highlighted in any study, are choices made by the scholar. Academics create and interpret the data of religion, but acknowledging that there is always a relationship between the scholar and the religious phenomena makes methodological demands particularly respectful to studies concerning Indigenous Peoples.

At the same time that students of Indigenous traditions are exploring their fascination with respect to these "*other*" cultures and peoples, they are also exploring their own urgent questions. Forming a relationship requires something more of the student besides simply

---

31. In *Patterns of Comparative Religions*, Mircea Eliade also appeals to material attributes of the phenomenal world, such as those listed in the text, as a morphology or language of the sacred. While Eliade is interested in how these material attributes *appear* cross-culturally in other religions, I am suggesting that his insights are much more usefully placed within the context of a methodological discussion about how to collaborate between different worldviews, religious and otherwise. The difference here is in where to locate these materialities rather than whether or not they are real or true. The point that both of us make is that religion is all about material life as opposed to those strands of intellectual work that would emphasize the ephemeral, spiritual, or immaterial nature of religion.

reading or studying; it demands that there be something of necessity that can be directly addressed within that intercultural exchange. One's worldview is risked in this exchange, just as aspects of an Indigenous worldview are being risked in confiding these traditions to outside investigators. As with the physical violence that accompanied the history of contact with Indigenous Peoples throughout the modern age, violence can likewise accompany scholarly activity—most pointedly when it comes to interpreting the central religious aspects of traditions on the brink of cultural destruction.

Several questions are asked in order to forge the relationship necessary to work in the category of Indigenous values. What would make it worth the violence necessary for interpreting an Indigenous tradition for those people who are devoted to its continuation? Why should they disclose their understanding of the sacred to anyone outside of their immediate community, no matter who they are, when the consequences of such a disclosure have been so disastrous in the past?

Rather than plying the worn-out perspective of being more objective, or more culturally sensitive, I want to suggest that we give up the illusion of having *any* objectivity whatsoever. Instead, all parties of the relationship that is implied in any academic study should calculate their risks. What is at stake in forging new alliances and new friendships? What makes the risk worth taking to engage another religious tradition? Only in the ways that Indigenous Peoples inform, challenge, and critique one's own cultural perspective can it be worth the risk. In light of past cultural relationships, Indigenous traditions, more than others, can create the most fertile arenas for cultural collaborations and critiques. It is, in that way, necessary work, as delicate as it may be.

Collaboration between people is most effective when, at the outset, the parties involved are clear about the need for the collaboration. This is not to say that the outcome of such work is known, or can even be predicted; indeed, the opposite is actually more often the case. The relationships that are developed take us in radically different and unpredictable directions. New layers of intractable problems are revealed and expressed. There is no end to the depth of these critical issues for those who are willing to dedicate themselves to exploring its possibilities.

Self-consciousness implied in the methodological work of the History of Religions has resulted recently in the charge of its being a quasi-theological enterprise. The charge of being "crypto-theological" has been leveled against the History of Religions by those scholars who embrace a social-scientific orientation to the study of religion. Such an orientation would want to see a more objective, less relational approach to the academic study of religion, in contradistinction to Smith's charge that there is no religion outside of the scholar's study.

My argument is that a move toward a more rigorous objectivity, whatever the justification, is a move toward a more neocolonial attitude within the academy. By leaving out the methodological return to a self-conscious critique with respect to studying other religious positions, one attempts to reify the authority of the scholar as the expert rather than emphasize their role as an active collaborator in the creation, continuation, and preservation of culture and religion.

If the interpreter of religion is coming to terms with the meaning of a given phenomenon, their work requires, at a minimum, a certain level of commitment to the phenomena by the interpreter. If one is an active collaborator, then one is attentive to the constantly shifting methodological positions that form those relationships. This, of course, requires constant attention to the data. The degree that one is committed to understanding Indigenous traditions is the degree to which one is committed to knowing one's own world.

I would not describe this method as "theological," as some have suggested, nor would I characterize it as a "postmodern," "postcolonial," or "cultural studies" model for studying religion. It is the History of Religions, as discussed, and fundamentally distinct from these methodological perspectives—because it goes to the nature of *religion* to get out of Tylor's conceptual boxes in such a way that it can reveal new dimensions of the world. As Eliade suggests, it is in its status as a cipher that religion has its most pernicious and long-lasting effects on cultural transformation. While this is the case for religion in general, it is much more important when working with Indigenous Peoples. It is attention being paid at a more than fair price.

4
Habitation

The primary characteristic of Indigeneity is knowing that human beings come from the Earth. We all share the same DNA and are related. We are as diversified as the landscape, and it is these defining characteristics of place that make us distinct from one another through language, diet, traditions, and ceremony. It is also what unifies us all.

Indigenous Peoples are not caretakers of the land. Instead, they know that the land takes care of its inhabitants—that is, if they are adhering to the responsibilities of living in proper relationship. Indigenous communities around the world are materially *and* spiritually supported by their distinctive physical environments. Theirs is a reciprocal collaboration with the natural world that has continued to develop for thousands of years that connects humanity to the regenerative life force. In this sense, Indigenous lifeways become ceremonial, and they perpetuate the ancient knowledge of deeply knowing a place and learning how best to inhabit that place as human beings.

What characterizes Indigenous values, therefore, is a *religious* orientation and connection to land itself. As I have shown previously, religious orientation means knowing and reconnecting through the origin stories to help locate the regenerative "center" of the world, where humans gain access to ancestors and the Creator. The religious orientation to that land is what shapes and determines everyday life and ritual relationships for humans. Activities such as hunting, gathering, and farming are primarily based on these relationships. My work with the Haudenosaunee has shown me that evoking the category of Indigenous values implies a spiritual, even religious, connection to a particular inhabited landscape.

Indigeneity involves both material and spiritual sensibilities regarding the economic familial, political, and aesthetic relationships with the land that emanate from the ceremonial and mythic understanding of inhabiting the land. The living landscape exerts, in the minds and hearts of Indigenous Peoples, a vital presence of an interactive nonhuman being who also serves as host for a variety of other living beings. Engaging and interacting with that living presence are at the center of Indigenous ceremonial life.

Indigenous Peoples realize that their vitality is regenerated from this reciprocal relationship with land. Maintaining the vitality of the land is a core value of Indigenous communities. This commitment is reflected in their human identity in language and as a member of a group, clan, tribe, and national affiliation.

The Haudenosaunee, for example, are comprised of thirteen matrilineal clans, with each clan representing one of thirteen different animals, birds, or fish. Each clan is represented by five title holders: 1) Clan Mother; 2) her chosen Hoyane (Man of a Good Mind); 3) sub-Hoyane; 4) female Faithkeeper; and 5) male Faithkeeper. Each member nation of the Confederacy—Mohawk, Oneida, Onondaga, Cayuga, Seneca, and Tuscarora—have some variation of this clan representation.

As I detailed in the introduction, this matrilineal clan system was installed well over one thousand years ago when the Peacemaker brought his message of peace and came to found the Great Binding Peace at Onondaga Lake. Each person, identified by their clan lineage, is given a special name by their respective Clan Mother, who has the responsibility of "holding" the names of her clan in her basket. Each name is unique to one child; upon that person's death, the name is returned to the basket, and, after one year's time, the name is reassigned to another child.

The natural world recognizes these children through this ancient lineage of naming. From this perspective, the Haudenosaunee are identified by their clan relationship to land, both as individuals and as clan families through their languages. These special relationships inform human beings as to how best to inhabit the Earth. This aspect of Indigenous values requires us to reorient ourselves to a different understanding of *habitation* as an attribute of religion.[1]

In this sense, religion is fundamentally *about how human beings meaningfully inhabit the world* in a way that combines the material and the mythic, the physical, and the spiritual—or, to use Long and Carrasco's phrase, *materiality of religion*.[2] In that spirit, the materiality of Indigenous Peoples is that the land is a living being upon which all life is completely dependent. Therefore, the land is not isolatable from other living beings or processes. The sky, underworld, air, water, animals, weather, etc. all participate in the integrative life forces of the natural world and thus the lives of Indigenous Peoples.

The centrality of the living land is a value often expressed by Indigenous communities. The Earth is called Mother Earth, Turtle Island, Pacha Mama—and characterized as a living being. In these formulations, the living *presence* of the land is emphasized as an obvious focal point upon which the community orients itself.

Indigenous Peoples often refer to themselves as "the real people," "people of this place," "people that were created here," or the "people who have the general quality of living in this place."[3] Every

---

1. My book *Eating Landscape* is an exploration of *religion as habitation*, as in the case of the Aztec, and *religion as occupation*, as in the case of the Spanish. It examines the distinctive ways that these empires controlled their places by means of conflicting Indigenous (for the Aztec) and Colonial (for the Spanish and Europeans) strategies.

2. See Carrasco, "Imagination of Matter." A remarkable study of Maya ceremonial architecture and their reception through time is Jones, *Twin City Tales*.

3. At first contact, Indigenous nations were given derogatory names by Europeans as a way to start the process of colonization through ownership, diminish their identity with place, and reflect the contentiousness of intercultural contact. Unfortunately, many of these names stuck because the primary sources of the time were usually written by antagonistic European explorers, priests, and other historians. Derogatory names tended to justify European dominance in lands not traditionally their own.

cultural orientation contains this connection to place. Knowledge of being Indigenous to a place is emphatically empirical from having exchanged knowledge with a living environment since the beginning of the world. In his book *Alpha: Myths of Creation*, Charles Long wrote that origin stories reveal how Indigenous Peoples originated from and therefore belong to a specific place that forever shapes their identity. The Tewa peoples tell how they emerged from beneath Sandy Place Lake and were guided to their new home by a spider. The Mixtecs painted scenes of their ancestors descending from the sky to find the central place on Earth to live. These myths are not fictions, as modern people tend to believe, but origin stories that orient these community values to their homelands.[4]

When academics—humanists, social scientists, or scientists—emphasize *human* ingenuity in the processes of forming Indigenous cultures, they tend to overlook the most important element of their identity: the land speaks to human beings by revealing that they belong to the land. The land, then, does not belong to them.[5] From the perspective of the History of Religions, it is quite acceptable, even common, that the land and its nonhuman inhabitants would speak and communicate to human beings in their Indigenous languages.[6]

▲ ▲ ▲

As discussed in the previous chapter, all religions have their origins in a hierophany. Ceremony and rituals tell the story of hierophanies that erupted into the world and then became fundamental values and foundational signs of how the material world came into being and operates. Fundamentally, the idea that the land communicates itself to human beings is a prerequisite for all human habitation. As Eliade says, the hierophany *founds* the world; according to him, a meaningful landscape is synonymous with an understandable world.

---

4. "The sui generis nature of religion must be maintained if the concreteness of man's history is to be understood and appreciated" (Long, *Alpha*, 6).
5. See Deloria Jr., *For This Land*; and Bastien, *Mountain of the Condor*.
6. Basso, *Wisdom Sits in Places*.

Scholars and journalists who take a human-centered, or anthropocentric, approach to Indigenous cultures erase the experiences of Indigenous Peoples and reduce their traditions to human creations. This approach deletes the autonomy of the landscape, ignores the innovative interactive forces of the natural world, as well as ignores the dynamic relations between the places and the peoples who learn through engagement with the land that it is a living relative. An anthropocentric approach to Indigenous values is simply not an adequate interpretive perspective to describe the religious features of these traditions. It is of critical importance to the viability and academic integrity of the category of "Indigenous" that the religious sensibility of the land as a living presence be maintained. Indigenous traditions belong to the land, not the other way around.

To state it plainly: an anthropocentric approach to religion is reflective of an immigrant, or settler-colonial, worldview. It places emphasis on human agency and therefore justifies human domination of the land. Indigenous religions are not projections of the human mind onto the land, nor are they merely inscriptions of human values onto the blank slate of a terra nullius, or an empty land. For Indigenous Peoples, the life of the land existed prior to any human community—which is empirically true. Land is the *total fact* of Indigenous values. Therefore, human beings are *totally contingent on the land, in all respects*. In order to understand and appreciate Indigenous traditions, modern people must begin to understand that land is the most active agent in the formation of human beings.

As discussed in chapter 2, some past theorists of religion (e.g., Tylor, James, Otto) saw that Indigenous Peoples expressed a primary reality in the evolutionary development of religion. I would like to argue here that widespread evidence shows that *religion as habitation* is fundamental to all religious orientations.

All religions have a homeland: a place that is regarded more highly than other places, or a sacred place which becomes the spiritual vortex, axis mundi, and center of the values of the society. Precolonial history, however, forced many religious communities into diaspora, limiting access to the homeland, the site of the founding hierophany and the appearance of divinities, the work of ancestors, and the origins of values. Displacements fundamentally change the nature of a human relationship with the sacred *and* with the land. It can be argued that, up until the fact of displacement, whether caused by ecological change, encroachment by others, or migrations of animals, all people were Indigenous.

Since the Age of Discovery, which, as Long recently showed in *Ellipsis*, is when colonialism impacted a huge percentage of Indigenous societies, there has been a monumental economic and religious elevation in the value of displacement. This profound change in the stories, rituals, and values associated with homelands and Indigenous Peoples comes, in part, in an exaggerated shift from understanding God as creator and the source of values in the world, to that of a God residing *outside the corporality of the world*—a God transcendent and almost totally at odds with the materiality of human life.

The Religious Value of the Living Land

"Every part of our culture comes from the Earth," writes Rigoberta Menchú. "Our religion comes from maize and bean harvests which are so vital to our community. So even if a man goes to try and make some money, he never forgets his culture springs from the Earth."[7] Menchú, a Quiché Maya woman and Indigenous women's rights activist, was awarded the Nobel Peace Prize in 1992 for her struggles for social justice and ethnocultural reconciliation based on respect for the rights of Indigenous Peoples. This passage appears in the context of a discussion about birth ceremonies and how these ceremonies connect the Quiché Maya to their natural world: how babies become one with the land and, especially, the plants of the Maya realm. The Maya grow because they eat the foods that come out of the Earth, their Mother, and, as they do, they become more and more a part of the land. Formalizing this vital relationship *is* the

---

7. Menchú, *I, Rigoberta Menchú*, 16.

purpose for having ceremonial events for the children through their various stages of life.

As previously noted, a healthy human body is an extension of the land. This relationship endures in multiple generations through what anthropologists and historians of religions call "rites of passage." The purpose of many Indigenous ceremonies is to reconnect human life, social relationships, and the expression of values with the living land. Connecting children with the land is the ritual work of the community, who direct and educate those next generations to carry out the responsibilities to a living Earth.

As Menchú states, this sense of responsibility is expressed through the understanding that, even if someone has to leave their Indigenous community either because it is under assault or to pursue their economic well-being, their Quiché identity remains intact because it is rooted in their connection with the land. Even though Menchú is discussing the Quiché Maya culture, the values she expresses are shared with Indigenous Peoples all over the world.

The Lakota of Rosebud, South Dakota, put the Indigenous value of the living landscape another way. In *Lakota Star Knowledge: Studies in Lakota Stellar Theology*, elders note that the primary way of knowing the land is with reference to the sky. The patterns of star constellations and activities of sky beings are intimately related to the patterns around the Black Hills and the activities of human beings. Ceremonies performed by sky beings are simultaneously performed on Earth by the Lakota people. For the urban geographer Paul Wheatley, this sense of connection between sky and landscape serves as an example of "cosmo-magical thinking," where beings of the sky are mirrored on the Earth and vice versa.[8] The difference between Wheatley's perspective and that of the Lakota is that "mirroring" is not the result of human construction but of the human recognition and respect for the natural attributes, dynamic patterns, powers, and gifts of the land—in this instance, the Black Hills. Understanding

---

8. Wheatley, *Pivot of the Four Quarters*.

and caring for the living Earth is likewise understanding and caring for the material attributes of the universe that surrounds and nurtures the land.

In *Lakota Star Knowledge*, the authors say that they are writing the book for both Lakota young people and non-Indigenous people, "so that they will be inspired to seek out and recover their own traditional ways of knowing the Earth—not as dead matter spinning in empty space—but rather, as our very mother, a living and holy being."[9] This is an urgent message. Developing a strong sense of the land as a living being should motivate humans of the modern world to grasp the awareness that the Earth is more than a dead "natural resource" there to be disinterred for profit and financial wealth.[10] This unhinged anthropocentric nature of our present abusive practices with land has brought us to the brink of global self-destruction.

The urgency here, then, of Indigenous values is twofold—not only spiritual but also ethical, with regard to the land we all inhabit. As we will discuss in chapter 6, success in transitioning to a more viable value system depends on the ability of human beings to realize that the world does not exist for them, but that they are part of a collaborative world. Modern people have forgotten this essential religious value. Modern existence has developed a worldview that is in near total opposition to the Indigenous values mentioned by Menchú, in spite of over five hundred years of intimate cultural contact.

Indigeneity: The Sacred and the Profane

Indigenous knowledge is directly connected with other kinds of knowledge, all of which communicate how the material world works. In this perception, traditional knowledge and practical knowledge are interconnected and interrelated, and the Earth is neither physically

---

9. Goodman, *Lakota Star Knowledge*, 1.
10. Or, as in the case of the sacred Black Hills, defacing Mount Rushmore to celebrate American domination across Lakota territory with the glare of four US presidents.

nor conceptually separate. Herein lies an important critique of past methodological assumptions in the History of Religions: according to Eliade, the sacred is categorically distinct from the profane.[11] In Indigenous traditions, however, sacred and profane realities are materially part of the same living landscape—that of being coinhabited. Categories of "sacred" and "profane" are specific to a certain place and time, and not necessarily permanent. What is considered sacred at one point may be regarded as profane at another. Put more pragmatically, a ceremonial precinct that is understood to be a sacred place at one time of the year may, at another time, be utilized as a place to hunt, gather, or grow food. The gap between the sacred and profane grows far wider when human beings feel the need to permanently designate places as either one or the other.

Also expressing Lakota values, Black Elk refers to the Black Hills as the most sacred place in the world. He also refers to them as a "food pack" and a place where people can be healed if they are sick. They serve as a site for acquiring sacred knowledge through visions, a place for hunting, and a place of great healing attributes. In the modern context, these could be characterized as a place of worship (i.e., church, temple, mosque), grocery store, and hospital—completely distinctive realities over which human beings seemingly exercise complete control. For Indigenous Peoples, however, these attributes of the sacred landscape necessarily imply their applicability to all aspects of human existence.[12]

The dichotomy of the sacred and the profane only works for Indigenous traditions in a limited way. While an expression of an opposition is important for a living landscape at specific times, it is

---

11. *The Sacred and the Profane* is one of Eliade's most popular books on the origins of religion. It has never appealed to me, however, because it tends to set up a false dichotomy between what he sees as polar opposites. To be fair, he does try to overcome the dichotomy in his analysis by appealing to the activity of religion. But the model tends to work best for the "great religions" of the West rather than for Indigenous traditions.

12. Neihardt, *Black Elk Speaks*.

equally important to appreciate that nothing in the material world is *essentially* sacred or profane. The Western tradition of isolating specific locations from all human contact because they are sacred or profane is contrary to Indigenous values. Sacred places, like profane places, require a human presence as well as an ongoing interaction with all living beings. Because the land is alive, it contains within it all dichotomous values, just like human beings: good and evil, sacred and profane, life and death, day and night. These reciprocal oppositions create the world and are not meant to be isolated or set against one another.

As Lévi-Strauss observed of myth, life is always involved in a series of bridging oppositions that creates the bricolage of life.[13] Likewise, the life of the land expresses itself to Indigenous Peoples as a series of ongoing interactive oppositions. This distinguishes Indigenous values from Western religions, where opposing forces are often seen as bifurcated and completely opposite from one another.[14]

It is the appreciation of the living nature of land, however, that brings oppositions together into a single reality. Celestial bodies oppose one another, for example, and the interaction of day and night, winter and summer, wet and dry, combine to promote the totality of a living world. Land, as an expression of life, makes material and comprehensible the more radically abstract theological concepts of the global religions.

It is not just individuals who self-consciously define themselves as being Indigenous and having sacred places from which they come.

---

13. For an early example of his thinking about oppositions, see Lévi-Strauss, *Savage Mind*. Unfortunately, Lévi-Strauss's early insights into the nature of oppositions became a school of thought that was later called "structuralism." It is unfortunate because becoming a school required a level of abstraction that removed his thinking from the living relationships discussed here.

14. According to Fernando Cervantes, the radical separation between God and the world, or the sacred and the profane, was a theological consequence of European colonization of the New World. This is a very important historical development that we will explore in chapter 6. See *Devil in the New World*.

Every human community has a place of origin—a homeland. All people have a sacred place that is home for them, where the land speaks so as to give them an understanding of who they are at the most profound levels.

Today, however, most religious people do not inhabit their sacred places of origin, where the hierophanies that defined their existence occurred. Most often these lands exist in some foreign land with which there is little possibility of ever making a physical connection. In addition, most religious people have not been connected with their sacred lands for long periods of time because they had been invaded by foreigners. The consequences are that most religions, particularly in the West, are *immigrant* and *itinerant* traditions. Over time, the global religions have developed strategies by which to understand the nature of the sacred as a reality independent of, and at times, even in opposition to, the land.

Particularly since the fifteenth century, religion has tended to deemphasize the sacred, the living nature of the land, and, in some cases, the material world altogether as a vital presence. Instead, land takes on a sacrality in its *historical* significance, as having *once* been the site of a hierophany, but not a site of a *continuous* hierophany. So, an understanding develops in immigrant and settler-colonial religions that the sacred had once revealed itself as a hierophany a long time ago in a distant place, not understanding that hierophanies are a series of ongoing revelations in the regenerative life of the land.[15] This historical hierophany can express and unfold itself in countless ways, the most ominous current examples including nationalism, fundamentalism, and millennialism. These are commitments to an *ideal* of the status of a human community in a place, rather than the living status of the place, or the Earth itself.

---

15. Vine Deloria Jr.'s *God Is Red* is the most potent critique of the historical orientation of contemporary understanding of religion that is in direct opposition to the geographical orientation of Indigenous traditions. In many ways it echoes and updates Mircea Eliade's *Myth of the Eternal Return*, in particular the section titled "The Terror of History."

Indigenous Peoples, however, have a distinctively different type and intensity of commitment to their sacred landscapes, whether or not they are currently residing in that place. Distinctions between Indigenous and immigrant religious orientations are not solely a matter of living in one's traditional lands, but primarily a matter of the degree to which land as a living presence enters into their understandings of themselves, or of how closely a place and a people are bound together in a living relationship. This distinction has been expressed as a difference between the status of "sacred texts" and "oral traditions," where more confidence is put in the global religious authority of the text.

Conventional sacred texts generally don't exist in Indigenous traditions, but, if they do, they have a much more performative emphasis.[16] Forming a distinction between Indigenous and Immigrant traditions around whether or not a given tradition has a text, however, tends to misconstrue the character of Indigenous Peoples as *lacking* the text—as deficient in something essential for authenticity. For my purposes, I would rather focus on another related criterion for illustrating the distinction between these types of value systems: on the *proximity of the sacred*.

In the History of Religions, the location of the sacred has played an important role in theorizing the nature and development of religion. Scholars such as Otto and Van der Leeuw all perceived that the origins of religion were in the immediate experience of the sacred, and that contemporary examples of this phenomenon were most clearly seen in primitive people. Similarly, for Indigenous Peoples, the sacred is in close proximity to human beings. Sacred beings, upon whom all life is based, exist in constant interaction with human beings. So close are the relationships between various kinds of beings that they are understood in familial terms. Names are exchanged between human beings and other kinds of beings, which underscores

---

16. There are numerous studies devoted to the issues of the function of text and orality in the History of Religions. A bibliography of the classics in this regard can be found at the back of this book.

the values of maintaining close, personal relationships with all manner of other than human beings. When it comes to the vitality of the land, the role of ancestors, for example, can be of fundamental importance to daily life. In death, they inhabit the land in different forms, even periodically visiting the living, often playing a role in the day-to-day activities of their descendants.

Immigrant religions have much less urgency in addressing the living status of land because, through various means and for various reasons, the sacred has more the character of having been removed from the world. I often pose a simple test in my classes to exemplify this idea. When I ask, "Where is God?," students often laughingly point upward. When I ask, "Why is God up in the sky?," students respond that it is because "He" is not in the world. Indeed, "He" is often understood to be opposed to the world, and everywhere, and nowhere, simultaneously.[17] In other words, God is *otiosus* (i.e., obscured or removed from the material world). God is less geographically proximate to human beings than even the stars, or any observable reality.

For itinerant, immigrant religions, *faith* is what bridges that gap between human beings and the sacred.[18] It is the proximity of the sacred that indicates the broad distinctions between Indigenous and immigrant orientations in a way that reflects the values of land, and

---

17. This is an American context, and the reaction would be quite different for students in other places. When I asked the same question in Japan, for example, it provoked a very different reaction. The Japanese have a more indigenous sensibility about the location of particular gods, or kami, and yet there is a greater ambiguity about the proximity of the sacred due to an excessive emphasis on modern economic development. Clearly, for the Japanese, maintaining Japanese values that uphold Japanese culture means having the ability to navigate a sacred landscape. Many in Japan are concerned about the culturally corrosive effects of Modern values that promote an abstract understanding of life.

18. An objection could be raised here that this reflects a particularity of American religious values that is not shared universally. To the degree that these values are involved with the materiality of the modern, global values, however, they can be understood to be universal.

the geographical arrangement that articulates a distinction of styles and motivations. It is not an absolute difference, because, as has been expressed throughout this book, everyone is Indigenous in some way. It takes shape through the process of becoming an immigrant to which people have had to adjust by virtue of religious ideas. Immigrant religions express both a sense of having lost one's Indigenous sensibilities and a sense of longing for a place lost, a yearning to return to a land where the sacred reveals itself: a holy *land*.

Religion as Orientation

As discussed in chapter 1, many Indigenous Peoples would object to pairing the terms "Indigenous" and "religions" together. They would wish to distinguish their traditions from the imperialistic religious expressions that have sought to destroy them by adopting the categories of "spirituality" or "tradition." Indigenous Peoples express a deep and abiding connection with their land—even if they are currently displaced from their traditional homelands—that is more than just economic. The term "Indigenous," therefore, implies a connectedness to the land that includes expressions and concerns for the sacred. I say it this way because in all religions we find the same (sometimes very distant) echoes of the primacy of the sacred land that arise in surprising ways.

As for Eliade, this is often expressed as nostalgia for a connection to place—pilgrimages, for example, to sacred sites, and trips to places that are religiously significant because of those historical hierophanies. But for Indigenous Peoples, sacred lands are still vitally active in their ceremonial traditions. The land speaks, and it still sends important messages.[19] While the distinctions between attitudes

---

19. According to Vine Deloria Jr. an Indigenous understanding of land has not been legally protected because of an immigrant understanding of the hierophany having taken place in the past. He writes: "Human beings must always be ready to receive new revelations at new locations. If this possibility did not exist, all deities and spirits would be dead. Consequently, we always look forward to the revelation

about land may be seen as one of varying degrees between those who practice a global religion and those who practice an "Indigenous" one, the place of land is a continuing religious sensibility that makes a sharp distinction between religious orientations.

One of the primary responsibilities of any fully functioning and morally and ethically motivated human being is to be properly oriented to the world. Orientation, as Long has pointed out, is a difficult process of adjudicating one's place with respect to a history, tradition, language, community, perception, and so on.[20] Indigenous Peoples embrace the process of becoming oriented to the physical world.

For example, the Lakota say that being aligned to the deities of the cardinal directions is the basis for all respect, interpersonally as well as with regard to the sacred. A variety of ceremonial strategies have been developed (fundamental among them the pipe ceremony) to address the sacred beings that reside in the different directions. For the Lakota, orientation is the basis of all respect. An emphasis on becoming correctly oriented to the cosmos is an overarching concern of these ceremonial practices. Orientation is not just a sentimental process of acknowledging a connection within the human being's heart or mind; in an Indigenous context, the process is achieved by dedicating oneself to physically knowing the cardinal directions, the movement of celestial bodies in the sky, the change of seasons, the movement of animals, and the currents of the sea. Spiritual beings associated with these natural phenomena form the basis

---

of new, sacred places and new ceremonies. Unfortunately, some federal courts have irrationally and arbitrarily circumscribed this universal aspect of religion by insisting that traditional practitioners restrict their identification of sacred locations to those places of historical significance, implying that, at least for the federal courts, God is Dead" ("Sacred Lands and Religious Freedom," 5).

20. Charles H. Long's definition of religion fits very well when considering the *religion as habitation*. "[Religion] will mean orientation—orientation in the ultimate sense, that is, how one comes to terms with the ultimate significance of one's place in the world . . . The religion of any people is more than a structure of thought; it is experience, expression, motivations, intentions, behaviors, styles, and rhythms" (*Significations*, vii).

of the material world. Neglecting to acknowledge and celebrate these sacred beings whose activities nurture all of material life would be not only disrespectful, but also impractical.[21]

Being oriented to sacred places goes deep in all religions, not just Indigenous traditions. Without sacred places, there would not have been "religion." In the History of Religions, a sacred reality *manifests* itself in material form to a wide variety of people. According to Eliade, practically every place of origin has been the site of a manifestation of the sacred: Jerusalem, Mount Ararat, Mecca, and in Onondaga ancestral territory, where I reside, at Onondaga Lake.

The significance of sacred places for Indigenous traditions and for the History of Religions brings up the dilemma of hierophanies for immigrant traditions. The religious status of sacred places for immigrant people is one that stands in marked contrast to Indigenous perspectives. Specifically, an understanding of the sacred necessarily accompanies an immigrant cosmology; as discussed, this is primarily oriented around the proximity of the sacred. In this context, however, the immigrant religious orientation is one where the hierophany is not where they presently reside. Their world is only habitable on a provisional basis.

Following from Eliade, therefore, immigrant religions necessarily inhabit *profane* space. For example, there are few, if any, sacred places for settler-colonial people in the United States, while, for Indigenous Peoples, sacred places are everywhere. This conceptual gap between immigrant and Indigenous orientations to the land highlights the problem of religion in modernity. It demonstrates why policies on land use and property rights are considered religious issues for Indigenous Peoples and economic or political issues for immigrant people—even though immigrants used religion to justify the theft of Indigenous lands.

---

21. Aboriginal people from Queensland, Australia, known as the Guugu Ymithirr learn an "internal compass" at a very young age. When they greet one another, they do so directionally rather than interpersonally, as with pronouns. Haviland, "Guugu Yimithirr Cardinal Directions."

Sacred Places in the History of Religions

According to Eliade, places in which a sacred reality has revealed itself are the center of the world, or the axis mundi. A dramatic example of this phenomenon is seen in Islam when Muslims kneel in prayer facing Mecca five times a day. Sacred places are quite literally the axis mundi because they are the physical location where a sacred reality has broken into material life.[22] These places thus become mediation centers between human beings and sacred beings.

Until recently, cities throughout the world were primarily organized with reference to hierophanies. The prestige of traditional cities, in contrast to modern cities, was directly related to their connection with the sacred. Rome, Beijing, Banaras, St. Petersburg, Jerusalem, and many others were prominent because of their ceremonial attributes, where mediation between human beings and sacred beings took place.[23]

Sacred places, however, have a distinctive character when contrasting the global religions with Indigenous traditions. Particularly with Christianity and Islam, sacred places orient people vertically toward a transcendent reality, or a reality removed from this material world. Places like Rome and Jerusalem, therefore, are isolated from the rest of the landscape because the sacred reality toward which they orient people exists above and outside the world. They serve as a shrine that facilitates this vertically oriented transcendent reality, where churches are usually adorned with spires, towers, and steeples that point toward heaven. In contrast, Indigenous Peoples are generally oriented horizontally, with respect to a sacred landscape. Therefore, sacred places for Indigenous Peoples are interconnected with

---

22. Mesoamerica is an excellent example of the dynamics of the Center. See Carrasco, *Quetzalcoatl and the Irony of Empire*; and Carrasco, *Religions of Mesoamerica*.

23. Paul Wheatley's seminal study of ancient China developed the foundational character of the hierophany of the ceremonial center in *Pivot of the Four Quarters*.

other attributes of the landscape because the sacred reality toward which they are oriented is embedded in the material world.

In Mesoamerica, Aztec and Maya traditional ceremonial centers are modeled from the natural mountainous landscape and surrounding skyscapes. When the Spanish overthrew these cities, they completely destroyed the ancient ceremonial pyramids that had stood for hundreds of years, and they used the rubble to erect Catholic churches with towering spires and turrets, which were intended to redirect attention from the Earth toward the heavens, where an imagined—or otiosus—God resided.

Indigenous, land-centered, or autochthonous traditions inhabit a living landscape. Ceremonies performed with respect to this living landscape do not hierarchically rank the importance of one sacred site over another or one sort of living being over another; rather, it is the interactive wholeness of the landscape that promotes life in all its manifestations. Through ceremonial performances, Indigenous Peoples are oriented to a living landscape. This understanding of the sacred character of land stands in marked contrast to sacred places among many global religions.

Are Indigenous Peoples Environmentalists?

While Indigenous Peoples and environmentalists share concerns regarding the vitality of the land, or cultural practices over which modern society exercises control, there is no direct correlation between the categories of Indigeneity and environmentalism.

As we have already discussed, for Indigenous Peoples the living earth of their homeland is a *total fact* of their lives, identity, culture, and traditions. They understand that humanity is materially constituted by the land and, therefore, that their identity is embedded and contingent on its health.

Environmentalism, like the History of Religions, is an ideological Western intellectual position developed during the Age of Discovery and the ensuing era of the Enlightenment. This complicated lineage includes the writings of transcendentalists, philosophers, travel writers, and others. It isn't my intention to make a judgment of environmentalism, but simply to note that it does not spring from the same kinds of cultural values that are expressed by Indigenous Peoples.

The different cultural values are often expressed in assumptions having to do with the proximity of the sacred, as discussed, and with the degree of control that human beings have, or should have, over the nonhuman world. Because environmentalism develops out of an Immigrant worldview and the otiose or sacred nature of God, it is sometimes assumed to share Indigenous values. However, the contrasting cultures of environmentalism and Indigenous values sometimes find their worlds at odds with one another—for example, over Native Alaskan whaling practices.[24] There are a great deal of overlapping concerns, however, between Indigenous Peoples and environmentalists. Critical issues regarding our shared environment is a potent area of conversation and activity because our mutual concern has become urgent.

A joke I recently heard illustrates this distinction. After meeting with environmentalists in the Longhouse at the Onondaga Nation, one Hoyane (Man of a Good Mind) recounted to another, older Hoyane, "I just learned that the Haudenosaunee are environmentalists! I never realized that until today," to which the other replied, "We are not environmentalists: *we are the environment.*"[25]

While it might first seem like this is a reasonable assertion to simply equate the two, reducing Indigenous values to "environmentalism" diminishes the integrity of both categories. Each of these perspectives has been developed from a particular cultural vantage point and has a cosmology by which each is continually informed and oriented. The assumption of the universal applicability of environmentalism is, perhaps, its most controversial and destructive aspect. However, by acknowledging that environmentalism has a lineage

---

24. Jones, "When Environmentalists Crossed the Strait."
25. Told in the Longhouse by Chief Irving Powless Jr., 2014.

and history that is tied to a legacy of discovery and conquest—that is to say, that it is a cultural creation that is therefore limited to a particular worldview—is to enable a more honest collaboration between environmentalists and Indigenous Peoples.

I regard myself as an environmentalist, in some part. I suggest that environmentalism is only made useful for Indigenous Peoples insofar as it is understood to be a particular cultural creation and not universally applicable to all people in all environments. There are numerous issues where environmentalists and Indigenous Peoples collaborate around the world. These are issues of *urgent mutual concern regarding place*. The notion of collaboration requires that one be keenly aware of one's concerns, one's influences, *and* one's limits of understanding.

I am arguing here for a *humble environmentalism* that is essentially open to the mystery of the world. This perspective has been expressed by many environmentalist leaders, too. With respect to Indigenous Peoples, however, environmentalists who wish to collaborate should try and stay clear of the excesses of some New Age participants who have been charged with woefully and wrongfully appropriating these religions. Assuming the limits of one's interpretive position, rather than its omniscient or omnipresent quality, inevitably leads to an overdetermined overconfidence that conflicts with *what is actually there, empirically, in the world*.

Even though one perspective cannot be reduced to the other, there is tremendous value in collaborating to address the most urgent issues facing human survival today. Put another way, "environmentalism," in some of its most extreme ideological, almost fundamentalist, formulations, should spend more time trying to *Indigenize* itself.

Locative and Utopian Religions

Defining religion as how one meaningfully inhabits the world changes the way modern people have conventionally comprehended the freedom of religion. In the United States, this is generally understood as being constitutionally guaranteed under individual rights. In other words, human beings are free to *believe* any religion they wish so long as it doesn't infringe on another human being's rights. Thus, religion is understood to be directly associated with a *faith* system that dwells within the human heart and mind.

So strong is the association between "faith traditions" and "religion" that often these terms are interchangeable for one another. The idea of religion as "faith" removes it from the material world and puts it into a world completely determined by human beings. For modern people, religion is a wholly human-centered reality within people's minds or bodies and therefore independent of how the world actually works.

Taking seriously the category of Indigenous values, however, transforms the nature of religion. On the one hand, Indigenous traditions require that one take seriously the material world—or, more specifically, the land—as a primary religious resource; material life is not just reduced to economic, scientific or political "realities." On the other hand, Indigenous values fundamentally alter the way we, who have been reared with immigrant worldviews, have thought about religion. They generate a critical self-consciousness about the religious dimensions of daily life.

For Indigenous Peoples, cultural identity is embedded in their ceremonial traditions, myths of origin, and the like, all of which are generated from their relationships with the land. This describes the *locative* values that orient these traditions.

With the Age of Discovery came a profound shift in how immigrant people, who had left their homeland, would create a new transportable and idealized utopian religion. Jonathan Z. Smith's distinction between "locative" and "utopian" offers us a critical point of entry into Indigenous traditions.[26] It is a critical point of entry

---

26. "For the native religionists, homeplace, the place to which one belongs, was *the* central religious category. One's self-definition, one's reality was the place into which one had been born, or understood as both geographical and social place. To the new immigrant in the diaspora, nostalgia for homeplace and cultic substitutes

because it communicates contrasting yet comparative values that are generated out of the gap between orientations to the material world. While his cases are largely taken from ancient Near Eastern urban centers, Indigenous Peoples inhabiting traditional cities, including the ancient ceremonial centers of Africa, Asia, the Americas, or where there was an exponential rise in the power and prestige of the urban center, also experienced a traumatic shift from locative to utopian worldviews. Most often, a shift to the utopian worldview was perpetrated by an outside force: an overconfidence in universalizing a local religious orientation and the ability, through conquest and domination, to subvert this worldview.

Locative religions acknowledge the inherent value of the land previous to human habitation. As Smith says, it is thus understood to be the homeland to which are tied the totality of the human community's sense of itself. Utopian religions must, for various reasons, understand their relationship with the sacred in fundamentally different yet analogous ways from locative traditions. Utopian traditions emphasize a memory of a place now distant, and the hope of the return to that sacred place one day; they focus on the possibility of an eventual return to the deity, to the land, to a heavenly place. With the diaspora, utopian traditions are detached from their original source, and thus from the center of the world. They wander in insignificant, profane space until the opportunity arrives for them

---

for the old, sacred center were central religious values. For the thoroughly diasporic member, who may not have belonged to the deity's original ethnic group, freedom from place became *the* central religious category. Projecting the group's diasporic existence into the cosmos, he discovered himself to be in exile from his true home (a world beyond this world), he found his fulfillment in serving the god beyond the god of this world and true freedom in stripping off his body which belonged to this world and in awakening that aspect of himself which was from the Beyond. Diasporic religion, in contrast to native, locative religion, was utopian in the strictest sense of the word, a religion of 'nowhere,' of transcendence" (Smith, *Map Is Not Territory*, xiv). This view is taken up by John Mohawk in *Utopian Legacies* as a way of interpreting the aggressive incursions of the West.

to return to their God. In fact, these oppositions are related to one another, but, during the Age of Discovery, the distinction between locative and utopian marks a radical disruption and trauma.

Nothing has been more traumatic for Indigenous Peoples and their traditions than the phenomenon of private property. As Rigoberta Menchú says, "We started thinking about the roots of the problem and came to the conclusion that everything stemmed from the ownership of land."[27] Owning the land is an inconceivable notion for an Indigenous community. The question often asked by Indigenous Peoples is, "How can human beings divide up a living earth into property?" Property violates the relationship between a human community and the living world. Since 1492, countless Indigenous Peoples have asked how can human beings own a living being like the land. It remains a good question that has largely gone unheeded by theologians of the West.

The Meaning of Land in the Modern World

If we take seriously the category of "Indigeneity," it turns the way that modern people tend to understand the general phenomenon of religion away from religion as faith or belief and toward the materiality of religion. Indigenous values allow us to interpret the world as religiously oriented in distinctive new ways.

For example, my academic orientations to Indigenous values have allowed me to reconsider my teaching about the *religious dimensions* of "colonialism," "consumerism," "whiteness," and "sports." Students at Syracuse University generally appreciate the opportunity to investigate these materialities of modern existence that have profoundly shaped their lives *as religion* rather as random activities of their existence. These interpretive approaches allow religion to

---

27. Menchú, *I, Rigoberta Menchú*, 116. There are, however, numerous examples of this sentiment that have been expressed in a wide variety of cultural contexts. It has also served as a point of entry into academic work. See, for example, Cronon, *Changes in the Land*; and Salisbury, *Manitou and Providence*.

be applied to cultural issues that have been restricted by economic, social, psychological, political, and biological perspectives.

At the end of this chapter, we will self-consciously reflect on the consequences of thinking about *religion as habitation* or *occupation* for modern, "civilized" human beings. This requires a certain ability to be culturally self-critical and yet not self-loathing. As I tell my students, "I'm not interested in self-hatred, but I am interested in self-improvement, and I am always the hardest on people and the things I care about the most!" The urgency of Indigenous values moves us out of the interpersonal, self-serving nature of our thoughts into an accounting of the detrimental effects of civilization on us all.

Real Estate Religion

The primary means by which people in the First World—the civilized world that drives the material realities of our present age—*meaningfully inhabit the land* is through the rubric of property. In fact, the concepts of private property and Western civilization's understanding of freedom are almost synonymous. To restate: there could hardly be a cultural phenomenon that has been more destructive to Indigenous Peoples and their lands than the idea of private property—that human beings can own the land. More violence has been done to Indigenous Peoples, and the lands that they have traditionally inhabited, in securing clear title to land than almost any other concept.

In most social contexts, it is considered absurd to regard property, or real estate, as "religion," and yet the consequence of regarding land as property has had a tremendously negative effect on Indigenous Peoples and can easily be seen in direct opposition to their values. Why has property been a devastating concept for Indigenous communities? What are some of the assumptions that follow from the cosmology of property? Does this say something about the materiality of religion in the civilized world?

Entire continents have based their growth and expansion on the displacement of Indigenous Peoples. Since the fifteenth century, this has largely been based on the promise of wealth and freedom in the form of owning land. The phenomenon of "real estate" is inherited from the aristocratic notion of a landed nobility that controlled the land as a matter of their divine right of inheritance. The notion survives today that land, as private property or real estate, is subservient to the will and rights of its owner. Someone who has bought the land is in control of it in much the same way as the noble was lord or lady of their estate.

This attitude of ownership, of course, has a theological legacy, one in which human beings, and particularly those in a more hierarchically elevated social condition, are the agents of God on Earth. The assumption in the phenomenon of property is that first, God is otiosus, or obscured and removed from the immediate circumstances of earthly life. Second, there are particular intermediaries among human beings who can impose the will of God on the world and thus render the world more acceptable to His image of heaven; in other words, private property is the material expression of a *utopian* vision. Third, real estate is not only about individualized ownership of land but also about putting the entire landscape of living beings under dominion—over the trees, birds, plants, rocks, water, and wind. Plainly, as a theology, the phenomenon of property is diametrically opposed to an Indigenous value system.

Private property or real estate had defined the land as fundamentally mute and empty, or terra nullius, until it was acted upon by human labor. Yet, for the modern world, this is the central attribute of freedom, because the owner is empowered through the acquisition of this insignificant medium called "land" as long as through its commodification he can apply value. Land can be rendered a home, housing, agricultural development, resource extraction, or all sorts of profit-generating activities. Instead of humans connecting with the regenerative power of the Earth, man becomes all powerful through his established dominion over the Earth. In this way, land must be regarded as dead, so that man can become all-powerful through his reconceptualization of the Earth as real estate.

Property is directly opposed to an Indigenous perspective that understands land to be not only alive but also the preeminent living being upon which all life is based. In sharp contrast to a cosmology of property, Mother Earth imparts power to human beings through her continuing communications, or hierophanies. Indigenous power for human beings is not due to total material control over the living earth, but in the ability to interact with the land, being to being, so that one can experience the totality of the living world. Power is directly connected with a person's ability to *pay attention* to the messages being constantly sent from the Earth so that human life can remain relevant and continue its course.

In the case of private property, God is necessarily seen as remote, removed from embodying and actively engaging in material life. Human beings are the only living beings that matter in this arrangement. For Indigenous Peoples, however, human life is always contingent on the larger living world that surrounds them. If the land were not alive, then human beings could not exist. There are distinctly different understandings of the proximity of the sacred and the agency of the sacred, as expressed through land, between cosmologies of private property and the living earth.

An illustration I use in my classes to exemplify this gap in religious dimensions of land is "the hierophany in my backyard." I am a property owner, and, as a citizen of the United States with a moderate income, I understand that my social power is directly related to my power as a property owner. I pay taxes and live in the suburbs and can sometimes be found working in my yard. If, for some reason, I were to begin to speak to my yard because I began to hear it speak to me, my neighbors would be very suspicious, even fearful that I had lost my mind. If, however, I were to go to Jerusalem or to Mecca to speak to God and returned home to talk with my neighbors about it, I would probably just be regarded as a fervent believer. My property, because it is *mine*, puts me in a specific sort of relationship with the land as its overlord. This makes it extremely difficult for me, or anyone who has committed to the theology of property, to hear and pay attention to the messages being communicated by a living earth.

In fact, there is nothing so disruptive to the fantasies of human power as hierophanies. If, by some strange coincidence, the sacred were to manifest itself in my yard or home (as with some Marian apparitions discussed in chapter 2) in such a way as to be unavoidable, then I could no longer regard it as *mine*. I would be forced to form another kind of relationship with the Earth, one that is Indigenous. I would be less able to think of myself as the only living being, or at least the most important living being, in the yard; I would become less anthropocentric, or at least my understanding of power would become less anthropocentric. Most importantly, I would have a more material sense of the sacred as in intimate proximity to my life. A hierophany in my yard would change everything, no longer allowing me to remain fixed to a theology of property.

Ecological Collapse and the Problem of Religion

I write this book because the world today is in peril. As has been expressed earlier in the book, empires have used religion to reorient people away from the natural world. The modern world's theological position with regard to the land is directly related to our current ecological crisis. The otiose nature of the sacred and the illusion that humans have dominion over the world are having devastating consequences politically, economically, socially, and environmentally.

The present analysis of environmental crisis is not to be understood as apocalyptic or millennial in the Protestant Christian sense, based on the return of God and the promise of a heavenly or utopian world established on Earth. My point here is that the escalation of devastating environmental collapse can be traced back to the Age of Discovery and the demonization of Indigenous Peoples, where land was determined to be terra nullius, belonging to no one, with Indigenous Peoples absent, pushing the possibility of the sacred out of day-to-day existence and creating an absolute value upon which the materiality of the modern civilized world is based.

So, the acceptance of a possible apocalyptic environmental collapse seems far worse than addressing the "end of times" fiction that has been propagated through the catalyst of religion since contact. Over the last five hundred years, this has wreaked havoc on the viability of our material world and on those who are Indigenous, who still retain the knowledge of how to live in proper relationship to the Earth. This is, of course, ironic in the extreme because "Religion" (i.e., the global Religions denoted with a capital R) has actually brought us to this state. The shifts and shades of religion as it folds into the basis of the modern material worldview, however, is what Indigenous values help us to delineate.

I am making a religious argument for the reasons behind such a collapse. Modernity is unable to see itself as contingent on any living being other than human beings; its religion is a theology of conquest, where habitation is more readily defined as "occupation." There are, of course, historical reasons for emphasizing a legacy of military style occupation of the land. We will discuss the Age of Discovery and its ties to private property in chapter 6, but it is also relevant here.

Religion came to constitute the occupation of land. Religion as occupation follows the direct lineage from colonialism and the material origins of modernity and Western civilization. As colonialism spread around the world, Indigenous Peoples stood in the way of "progress" and became the target for removal. Due to the care with which Indigenous Peoples interacted with the living Earth, their territories had an abundance of resources. Colonialism morphed into today's global capitalism, where an extractive economy is predicated on the hierarchical patrimony passed from a Supreme God who holds dominion over the Earth and those subordinate to his command. Moreover, certain human beings were appointed to be His representatives on the Earth in His absence. The theological legacy of colonialism has led us to the devaluing of Indigenousness and, among other things, to the brink of environmental collapse.

I am far from the first person to have noticed these relationships; many people in the past and present are and have been fully aware. These are predominately Indigenous Peoples, who have remained as critical today as they were at first European contact. Not many academics or modern civilized people seem to make these connections, but the emergence of the category of "Indigeneity" does pose promise, if we are to listen and pay attention.

Urgent Issues of Collaboration between Locative and Utopian People

As I said in the preface to this book, I wouldn't characterize myself as an Indigenous person. In fact, I come from a long line of immigrant people (which is an ironic statement in itself) that can be traced to the Pequot Massacre of 1636, the event that established Hartford, Connecticut.[28] Enough time has elapsed from immediate family history that I am able to work through that sore spot of conscience. There is now an urgent sense in acknowledging that my family came to occupy inhabited lands to help establish a New World order that involved the extermination of Indigenous Peoples and commodification of the land. There has yet to be compensation, and we never escape the enormous consequence in setting forth those kind of genocidal actions by our ancestors.

The category of "Indigeneity" can clarify the cultural appropriations of land by settler-colonial people; put more personally, Indigenous values helps me to clarify the processes by which European Americans, my forefathers and foremothers, came to occupy this land. From my vantage point, this is not a nice, optimistic, or triumphal history; it is a genocidal history, full of self-hatred and fear. However, in spite of its overwhelming negativity, the meaning of being an immigrant is clearer to me now, having studied Indigenous Peoples with appreciation and enthusiasm. The religious orientation of my cultural heritage, as an immigrant American born out of a colonial legacy, is clarified by having considered it in contrast to and in cultural contact with an Indigenous orientation. So, even though I

---

28. See Cave, *Pequot War*.

have academically and personally committed my work to the continued survival of Indigenous Peoples and traditions, I can only claim myself to be an immigrant American. I can never *convert* to being Indigenous because I cannot ever give up who I am. This is another sense in which Indigenous traditions are not "religion." In the History of Religions, this could be regarded as being methodologically committed to the other of one's study, but, of course, it is more than merely an academic or descriptive endeavor. What is clear, in the end, is that I have a culture and am not Indigenous. My aim, however, is to promote Indigeneity by fostering an ability to meaningfully pay attention to the world and all its inhabitants both human and nonhuman alike.

Having a culture and knowing some of its limits is the first step in all collaborative enterprises and the basis for having respectful intercultural exchanges. Rather than objectifying one's study, or assuming that the academic location allows for some sort of omniscient knowledge outside of one's cultural creation, collaborative methodologies create knowledge interculturally. Knowledge of another interpretive location, such as an Indigenous values perspective, will exert an influence on one's own interpretive position. Out of these exchanges, new understandings are required. At best, historians of religions collaborate with the other, as opposed to objectifying the other, so that new interpretations of the world can be made available. Descriptions of other religions—in this case, Indigenous traditions—imply, necessitate, and demand a collaborative method.

Collaboration, however, is more than an academic methodology. For Indigenous Peoples, it is the primary means by which human beings can meaningfully co-inhabit the world. No single being can control the whole world; no single being can make itself live. Life is a coordinated, integrative effort on the parts of a myriad number of beings that intersect at different points. Inhabiting the world is the process by which human beings can interject themselves in proper ways into this web of life, and Indigenous Peoples use numerous metaphors, stories, and symbols to articulate the living web of relationships that form the basis of inhabitation. It requires the total attention of Indigenous Peoples to remain aware of the constantly shifting yet stable conditions of their existence. In other words, *religion as habitation* requires a collaborative interpretive methodology. Indigeneity assumes that adjudicating one's interpretive position cannot be omniscient or all-knowing, but contingent, limited, and, by necessity, collaborative.

The Future of the University

Academic work, particularly work among Indigenous groups of people, has been turning more and more to collaborative models. This turn has largely been defended by those who are ashamed of past interpretations that tended to objectify and reduce the profound nature of Indigenous values to dim reflections of their true power. Anthropologists and historians of religions, for example, aim to overcome a legacy of colonization and missionization that have wedded the interpretation of Indigenous Peoples to conquest, genocide, and world domination.

To escape our past, we as academics have employed new interpretive strategies. We have befriended and have been reconstituted by those who were once mere objects of study; we have become allies in taking on their fights against global forces such as deforestation, environmental racism, racial intolerance, sexism, poverty, and disease, as an expression of our commitments. Relationships once viewed as contentious can now become more intimate. Thus, the shift in interpretive positions over the last few generations of academics has been much more than just "political correctness," as some would have it. University culture, in some quarters, is undergoing a change in the way it creates knowledge. The change can be characterized as a turn toward Indigenization. Academics are making more fine-grained judgments about their own interpretive positions, which enables them to engage in an intercultural exchange in a respectful and disciplined manner.

I am not describing some form of interpretive relativism. The point of locating one's interpretations in one's own cultural position is not solipsistic, as some might suggest, nor is it an attempt to minimize academic standards. The reason for scrutinizing one's own interpretive location is to test it with respect to another human position. Together in collaboration, academics, Indigenous thinkers, and others can determine what needs to be done in the world.

There is no shortage of issues, problems, dilemmas, and misunderstandings that could use the collaborative efforts of a number of good thinking people. Not only does a collaborative method solve many of the extreme negativities of the past but it can also address some of the problems that face human beings today. Why should it only be the trained experts that can confront the urgent issues that we face today? Don't Indigenous Peoples, who have survived the devastations of the last five hundred years, have something to offer? Can we imagine the amount of cultural creativity that could be released if only we could drop the fiction of expert knowledge and cultivate a collaborative method?

The History of Religions has the interpretive tools to promote a sustained collaborative relationship between an academic discipline and Indigenous Peoples—those who were once thought to be the farthest away from university culture. This is a move that the entire university, which is still the site of knowledge production and innovation, must make to remain relevant. As Oren Lyons has said, "We wonder, how do you instruct seven billion people as to the relationship to the Earth? Because unless they understand that and relate the way they should be, future is pretty dim for the human species."[29] In this case, a true and respectful collaborative methodology is still greatly needed. The emergence and vitality of this category, however, is a step in the right direction, for it is in our collective habitation that we truly become cohabitants.

---

29. Onondaga Leader Oren Lyons, 9 August 2013, on the radio show *Democracy Now!* with Amy Goodman, www.democracynow.org.//AU.

5
Exchange

While "religion" may be absent from them, religious exchanges are essential features of Indigenous traditions. Exchange is a central organizing feature of material life and therefore a point of comparison and contrast with global religions and economic realities. Exchange practices directly involve how human beings exist in relationship to other beings, whether spiritual, human, or nonhuman. Exchanges between oneself and others comprise fundamental features of what transpires in all ceremonial activities. Allow me to submit that the nature of "the person" for Indigenous Peoples is in complete contrast with the Self, or the individual which is at the center of Western traditions, and that by understanding this difference we come to understand the necessity of exchange as a material, and empirically universal, human phenomenon.

The Indigenous Body

To begin with, Indigenous reflections on exchange are intimately connected to the human body. It is quite difficult, of course, to discuss the body as a generalized phenomenon without sounding as if one is universalizing. Although the human body appears to be the same across cultures, its *meaning* tends to be specific to its cultural context and location. This is a point of emphasis for Indigenous values. The location of the human body affects its makeup in profound ways. For example, Sherpa or Aymara bodies from the Himalayas and Andes high-altitude regions can endure extraordinary deprivation of oxygen and water for longer periods of time than most other human beings who inhabit lower, more temperate regions. This fact reveals that Indigenous Peoples have clear, profound local knowledge: they are aware of the wide constellation of living beings that coinhabit their world. More importantly, they know what these beings require of them to survive in their worlds. Sherpa and Aymara literally embody their local ceremonial knowledge.

From an Indigenous perspective, human bodies and the societies that they develop are directly, materially connected to the places they inhabit. As material expressions of the world, human beings articulate the cosmos in all its subtlety and complexity. Human beings are not self made in any sense, but entirely comprised of the world that surrounds them for everything that grows their bodies. Human bodies are an intersection of forces, beings, and elements; there is no durable self that exists previous to this intersection of matter. This is reminiscent of the Buddhist notion of anatta, or "no-self." That said, this is not only a philosophical concept for Indigenous Peoples but also a material one.

In many respects, this sort of knowledge is not too far from scientific knowledge. For example, we are not philosophically carbon life forms, nor does our faith or belief determine whether we are carbon life forms—we *are* carbon life forms. Since hydrogen and helium are the only elements in the universe that create carbon under the extreme heat of the sun or stars, then all life, including our own, is a remnant of the activities of stars. Being "stardust" is more than a concept: it is scientific, material, and meaningful.

▲ ▲ ▲

The totality of human existence is based on things, people, and beings that are external to the self. Human life cannot sustain itself, but is upheld and coordinated by all kinds of relationships. I'd like to explore this idea in two ways. First, the human body is a reflection of the dead: the ancestors. Second, the human body is made possible by food. In both of these ways, the human body survives by means of ceremonial exchanges. Although presented here as Indigenous values, I have focused on these aspects because they can be easily comprehended as attributes of all human bodily existence. The difference between an Indigenous and settler-colonial sensibility in all of these examples is, of course, the degree to which the human being is seen as contingent on, or dominant over, all other living beings. Nevertheless, they were chosen for their obvious and more universal qualities.

The Body of the Ancestors

Everyone is a reflection of the people who have gone before them. When a baby is born, it is a material expression of its mother and father. The human body comes into existence as a result of the lives of people who are now long dead and gone. A baby is the manifestation of an unbroken chain of life that includes the dead. Human life, then, is not a discrete phenomenon, but necessarily includes the actions of those who are not living *but still present in the body.* In this way, a baby is the presence of the potent absence of the dead. Often people look for physical signs in the baby, such as noses, eyes, smiles, that reveal its family ties. This gives the line continuity: a past, a present, and a future. These factors might be relevant for naming the baby, identifying how the baby should be dedicated or how the baby will become responsible to its community throughout its future.

If, as science tells us, we are an assemblage of DNA that has been given to us by our forefathers and foremothers, then we are, in fact, the material evidence of who came before us. If we take seriously the fact that we are completely organized materially by our genetic code, then the dead are directly active in our lives. Our predisposition to disease of various kinds, and even some features of our lifestyles, are said to be the product of genetic factors that we have inherited.

In fact, the growing body of evidence suggests that our bodies are more of a reflection of our ancestors than of our environment. For example, I just got my cholesterol level checked by the doctor; he called me into his office to discuss the fact that it was too high. I made a deal with him that I would try some lifestyle changes before he would have to put me on medication. He agreed, but then went on to say that I probably won't be able to bring the cholesterol score down more than 20 percent because this health condition is almost entirely due to genetic factors. In a panic, I phoned my mother, who said that her cholesterol was also high, and that it was, in fact, genetic. She also said that, in spite of her high cholesterol, she refused to take the drugs; instead, she chose to accept that the condition was genetic, but to use that knowledge to motivate her in to making better lifestyle choices. She told me not to worry because she was able to lower her cholesterol. As usual, she was able to calm me down.

Neither here nor there, perhaps, but it does raise the question: To what degree are we really in charge of our own bodies? Genetically, we are a kind of expression, the "spitting image," of our ancestors, who are the most important beings in our bodies. It only makes sense that we would try and learn as much as we can about them, to regard them, to think about them periodically, to consider our dreams about them.

The obvious knowledge that the ancestors are active in our bodies is of little *religious* importance for modern people. However, for Indigenous Peoples, this is of great importance. How one regards the body is directly connected with how one regards the dead. A healthy body is an expression of the degree to which one regards the ancestors. Indigenous Peoples have associated ceremonies for the dead with bodily healing, an association that academic interpretations of the past have regarded as "superstition." As I have indicated, however, a connection between the dead and healing is not superstition, nor is it an example of flawed, quasi-magical thinking; this connection is actually a natural fact of bodily existence. A regard for the ancestors, as active beings in the processes of the body, is necessary in order to understand and appreciate one's own physical health. The materiality of this connection is an expression of its Indigenousness.[1] Much

---

1. See Sullivan, "Terminology," in *Icanchu's Drum*, 467–614, which introduces the diverse ways that Indigenous Peoples from South America conceive of death and ancestor ceremonies.

like our discussion in previous chapters, to value one's self, one's own body, is to value one's family, one's history, and one's place.

Respect for the ancestors is expressed largely in ceremonies. Ceremonies for the dead are not confined to Indigenous ceremonies, but, from an Indigenous perspective, they are sacred occasions that are vitally necessary for the continuation of material life. The dead and the living stand in direct material relationship with one another. Ceremonies to the dead are not only sentimental occasions but are also events where something real is transacted between living and dead human beings.

Illness, unhappiness, and bad luck, among other problems, that express themselves in the physical body and the community can be seen as tied to transgressions with regard to the dead. Insulting the dead can come in many forms, so people are sought out and consulted who are more keenly aware of, who are better able to pay attention to, those subtle signs and signals that emanate from the spirit world. Experts at paying attention are called by many names. In the History of Religions, they have been referred to as "shamans."[2] Shamans are the healers in Indigenous traditions. They are not priests, because their authority is vested in their knowledge of the spiritual world and not necessarily in an institution, lineage, or textual tradition, but they do conduct ceremonies and usually have extensive ceremonial knowledge. Oftentimes, their interpretations of the cause of disease is negotiated between themselves and the patient, family, or

---

2. This term originates from Siberian peoples but has been applied to Indigenous spiritual healers the world over. There is considerable controversy about the applicability of this term to people who have their own titles for healers, having their own unique practices and traditions. The term "shaman" has become widely recognized by students as representing an expert in Indigenous traditions. So, even though it was coined by Eliade and artificially represents a tremendous diversity of healing strategies across the world, it is still viable in communicating something of importance to a non-Indigenous audience. It is unfortunate that Eliade emphasized the ecstatic nature of shamanism, rather than its healing dimension. Nevertheless, there is still some utility in the term as a mode of thinking about healing outside the conventions of the West. See Eliade, *Shamanism*.

community. In other words, the shaman's interpretation is not prioritized above the interpretations of others. This reflects the fact that the sacred is a part of the world that can express itself in a myriad number of ways. The sacred does not speak just through one person or place at a time. All sacred utterances, whether perceived by the shaman or someone else, have to be scrutinized and interpreted by the listener. There is no police force of the sacred; there is no way that someone purporting to represent the sacred, like a shaman, can forcibly urge people to do what they say.

These comments about the status of the shaman are important because I find that students generally have a negative, suspicious, and flawed view of the shaman's position vis-à-vis an Indigenous community. They see him or her as a charlatan, someone who dupes poor and ignorant people out of money and goods for bogus services rendered. This mistakenly reflects a belief in the general gullibility of Indigenous Peoples, who, stereotypically, are thought to believe every fantastical story that they are told. In European fantasies, like the stories of Captain Cook or Robinson Crusoe, the Indigenous Peoples of a place are understood by Westerners to be credulous enough to regard white people as Gods, largely due to the activities of shamanic charlatans who have operated among them for such a long time. These stories have effectively diminished Indigenous Peoples and their traditions while enhancing the superiority of Europeans as "natural."[3] The deficiencies of the phenomenon of the shaman that I experience in class, however, are almost totally tied to European fictions, which are expressed as a simultaneous fascination and revulsion for this social position. Most often shamans have to be discredited by colonial authorities because of their threat to their religious authority.

While it's true that a shaman's ability is tied to some kind of unusual insight into the spiritual world, that insight is not more or

---

3. The great debate between Marshall Sahlins (*Islands of History* and *How "Natives" Think*) and Gananath Obeyesekere (*Apotheosis of Captain Cook*) has been immensely productive in discerning the fact that mythmaking is as prevalent among colonizers as it is among Indigenous Peoples.

less valid than any other human insight. The shaman acts as a point in the conversation about the possibilities of violations between beings. The fantasy about shamanism is the result of a categorical confusion in the misapplication of one form of religiousness on to another.

In the West, religion has been policed by various kinds of religious authorities who have coerced human beings into following the pronouncements of a sacred leader, who claims to be the only and true intermediary between human beings and God. Today, this is largely accomplished through the fear of personal condemnation. In other words, the non-Indigenous stereotypical understanding of the shaman as part con man and part mystic is much more reflective of a Western understanding of the religious expert than it is of Indigenous practices. Unlike Western religious institutions, there is no way a shaman can force the people who enlist his services to follow his directions. In fact, unlike any other aspect of Indigeneity, the shaman seems to be a symbolic flashpoint for disparaging attitudes held by academics toward these traditions and the people who practice them.

My intention here is to suggest that the activities of the ancestors in the body are physical processes that are mediated by living human beings who are regarded as experts in the ways of the dead. The presence of the ancestors in the body are evident and necessary for all living beings. The activities of the dead are not superstitions or phantoms. We are alive, and, therefore, so are our ancestors. This is an element of human life upon which many aspects of Indigenous values are based. Death, then, is a shift in the nature of human existence—one that is not the opposite of living, but another sort of living, and a transition that is organized by means of ceremonies.

The Body That Eats

Food is a general reason Indigenous Peoples perform ceremonial exchanges. As was emphasized earlier, Indigenous Peoples are pragmatic: they have developed strategies over a very long period of time for living in the world they coinhabit. In fact, Indigenous Peoples have not only survived the colonial displacement from their homelands but also adapted by learning how to inhabit some of the most inhospitable places in the world. Based on their observations over millennia, they have developed the most effective ways of living successfully in a place. Indigenous Peoples are keenly aware of the spiritual attributes of their locations that undergird their phenomenal world; they have committed themselves to paying attention to those processes that support life in its wide diversity of ways.

Food is a complicated phenomenon. We all know that what people eat is highly variable from society to society. While some, like the Japanese and French, relish foods as a delicacy (e.g., seaweed and snails) others connect their food to their geographical locations and history. The particularities of a diet—what is and what is not food—are directly related to a cultural or ethnic identity, nationality, and religion. As the saying goes, "You are what you eat." I don't know why academics don't spend more time on the phenomenon of food. It is much more relevant to theories of subjectivity and identity than are ideas and systems of belief. I'd like to spend that time here, because it is well worth it.

For Indigenous Peoples, food is more likely to be fully spiritual in nature than for other cultures and to be the basis of regular ceremonial activity. The 365-day calendar year, or agricultural year, is punctuated by regular ceremonial cycles around the moon that are directly connected with sacred beings and phenomena that appear at regular intervals. The seasons bring rain, snow, sun, heat, cold, thunder, and lightning—hierophanies that are met with ceremonial events that welcome their appearance. The periodicity of the seasons is a cause for ceremonies that are directly reflective of the continuing life of the community, the land, and the world.

Therefore, something tangible is being transacted between human beings and a sacred world during the periodic ceremonies that happen over the course of the seasonal calendar and the cycles of the moon. The perpetuation of these cycles is incumbent on the reciprocity of gifts given in exchange for the gifts that have already been received.[4]

Human beings receive the gift of food from a sacred reality, and the gift must be reciprocated by exchange. To put it in more modern terms, consumption has a price. What people eat or consume in order to live creates a debt that must be met with a required payment that reinforces the perpetuation of a regenerative life force. The phenomenon of food also contains the intimate interaction of life and death. It is a basic feature of human existence that some living beings must die in order that others might live. It doesn't matter if the life sacrificed is vegetable, animal, or mineral; the simple fact of eating food is that the life of one being is exchanged for the life of others—in our case, humans.

The problem of human consumption is a regular feature of religious life. Vegetarianism among Hindus and Buddhists, fasting practices among Christians or Muslims, or adhering to kosher rules for Jews are, from an Indigenous vantage point, all reflections of this issue of human consumption and violence. So, how does one push away the consequences of violence in the process of consuming food? Some do so by following strict dietary rules, but even eating rice or vegetables, or an animal that was killed in a sacred or humane manner, doesn't negate the equation that some living being must die in order for human life to flourish. In this respect, ceremonial activities that deal with the life and death exchanges in the process of creating food are just as necessary as the process of cooking and eating.

---

4. One spring, when I first began teaching at Syracuse University, the Haudenosaunee were invited to hold a social dancing demonstration outside on our Quad. As they danced, the sky darkened, threatening a heavy downpour. This change in weather made us all nervous, especially with that initial loud clap of thunder that was followed by several others. Most of us cowered, scrambling for nearby shelter. The lead dancer, whom I will call Debbie, and who has become a very good friend of ours, laughed into the microphone and directed thanksgivings to the Thunderbeings. This was followed by a general celebration by all of the dancers.

Human beings are necessarily receptive to the world. They cannot operate as closed biological systems because by its material nature the human body is completely contingent on forces beyond its control.[5] The problem is even more acute for Indigenous Peoples because all living beings are essentially equal in stature to human beings. Myths of origin and creation reflect this fact. Human beings are sisters, brothers, uncles, aunts, to animals, plants, trees, rocks, mountains, water, insects. Eating is, in essence, a cannibalistic act of killing and consuming a sibling or a relative. This is the case whether the group's primary food source is plant or animal. The need for a gift to compensate for food is felt more intimately.

Thus, it is of greater pragmatic concern that ceremonies address the living beings associated with food, and that they be regularly performed in a correct manner. It is also important that, after a ceremony is performed, the entire community observe signs or signals that express the acceptance of the human gift. All manner of things can indicate this acceptance, but receiving this sign is crucial, because it indicates the corrective measures that must be taken to maintain the vital relationship between human beings and other living beings within the cosmos.

To sum up, food is given to human beings: it is a gift from a living cosmos, and a debt that requires compensation. Because mythic values reveal that all living beings are related, food represents violence against one's family and, simultaneously, the necessity of all human life and growth. As complex as it may seem in a Western/colonial context, this fact of food in the development of the human body is central to Indigenous values. Food is a clear referent in determining our interaction within a connected world and, for this reason, is central to the ceremonial life of the community.

Food, more than other aspects of human life, is the day-to-day reality that affirms the notion that all human societies have a value

---

5. For a view from Theravada Buddhism, see Arnold, "Religious Dimensions of Food"; and Arnold, "Eating and Giving Food."

system that defines the ways in which humans are engaged with the material world. This fundamental expression of life has been contextualized into the category of study called "religion."[6]

Ceremonial Exchanges

Ceremonies are occasions of exchange. In spite of its variations and indecipherability, the phenomenon of religion is really quite simple to understand from an Indigenous perspective: it is based in an economy of exchanges.

Ceremonies are understood as events that stimulate exchanges between various living beings for the purpose of perpetuating the material world. For Indigenous Peoples today, wealth abounds from the primary source of power, prestige, and identity that is regenerated through their ceremonial obligations. Without ceremonies a community would cease to exist.[7]

This presents two fundamental realities about Indigenous values. First, what scholars have determined religious about these traditions is based in human activity, and more particularly on community activity expressing ceremonial gratitude to that which is valued. This contrasts with the concept of "religion" as individual human thought: what people *think, believe, aspire to, or experience*. Global religions have been textualized to serve as the reference for "talking about God" and establishing theological traditions.

The second reality is that Indigenous communities are committed to the continuation of the material world as it pertains to the spiritual values undergirding material life, whereas ceremonial life in the global religions center around a human petition to God, usually searching for an individual human experience of the sacred.

---

6. See Arnold, "The Matter of Understanding," in *Eating Landscape*, chapter 1.

7. For a viewpoint from the Haudenosaunee, Wall, *To Become a Human Being*, is an excellent resource.

To paraphrase Oren Lyons, Indigenous ceremonies are not fundamentally about generating human experience, but about fulfilling responsibilities in giving thanks to Creation for all the gifts of life.[8] As we will discuss later, ceremony is rooted in Indigenous value traditions that promote a *gift* economy, rather than the *monetary* or *profit* economy of settler-colonial cultures. Each of these economies has a distinctive set of values that are, most often, diametrically opposed to one another.

Indigenous ceremonies transact materially between human beings and other beings. This very important distinction goes overlooked for two main reasons. First, when Indigenous ceremonial practices are culturally appropriated (i.e., through the Church, or with the New Age movement), it is used for the purpose of promoting a sense of personal euphoria or empowerment. This accentuates the interpretive gulf between Indigenous understandings of a gift exchange economy with the Earth and the settler-colonial concept of a profit economy culminating with personal empowerment over the Earth. The second reason is that "religious experience" and "personal empowerment" are likewise traditional bailiwicks of the academic study of religion. An emphasized elevation of personal consciousness over and above the material exchanges between sacred beings that constitute the Earth entirely misconstrues Indigenous ceremonial practices. In effect, Indigenous ceremonies are used as a disguise to further promote anthropocentric religious values of the "great religions."

Mythic Paradigms to Ceremonial Processes

Contemporary use of the term "myth" in modern or civilized societies is synonymous with "fiction" and "falsehood." In the History of Religions, however, myths are "true" stories. Indeed, myths are truer than facts.

---

8. Personal communication.

Myths communicate to human beings the essential nature of reality. Models of and models for reality, they impart what is really "real" about the world. Another popular misconception about myths is that they are the creation of human beings. However, even a cursory examination of the regard with which myths are held in a variety of traditions reveals that they are more properly understood to be revealed to, or discovered by, people in the past. From a religious community's point of view, myths are *in and of the world*, existing previous to human beings, and an intrinsic part of Creation. They are the blueprint of how the cosmos works and how it should, at all costs, be heeded. Myths are enacted, or performed, in a ceremonial context so that human beings can be properly oriented to the underlying structure of reality. Myths are not so much stories as they are accounts of how the world has come to be.

Indigenous creation myths undergird ceremonies of regeneration, rather than the biblical apocalyptic myths that generate fear with the hope of salvation from the destruction or end of the world. The latter is central for settler-colonial mythologies; in fact, millennialism and apocalyptic mythology have been very significant in the development of modernity since the Age of Discovery. We will discuss later how echoes of this apocalyptic mythic history continue with us in all sorts of ways.

Creation myths, however, are essential features of Indigenous values. Key elements like kinship with various animals, connection with other worlds, and the origins of the world reveal to human beings the appropriate ways in which to interact with a regenerative cosmos and all life on the Earth.

According to Charles Long, there are several types of Creation accounts that contain central orienting values for the traditions that hold them.[9] For these reasons, Creation accounts are told and retold, ceremonialized and receremonialized, over and over again. They are not just stories about the beginning of the world, about the distant past; they are also contemporary accounts in the sense

---

9. See Long, *Alpha*.

that *Creation is happening all the time.* The model for staying connected to a regenerative cosmos is always about Creation because every moment is the creative moment par excellence.

As Vine Deloria Jr. has pointed out in *God Is Red*, creation stories are understood in temporal rather than spatial terms.[10] In Christianity and other global religions, Creation is generally seen as occurring at the beginning of time and therefore, like God, remaining at great distance from human beings. Only at the end of time can the return to God be possible. The drive to reunite with a God otiosus, removed from the world, exemplifies why the hope of an apocalypse was the propelling force behind the Age of Discovery and world domination. Eliade referred to this understanding of time as the "Terror of History."[11]

The real point of contrast emphasizes the different mythic orientations between settler-colonial and Indigenous Peoples. As with sacred lands, Indigenous ceremonial practices emphasize the close proximity of the sacred in the regenerating processes of creation that are prevalent in the world around them. In this way, Creation myths serve as a model of spatial rather than temporal reality for settler-colonial people.

Indigenous ceremonial processes are connected to the ways that human beings are responsible for perpetuating life. Ceremonial life is based upon the structures of reality that are revealed to Indigenous Peoples in Creation myths. Each ceremony *transacts* with the

---

10. "Western European peoples have never learned to consider the nature of the world discerned from a spatial point of view. . . . The very essence of Western European identity involves the assumption that time proceeds in a linear fashion; further it assumes that at a particular point in the unraveling of this sequence, the peoples of Western Europe became the guardians of the world . . . Western political ideas came to depend on spatial restriction of what were essentially non-spatial ideas" (Deloria Jr., *God Is Red*, 63).

11. "There is also reason to foresee that, as the terror of history grows worse, as existence becomes more and more precarious because of history, the positions of historicism will increasingly lose in prestige" (Eliade, *Myth of the Eternal Return*, 153).

surrounding world; a constant exchange of gifts is necessary between human beings and other beings so that the world can continue. Creation myths are an essential factor in this ceremonial transaction, but it is not always a literal transference of the Creation story into a ceremonial framework that orients the activity. Sometimes the logic of Creation, or the values expressed in the Creation myth, are utilized and elaborated within the context of the Indigenous material world that grounds the ceremony. From the time of Creation forward, the material world is nothing but an elaboration of the values set in motion by the activities of sacred beings and forces.[12]

The emphasis of ceremonies is to promote good health, good crops, good hunting, and good relationships between human beings and the natural world. The Earth is alive: food grows, animals grow, human beings grow, everything alive grows, so ceremonies dedicated to orienting human beings to this process, and to the participation in this process, look to Creation myths as a model. In other words, Creation myths are not ideological constructions of reality by human beings that are then projected onto the world. They cannot be part of any adequate scholarly interpretation, and an adequate understanding of Creation myths in Indigenous traditions requires that they be seen as guides for the ways human beings *act* in the world, not just how they *think* about the world.

It would be more convincing to interpret Creation myths as ideological constructs if they were taken from written text. In Indigenous practices, however, Creation myths have been passed down for millennia through oral tradition. A few important consequences follow from an oral orientation to myth. First, myths are essentially performative activities—that is to say, they are recounted from human activity through important ceremonial events in themselves.[13] Without a

---

12. The example of Kinaaldá, the Dine' women's puberty ritual dedicated to Changing Woman, is a ceremony that connects becoming a woman to Creation and regeneration. See Roessel, *Kinaaldá*.

13. The performative nature of Native American religious traditions is the thrust of Sam Gill's *Native American Religions*.

written text, the myths are best recounted in the original language of their transmission by those who have the talents and abilities to pass them along. They mark a coming together of the people, in a physical place, to listen and share their interpretations. Indigenous myth-telling is a community-affirming event that calls on a host of factors that have been encapsulated by the category of "oral tradition."

In considering oral traditions, it is important to emphasize that there is little expert knowledge of ceremonies, but there are, of course, people who are more or less devoted to directing them. There are also people who have undergone visions or experiences and are marked as being predisposed to having intimate knowledge of sacred realities that are useful in the ceremonial transactions, but, because they are events of the entire community, there are no single experts. Every participant must share in the responsibilities of making the ceremonial event a success. Different people have different roles, but all are contingent as a whole. There is no hierarchical arrangement, as in global religions.

Ceremonial life, by contrast, is a series of ongoing collaborations between human beings and other sorts of beings that inhabit the world together. Ceremonial knowledge is collaborative knowledge. This sort of knowledge is not just discursive (i.e., about different people or beings talking with one another), but is more fully a material collaboration of living together with one another, inhabiting the same place, and consuming the same things in kinship.

Ceremonial Gift Economies

Everyone has given or received a gift at some point in their lives. Therefore, everyone knows something of the elaborate ceremonial events that surround the giving and receiving of gifts. As discussed, these ceremonial occasions usually involve a rite of passage—for example, birthdays, weddings, and funerals. Sometimes gifts are welcomed, and sometimes they are not. This is because gifts carry with them a responsibility of reciprocating and paying attention. Because it involves reciprocity, giving and receiving a gift can be interpreted as an act of kindness or of vengeance, depending on the context.[14] Whether the relationship is friendly or antagonistic, in order for a relationship to flourish one must respond with giving a gift in exchange for a gift already given.

Gifts are for maintaining relationships of love and bonds of affection, relationships, and community, among other things. They can also be given between sworn enemies, opposing teams, or rivals. Both positive and negative gifts create community.[15] A gift between people always simultaneously carries with it a multitude of meanings, and ceremonial events are times for gift exchanges that involve human and nonhuman beings. While most people think of gifts as being confined to interhuman exchanges, the focal point of gifts in ceremonial practices of Indigenous Peoples is primarily exchanges with nonhuman beings, upon whom human beings depend. Gifts are not just exchanged between people but are more often exchanged between human and sacred beings.

Ceremonial events acknowledge and celebrate gifts that have already been given to human beings by a living sacred presence in the world. As for the Haudenosaunee, they can be as simple as reciting the "Thanksgiving Address" or as elaborate as a potlach ceremony among the Kwakiutl of the Pacific Northwest.[16] Without

---

14. Derrida's *Specters of Marx* goes into the relationships around the giving and receiving of gifts with great benefit. He states that it is impossible to give a gift because a gift must be unencumbered by a desire for the return.

15. It's very important to see that rivalry, as in sports, is also an opportunity for an exchange of gifts. Although there is an intensity in ceremonial sports games, the exchanges do not lead to violence, nor even to negative values in the rival communities. Therefore, gift exchanges are not always nice or friendly events, but they are always about forming and making explicit relationships. This is why sports have always been an important aspect of Indigenous ceremonial practices. See Arnold, *Gift of Sports*.

16. For a profoundly simple and intimate look at the gift economy among the Haudenosaunee, see Kimmerer, *Braiding Sweetgrass*. For an example of the elaborate ceremonies of the Pacific Northwest, see Jonaitis, *Chiefly Feasts*; and Goldman, *Mouth of Heaven*.

these gifts, life would not be possible. A gift economy, as it is most potently expressed in ceremonies, is an economy between beings that are understood to be constantly in shifting roles of debt and credit relationships.[17]

Through the lens of Indigenous values, the most important fact of life is that one is always in a debtor relationship with the world. Ceremonies help Indigenous Peoples overcome their debt of life in order to restore proper relationships of balance to all living things. So, while ceremonies are expressions of traditions that have sustained the community in the past, they are performed so that there might be a viable future. Ceremonies are like "life strategies" in which Indigenous communities perform actions on the future material well-being of their children, grandchildren, and generations of descendants beyond.

A big part of paying attention is being keenly aware of these shifting debtor relationships. The debtor relationship with the world grounds one's interpretive location and is therefore a central feature of one's human identity. Adjudicating relationships with the world is a key feature of understanding debts to the ancestors, family (which includes extended family), animals, plants, planets, stars, and so on. The debt incurred by being human is infinite, and yet the life of human beings is finite. An attempt to acknowledge and "make good" on that debt is the "religious" response most evident in all Indigenous values.

While the effects of a gift economy are evident in social and psychological lives of human beings, like any coherent community and sense of self necessary for human health, gift economics are actually religious in orientation. They are based in the ceremonial connection

---

17. It's no accident that "economics" was originally under the purview of the Church in Europe. This is because economics was explicitly understood to be central to the human relationship with God. With the development of modernity, however, there was a marked shift to the secularization of economic processes along with the rise of a profit economy in the West. See Little, *Religious Poverty and the Profit Economy*.

of human beings with the sacred reality. It would be a mistake to confine gift exchange practices as being purely anthropocentric.

Ceremonies return the gift of life to those beings that are responsible for human life. It is a precisely determined gift that is given to a specific being or beings that are well known to the Indigenous community. A specific material reality is always being transacted, always being shared between human and sacred beings.

Ceremonies, then, are *economic* activities, in the religious sense of the term, and ceremonial practices are the "total fact" of Indigenous values—the occasions when real relationships are actively established between various types of beings. A ceremony is not, fundamentally, a sentimental or gratuitous activity meant to shape human experience and human community, as many have suggested. Rather, it is most easily understood as a system of reciprocal exchanges that transpire under the influence of a sacred reality that permeates all of material existence. Simply put, Indigenous ceremonies are gift exchanges.[18]

Gift economies are based in relationships between living beings. Everything for Indigenous Peoples is alive and exerts an influence on the daily lives of human beings. The influences of "things" as gifts are alive in the world and constantly make themselves known. As Marcel Mauss has pointed out, the medium of the exchange—whether it be shells, stones, animals, or human beings—can be understood as a vital presence in the practices of exchange.[19] Ceremonies where

---

18. The respected Haudenosaunee speaker Tom Porter frequently notes that the central feature of the Great Law of Peace is making a home. This echoes the original meaning of "economics" from the Greek. Gift exchanges are part of the nurturing structure of the home and the intended outcome of ceremonial activity. Regarding the importance of a gift economy, see Kimmerer, *Braiding Sweetgrass*.

19. Marcel Mauss's *The Gift* is still the best initiation into "exchange theory." Even though he never actually went into the field to meet any of the people he discussed, he could apprehend the general principles of exchange from his place of study in Paris. Of particular importance was his interpretation of the "living status of the medium of exchange," and not just the persons in the exchange process. Mauss's insights were to inform his contemporaries, like Malinowski, who championed fieldwork methodologies, as well as those who followed him.

gifts are exchanged are subtle events in which living relationships between beings are emphasized or shifted in ways that are necessary for material survival.

The relationships being transacted in ceremonies are an expression of the presence of the sacred. Therefore, the medium of the exchange, the gift, embodies the presence of the sacred, or displays a *sign* of the deity. The gift and the medium of exchange operate as living beings, like human beings, sacred beings, and others who are involved. The medium of exchange (e.g., shells, stones, seeds, legumes, human energy as in dance, games, songs) is an active presence.[20] Human beings are not the sole active agents in ceremonial exchanges, and perhaps not even the most important ones. For Indigenous Peoples, it is often expressed that human beings are dependent on other sacred, spiritual forces in the world upon which their lives are contingent.

It should be mentioned again, however, that an understanding of the gift as central to ceremonial life is not very far away from all religious activity. Normally, anyone who performs a ceremony does so in the hope that something, materially, will be transacted between themselves and a sacred reality, like God, a deity, an ancestor, or some vital spirit in the world. This is a consistent notion throughout all religions. The understanding that human beings can engage in material exchanges with the sacred gets a very bad rap in modernity; it has been attributed to "superstition," "witchcraft," "religious fundamentalism," or fanaticism. Even though these terms are regarded as intensely negative by most academics, these understandings amount to Indigenous survival within modernity. The persistence of superstition in spite of confidence in the ability of modern science to explain the entirety of the world persistently vexes many academics. The fact that religion, in all its forms, exerts such a tremendous influence over world events is a great mystery to people who believe in the promise of modernity.

---

20. Shells are used as an item of exchange in many Indigenous contexts around the world. One important example is the Kulu shell in the South Pacific region. See Munn, *Fame of Gawa*.

As an analysis of the gift economy, Indigenous values indicate that human beings are materially predisposed to be involved with the sacred. Mircea Eliade refers to this as "homo-religiosus": as a cultural condition that is based on the material makeup of human life.[21] Modernity, however, privileges another economic system of exchange: the monetary or profit economy. It's not so much that intellectuals or cultural leaders are anti-religious, but, rather, that a monetary economy is considered more important than that of a gift economy in establishing the "appropriate" medium for guiding human relationships. It is this collision of materialities that creates the cultural bias of the Western academy, and modernity in general, against the Indigenous values that challenge the free-flowing monetary economy that fuels Western/global expansion. It is not my intention to reduce "religion" to "economic realities," but to do the reverse: to expand our understanding of "economic relationships" in order to reveal the activities of "religion."

The Religion of Money

A primary reason for writing this book is to better understand how Indigenous values could help me—as a non-Indigenous white male cisgender descendant of settler-colonists—systematically reevaluate how my own cultural underpinnings continue on the destructive path of domination. "Indigeneity" is such a vast and unwieldy category that I am bound to get it wrong, but I'll take the risk, and at least begin the necessary conversation. The risk of misinterpretation has consequences for the interpreter (i.e., this author) and for the interpreted (Indigenous Peoples). However, these traditions, more than all the others I could have studied, reveal the most devastating, negative realities about my own cultural heritage.

In fact, Indigenous values clarify what is of most urgent concern for all human beings and indicate a way toward restoration. Just as religion "as habitation" in chapter 4 brought out the religious

---

21. Eliade, *Sacred and the Profane*, 15.

dimensions of land, real estate, and private property, so, too, can defining religion as "exchange" expose the religious dimensions of money and the global profit economy.

Money is the total fact of modern existence: it demands that we pay constant attention. Money determines power balances, health, morality, life, and death. People worry about it incessantly, whether they have it or not, because all meaningful human life today is based on money. It accounts for most of the violent crime and war in the world, creates fractures in families and between neighbors, and is the basis of individual and corporate empowerment, greed, and corruption. In fact, money is so much a part of the daily life of human beings today that it is regarded as a natural attribute of the human condition.

As with the cosmology of property, money has historically been at odds with Indigenous values. Indeed, it would be difficult to find a more destructive force over the last 530 years than money. Money is not a more "evolved" form of social organization, but a fundamentally different one. Operating within the monetary economy implies a distinct theology of values. As with the religious dimensions of private property, the religious dimensions of a monetary economy move all humans toward an anthropocentric understanding of exchange. It is imperative to understand this as we move forward with our discussion of Indigenous values around the idea of "exchange."

A Theology of Money

Money is based completely on a system of faith and, as with all belief systems, is a complete and utter mystery. People regularly lie, cheat, steal, and kill one another over money, and yet it has no intrinsic worth. People will do everything they can to acquire money; in fact, it articulates the cosmology of modernity.[22] Money is a system of

---

22. One of the best books on the meaning of money was written over one hundred years ago by Georg Simmel: *The Philosophy of Money*, which was originally published in 1900 and revised in 1907 and is best at capturing the importance of money in the day-to-day operations of people's lives.

faith because it *has* no intrinsic value. It effectively symbolizes the use value of anything to which it refers at the moment of a transaction. The effectiveness of the monetary economy is wholly contingent on the degree to which humans have confidence in its value.

In the early history of the United States, money used to be backed up by a "gold standard." Today, however, all currency is evaluated purely by its exchange value. Money is a direct reflection of one country's status, prestige, and power vis-à-vis all other countries in the world. Purchasing power emanates from the symbolic act of exchanging money for something of human demand or necessity (i.e., a car, a meal, a home). Whether a given item is affordable or unaffordable determines the measure of how much power or control one can wield using the monetary symbolic system. One's purchasing power is directly tied to the degree of confidence that a given nation has in its ability to back up its money. Thus, the value of money is completely dependent on a population's "consumer confidence." Money can operate only if everyone believes that it has the power to determine the comparative value of the material world.

As Marx says, however, the world of commodities, of which the symbol of money is a part, is really just a constant competition between different use values. The amount of labor invested in the material world is what is actually being exchanged in all monetary transactions.[23] For Marx, the commodity is the bedrock of the world monetary system; it is defined as a unit of labor that renders an element of material life into something suitable or necessary for human consumption. This definition of the commodity is more abstract, however, in the contemporary context, where the meaning of the commodity is less and less tangible. Today, though, money is the measure of human labor, or the time required to produce a product. As they say, "Time is money," and this seems to remain true although the nature of the commodity has shifted.

---

23. "Hence the mysteriousness of the equivalent form, which only impinges on the crude bourgeois vision of the political economist when it confronts him in its fully developed shape, that of money" (Marx, *Capital*, 149).

If, for some reason, human confidence were to wane in the value of a country's currency—say, due to environmental collapse or a war—then the currency would be devalued. If faith in our currency were to sink, then the US economy would sink as well, likely affecting the world economy. Thus, great attention is given to promoting and selling confidence in the money economy. Entire governmental offices have been created to increase the confidence with which we, as citizens, invest in the symbolism of money. A potent example is how, after the attacks on the World Trade Center and the Pentagon on September 11, 2001, President George W. Bush quickly urged all US citizens to spend money to show that the terrorists did not win. President Barack Obama also urged us all to buy more goods in response to the Great Recession of 2009. The symbolic value of money is directly tied to its circulation; therefore, not spending it would decrease the overall value of US currency. Hoarding money would have violated its symbolic value. Money is only of value when it is circulated among human beings.

Money determines the worth of our contemporary material life. It is a total symbolic system which requires that every human being be involved. No group can opt out or start their own system, because this would violate the symbolic system of equivalents that money encompasses. While everyone must participate—as mandated by force—money also determines the worth of every other life form in the world. Animals, plants, and stones, for example, are all evaluated monetarily with respect to their use value, or resource value, for the benefit of human beings. Money reduces all living things to symbols that become operative in evaluating everything in the world. It is completely anthropocentric because it compares the relative value of material life to a human need or desire. Even though it is often said that "money doesn't buy everything," it is more often the case that money *tries* to buy everything. As an abstract system, money represents the total measure of value for everything in life.

▲ ▲ ▲

It would be hard to imagine anything more detrimental to Indigenous values than money. As discussed, ceremonies are gift exchanges that are performed by human beings to address the sacred beings that comprise the material world; conversely, monetary exchange practices between human beings aid in the human consumption of the material world. Dividing a living earth into private property has been traumatic to the Earth and Indigenous Peoples. This theology of money is a direct assault on Indigenous values and an Indigenous cosmology.

The god of money is otiosus; this is why the American currency reads, "In God We Trust." We are to have faith in God *removed* from the world, rather than having a concrete knowledge of Him *in* the world. There is no material sensibility of the sacred in the God of money—only transcendence.[24]

In a monetary economy, spirit is opposed to matter, and matter is opposed to spirit. So, God is removed from a material world that he created in some distant past, and the world is no longer divine, but wholly placed under the control of human beings, who act as His divine agents over and above all other nonhuman beings. While the monetary system of exchange places its faith in this divine priority of God, human beings have been placed in charge of all life on Earth. Money represents and puts a number to human desire, need, and monetary value in the material world. Everything, then, is reducible to a value relative to human consumption.[25]

Consumerism, as an ideology of monetary exchange practices, articulates many of these religious ideals. The singular human being,

---

24. This is why I choose not to use the term "Indigenous spirituality." In the West, "spirituality" has a peculiar legacy that is sharply contrasted with "materiality," but many Indigenous Peoples utilize the term "spirituality"—as opposed to "religion"—to characterize their traditions. Their understanding is reasonable, given the history of contact between Indigenous and immigrant people. My point is that it can easily lead to some categorical confusion. Instead, this book is proposing that "religion" can be both descriptive and critical.

25. Herman Melville, in his 1857 masterpiece *The Confidence-Man: His Masquerade* (London: Penguin, 1990), best articulates how a monetary economy is continually in danger from the "con-man." In chapter 26 on the "metaphysics of Indian-hating," he puts his finger on why there is a deep-seated hatred of Indigenous Peoples and their values by settler-colonial people.

the capital-S Self, is the central focus of exchange activity. The Self is a closed system toward which flow all worldly goods, the ceremonial center or "axis mundi" of Modernity. The Self, in many ways, replaces the absent God and becomes the omniscient, omnipresent force in the world. Money makes these religious attitudes and assumptions physical, if not material. The Self is the bedrock of consumer culture: its value is supreme, above the survival of all other living beings. With the dissolution of the world, the human Self will reunite with the otiosus deity that exists outside this Earth. In rough terms, this highlights the prominent features of the theology of money as apocalyptic, which helps to theoretically clarify how monetary economies stand in sharp conflict to gift economies.

Monetary Economies, Gift Economies, and the Future of Religion

While Indigenous Peoples have had to deal with money in their various cultural contexts over the last 530 years, this has always had a profound effect on Indigenous values. Indigenous Peoples and governments have had to acclimate themselves to money. It would be naive to think that there is a group today that has not felt the effects of the monetary economy of global capitalism within their community. These enterprises have been active around the world with mixed results, but most Indigenous communities have gotten themselves involved in the global monetary economy at great risk to their traditional practices and lands. Making money on Indigenous nations has most often been met with controversy.

The nature of monetary exchanges undermines the nature of familial exchanges that are basic to Indigenous values. For example, progressive Native American governments that had been reconstituted and placed under the "guardianship" of the United States through the Bureau of Indian Affairs were encouraged to bring gaming casino enterprises into their territories as a way to help alleviate intense poverty. Opposing factions that remained traditional in their values warned that casinos would erode their treaty status as sovereign nations. These business initiatives have had some regional success in getting money into the hands of progressive Native Americans, but, at the same time, they often create discord between progressive and traditional people.[26] It's important to note here that traditional people are rarely listened to, for they rarely vote in BIA government elections they refuse to "recognize." Casinos have not had any appreciable effect in promoting traditional or Indigenous values. Casino profits have polarized Native American communities between "progressive" (i.e., those who support casino development) and "traditional" (i.e., those who support traditional cultural values) groups in the community. Whatever side one may take—and one must always take a side—it is clear that big money ventures, such as state-sponsored casinos, have been extremely controversial within Indigenous communities. Among the issues most intensely debated is the effect of these money-making exploits on their culture—or, in my parlance, on the gift economy of Indigenous values. Today, as people are becoming more knowledgeable about the Doctrines of Christian Discovery, there seems to be a shift in reevaluating the deeply insidious role Christianity played in colonization. A growing movement gives more credence to the Indigenous voices that have been silenced through the BIA. This serves as evidence that many communities are beginning the process of healing the colonial divide that was forced upon their people.[27]

Indigenous values, and their emphasis on ceremonial gift exchanges, dramatize and clarify the religious nature of the monetary exchanges of the modern world. The cosmology of money compares

---

26. This conflict between "progressive" and "traditional" Mohawks erupted into a civil war in the early 1990s when the first Indian casino was built under the "protection" of armed warriors. Sandy and I were at Akwesasne when this conflict moved to gunfire. Reading old issues of the world-renowned *Akwesasne Notes* can give anyone a good sense of the depth of this conflict that began with settler-colonialism. See "Items in the *Akewsasne Notes* Collection 10/85," American Indian Digital History Project, http://www.aidhp.com/ (accessed 2 January 2023).

27. See Bigtree and Arnold, "Why Removing Columbus Matters."

and contrasts at several levels with the Indigenous meaning of exchange. Both are the total fact of their respective cosmologies, and they each require the total attention and participation of human beings. Success in life requires complete involvement as a ceremonial element. Both gift and monetary economies express central religious orientations of human action rather than belief, as well as the contrasting ways that Indigenous and Immigrant communities understand the materiality of "how the world works."

Gift and monetary economies, of course, orient human beings to the cosmos in fundamentally different ways. Ceremonies and performances of Indigenous values are organized around the return of a gift of life that has already been given by Creation. Among the Haudenosaunee, ceremonies are referred to as "Thanksgivings." Ceremonies are expressions of gratitude for gifts already given. In other words, as previously discussed, human life is completely contingent on the surrounding living world and dedicated to the continuation of the regenerative cosmos. This is also demonstrated in Indigenous sacrificial and sporting events among Nahuatl-speaking people of Mexico. *Nextlahualli*, their word for "sacrifice," which has been translated as the "payment of debt," emphasizes this idea of a ceremonial gift economy or the rendering of a life in exchange with the natural world for the life of the community. It would be shortsighted, greedy, and disrespectful if Nahuatl-speaking people were to understand a human relationship without the world.

Further, the theme of the way money corrupts human society is not new; understandings of this tendency are as old as religion itself. Prophets, preachers, priests, and shamans, among many other moral leaders throughout all the religions of the world, have warned that valuing human life over what is regarded as sacred will erode any human relationship with a God or the Creator. In other words, the values expressed in the gift economy of Indigenous Peoples are closer to the essential features of all religions, including the global religions.

In chapter 3, we discussed how Indigenous values were closest to the original values that pre-dated religion. Similarly, the values expressed in a gift relationship with the world are closer to these values. The distinction between gift and monetary evaluations could be understood as the essential distinction between religious and secular values, but in this scenario the "secular" is derivative from religious understandings. Indigenous values express what is essential in all religious understandings that promote community cohesion.

This begs the question: Why have these traditions been disparaged, harassed, and systematically destroyed over the last five hundred years? Why have these ceremonial practices been subjected to attack by religious institutions through processes of missionization, education, and forced assimilation? Why are Indigenous values still considered by some to be detrimental to progress? An examination of Indigenous values reveals the dangerous oppositions at work in religion. On the one hand, the global religions claim to promote peace, justice, health, wealth. But, on the other hand, these religions want these values at the price of reducing the plurality of local religious expressions to their monolithic God. How can the values of a gift economy, which intimately relates human beings to a living world, be consistent with the values of global domination and an intolerance for religious diversity?

The category of Indigenous values reveals numerous opposing values that run through modernity. Studying Indigenous values shows us a great deal about other, local religious orientations, but even more about modern existence. As maintained in the History of Religions, an examination of the other is always, simultaneously, an examination of oneself and the culture from which one sprang. Almost all successful writings about Indigenous Peoples have included this self-reflective aspect. These studies measure the consequences of the academic study of religion.

Religious ceremonies are always intended to relate human life to the sacred. The primary difference between Indigenous and global religious ceremonies comes down to the proximity of the sacred. While Indigenous Peoples understand themselves to be completely engulfed at all times by a sacred spiritual presence, most global religions see the sacred as very distant. In all cases, the fervent practitioner—who is regarded as a saint, or teacher, or prophet—operates as if always surrounded by the sacred. The fervent practitioner, or community of practitioners, seem to desire and embody a close relationship to the sacred. On the one hand, this expresses how Indigeneity can be understood to be an essential feature of all religious understandings; these traditions articulate where religious creativity and innovation flourish, and why religion can never remain stagnate or fixed to unchanging criteria because there is always the possibility of another hierophany. On the other hand, the fervent practitioner or community is also antagonistic to Indigenous sensibilities, particularly when that fervor is more attached to an ideology than to the materiality of life.

Religious fervor is often connected with the intolerance of religious plurality, or fundamentalism. Religious fervor in the global religions has also expressed itself before as nationalism, the belief that the most unambiguous expression of God is through a nation-state or national figure. Since the fifteenth century, Christian religious fervor has manifested as a missionary zeal to convert Indigenous Peoples to Christianity and been informed by absolute confidence in the Christian orientation to God, understood to be over and above all other religious formulations. This overconfidence has inspired people (now, more than just Christian people) to travel to far-off places around the world to reach "untouched" Indigenous Peoples in order to spread the Gospel.

Fundamentalism, nationalism, and missionization are expressions of religious zeal and fervor. They combine a sense of being enfolded in the sacred, but with a settler-colonial sensibility of being excessively certain of the universal nature of their own religious faith, establishing that the essential nature of the sacred has finally been revealed within the sacred texts for everyone. Their religion is the "seal," or final prophetic utterance, of God for all human beings. The extent to which a sacred text is the final word of God is the extent to which intolerance for religious diversity, fundamentalism, nationalism, and missionization can flourish. Sacred texts funnel a human relationship with the sacred through a particular medium of expression that excludes other religious expressions in the world. The degree to which a sacred text is determinative of all religious meanings among the global religions is the degree to which there is a generalized intolerance of Indigenous values and a persecution of Indigenous Peoples. In either world, the depth of religious conviction is an attribute of the proximity of the sacred. For Indigenous Peoples, however, expressions of the sacred can occur regularly in the material world. For immigrant people, expressions of the sacred happened in the past at a particular time and place and it was determined equally valid for all people everywhere, because it was primarily revealed through a book.

Often, a difference between Indigenous and global religions has been expressed as the difference between oral and textual religions. Indigenous values are understood to be oriented around oral traditions and performative myths through ceremony. In contrast, global religions are oriented around sacred texts and are traditions of ideas and faith. Judaism, Christianity, and Islam are closely identified by their sacred texts and are often called "religions of the book." The difference between oral and textual religions, however, transforms into a kind of socioreligious evolutionary model of religious development.

This, I would like to submit, is a problem: rather than a difference, this tends to convey a sense that the textual tradition is more valuable, more dependable, and somehow more "real" than the oral tradition. I'm suggesting here that emphasizing different exchange practices in the distinctive religious orientations helps to clarify a real difference between Indigenous and immigrant traditions. The gift economies of Indigenous ceremonial practices are constantly shifting, but are always connected to the traditions that take place in a variety of living landscapes. A monetary exchange system is rooted in the textual traditions of the West, where the sacred is much less proximate and outside—in other words, otiosus to the world.

These are two fundamentally distinctive ways of being in the world. While both involve human activity and the way human beings value the world, they are completely distinct in their understanding of the relationship of human beings to the sacred. The question, of course, becomes *how* we value what it *is* that we value, and the ways of exchanging that value within that framework. The answer, I would argue, is complex, but quite clear.

6

Discovery and Indigeneity

> We were planting corn; they were planting crosses.
> —Oren Lyons quote at the Skä·noñh—
> Great Law of Peace Center

Today, most historical demographers agree that between fifty million and one hundred million Indigenous People died throughout the Americas in the years after 1492.[1] Disease, epidemics, warfare, enslavement, forced removal, and imprisonment by the Old World are to blame. Along with human populations, other living beings suffered, including the American buffalo, which was slaughtered in the millions to starve out western Indigenous nations, as well as the carrier pigeon, which was said to have lived in such numbers as to blacken the sky.[2] According to scientists, we are entering the sixth mass extinction, where up to two hundred species of living beings, relatives to Indigenous Peoples, are disappearing every day.[3]

My question here is: What is the root cause of this mass extinction that threatens the survival of all living beings on the Earth? Is

---

1. The science of estimating human populations of the past is highly speculative. Alfred W. Crosby's *Columbian Exchange* transformed this area of research. David Stannard's *American Holocaust* created an eye-popping awareness of the enormity of this devastation, after which Charles Mann's *1492* tried to answer some of the fundamental questions. William Denevan's work has tempered the numbers, but is still sobering in its scale.

2. See Cronon, *Changes in the Land*; and Stannard, *American Holocaust*.

3. Cowie, Bouchet, and Fontaine, "Sixth Mass Extinction," 97.

it bad actors like Columbus? No—not only that, but the fact that our current crisis is rooted in a worldview based in a theology of Christian settler-colonialism that has been operative since the Age of Discovery. Our continued survival, therefore, depends not just on moving toward technologies that ensure a carbon-neutral future, but, more critically, rethinking our relationship to the Earth by supporting Indigenous Peoples' values.

This chapter is dedicated to exposing a settler-colonial religion that celebrates the end of all things, from an Indigenous values perspective. Religion, and Christianity in particular, combines with political, military, and corporate power to create the material conditions of an apocalyptic reality based in the Doctrine of Christian Discovery (DoCD).[4]

Where Is the Spiritual Home for Human Beings?

Our 501c3 nonprofit, Indigenous Values Initiative, also sponsors the work of the American Indian Law Alliance (AILA). When we accompanied AILA to the UN Permanent Forum on Indigenous Issues in New York in 2008, Oren Lyons, Faithkeeper and member of the Chiefs Council of the Onondaga Nation, discussed religion with noted author, environmentalist, and student of mythology Phil Cousineau. Lyons pinpointed the destruction of the environment as coming from the global religious orientation toward heaven rather than the Earth. As he said: "If you grow up with the idea that there is always a better place, always another place [i.e., heaven], then this place here [on Earth] suffers the consequence of this kind of thinking. Now, not only this place, but everyone and all humanity is suffering

---

4. I realize that there are many Christians who are Indigenous and many non-Indigenous Christians who are working on social justice and environmental issues (to be discussed later in this chapter). My interest is not in criticizing anyone's faith tradition, and certainly not in reforming Christianity. Rather, my focus is on applying a "materiality of religion" approach from the History of Religions to the more textually obscured elements of Indigenous Peoples' values.

the consequences of this kind of thinking. Now, we are facing the reality and consequences of our disregarding the laws of the Earth."[5]

If we look back to fifteenth- and sixteenth-century papal bulls (letters from the pope to the Church), we can clearly see that Christianity had been used to justify not only the colonization of Indigenous Peoples in Africa and the Americas but also the theft of land. The phenomenon known today as the Doctrine of Christian Discovery (DoCD) has espoused a value system that is diametrically opposed to Indigenous understandings of being human and inhabiting the Earth. These ideologies were used to effectively destroy an Indigenous identity with the land so that it could be more easily commodified.

It is this dominion over the land that has brought us today to the brink of environmental catastrophe. These documents, with others, were instrumentalized to reorient all human beings away from the understanding that land is sacred and significant. Examining the fifteenth- and sixteenth-century texts regarding the DoCD and its negative effects on Indigenous Peoples will help us better understand how religion was used both to reorient us in opposition to the Earth as well as to define Indigenous Peoples as being enemies of Christ and opponents of the Catholic Church. Steven Newcomb has painstakingly assembled a sequence of papal bulls written between 1452 and 1493 outlining the Vatican's justification of the conquest of non-Christian people and taking possession of the New World.[6] By March 5, 1496, English king Henry VII incorporated the DoCD ideologies into British colonial ambitions through the Cabot Charter so England could also lay claims to non-Christian lands. By 1823, these same ideas were codified into US federal law. The DoCD is now understood to be fundamental to US property law. Today, these issues remain systematically active in areas of law, politics, economic development, and religion, with the DoCD most recently being referenced

---

5. "Earth Wisdom: For a World in Crisis," Global Spirit Series, LinkTV 2009, https://archive.org/details/linktv_special-global-spirit-earth-wisdom20090917 (accessed 3 February 2023).

6. Newcomb, *Pagans in the Promised Land*.

in Ruth Bader Ginsburg's notorious opinion in 2005's land claim dispute *City of Sherrill v. Oneida Indian Nation*.[7]

For these reasons, Indigenous Peoples have sought to expose the history and policies of the DoCD before the UN. They have made further requests that the Vatican repudiate and revoke these papal bulls.[8] For Indigenous Peoples, it is of high priority that the public be educated about how the DoCD perpetuates the code of domination through the Vatican's member status on the world platform at the UN. Cayuga Chief Deskaheh first addressed the League of Nations in Geneva, Switzerland, in 1923 regarding US and Canadian treaty violations; in 1977, Indigenous leaders took those same concerns back to the UN. The Haudenosaunee have continually presented these issues at the United Nations; since 2001, the focus has included the DoCD, which had defined Indigenous Peoples as barbarians, heathens, and enemies of Christ. Prior to the United Nations Declaration on the Rights of Indigenous Peoples (UNDRIP), which was adopted in 2007, Indigenous Peoples were referred to as "populations"—the same designation given to Norway's herds of reindeer. The UNDRIP finally designated Indigenous Peoples as being human and gave them a seat at the table.

As we have discussed, "Indigenous values" is not a natural category (i.e., one that emerges organically from a particular community of people), but one that comes out of the necessity of bringing disparate communities all over the world together to oppose the cultural forces that are bent on their destruction. The intense cultural clash of worldviews that was implemented by the DoCD with Columbus's voyages has created the need for an awareness of Indigenous values.

---

7. *City of Sherrill v. Oneida Indian Nation*, Oyez, https://www.oyez.org/cases/2004/03-855 (accessed 3 February 2023).

8. In 2001 Oren Lyons introduced the harmful effects of the DoCD for Indigenous Peoples in a speech at the United Nation in Geneva, Switzerland, for the first time. The Holy See, holding the UN papal seat, heard his speech.

An understanding of Indigeneity, therefore, requires that we appreciate the depth to which these different values have been articulated by Christian authorities. Because the DoCD threatens Indigenous Peoples all over the world, these religious discussions continue to remain central at the UN between the Holy See (Vatican authority of the Catholic Church) and Indigenous Peoples.[9]

Although there are rarely clear oppositions in the area of religion, the DoCD comes closest to articulating what has become a nearly complete rejection of what we now have come to call "Indigenous values." The cultural-religious forces unleashed upon the world during the Age of Discovery gave rise to the modern age of the West that was built on the demonization of Indigenous Peoples and their traditions. This age brought unimagined wealth and power to the Church and European empires as well as unimagined devastation and misery to Indigenous Peoples all over the world. The DoCD established a New World paradigm ordered around the commoditization of non-Christians' bodies, material lives, and land. From an Indigenous perspective, the DoCD paradigm continues to wreak havoc today. Among other issues, it underlies the justification for Christian superiority over other religions, while serving as the impetus for converting

---

9. I have been conducting research in the area of religion and colonialism for over thirty years and teaching on the subject for over twenty. It wasn't until I attended a special session of the 4th Session of the UN Permanent Forum on Indigenous Issues in New York in 2005 that this work was galvanized under the heading of the "Doctrine of Christian Discovery." The panel was organized by Tonya Gonnella Frichner (Snipe Clan), who was a citizen of the Onondaga Nation, founder and director of the American Indian Law Alliance, and the North American Representative to the UN Permanent Forum on Indigenous Issues. The panel was comprised of Oren Lyons, Onondaga Nation Faithkeeper; Esmeralda Brown, United Methodist Office for the United Nations; Alex White Plume, Oglala Lakota; Steven Newcomb, Indigenous Law Institute; and Birgil Kills Straight, Oglala Lakota and Indigenous Law Institute. This panel completely reoriented my understanding of the issues underlying Indigenous religions and colonialism. In 2012, the UN Permanent Forum on Indigenous Issues focused on the DoCD as one of their primary issues.

and holding dominion over others. In its legal formulation, the DoCD justifies the commoditization of the natural world allowing multinational corporations to channel enormous wealth into the hands of a few, which continues today. In short, nothing articulates the opposing values between settler-colonial and Indigenous worldviews more clearly than the DoCD.

From Christendom's Theology of Conquest to the Doctrine of Christian Discovery

In December 2009, I accompanied a delegation of Haudenosaunee representatives to a meeting of the Parliament of World Religions in Melbourne, Australia. The parliament, which was founded in 1893, is the largest interfaith organization in the world dedicated to bringing the world's religions together through dialogue. The first Parliament of World Religions was held in 1893 at the World's Fair in Chicago. This was a time when Indigenous Peoples were treated as oddities, exhibited in caged spaces and displayed like some kind of freak show. The general spirit of the day was in celebration of the promises of progress through the achievements of manifest destiny and the show titled "March of Civilization in Settling the American Wild West."

This was exemplified by pairing the parliament with Chicago's World's Fair, which was aptly titled the Columbian Exposition of 1893, commemorating the four-hundredth anniversary of Columbus's landing. To draw greater attention to the event, President Cleveland ceremoniously flipped the electrical switch from the White House and inaugurated the first use of light bulb illumination throughout the fair.[10]

Much has changed since the inception of the Parliament of World Religions. In Melbourne in 2009, Indigenous Peoples were not seen as

---

10. These events also correspond with the founding of the University of Chicago and with the beginning of what has come to be known throughout the world as the "History of Religions" or "comparative religions." See Kitagawa, *History of Religions*; Rydell, *All the World's a Fair*; and Burris, *Exhibiting Religion*.

the exotic curiosities and carnival freaks of the inaugural 1893 event. Instead, they were invited to act as consultants on the world's deepest and most intractable problems regarding environmental crisis and social injustice and to collaborate on several panels that addressed major topics such as "Healing the Earth with Care and Concern" and "Reconciling with Indigenous Peoples." An Indigenous caucus, led by Oren Lyons, Tonya Gonnella Frichner, and Steve Newcomb, created a document highlighting the urgency of the Parliament of World Religions in addressing the DoCD as the root cause for the world's problems. It reads in part:

> Unfortunately, certain doctrines have been threatening to the survival of our cultures, our languages, and our people, and devastating to our ways of life. These are found in particular colonizing documents such as the Inter Caetera Papal Bull of 1493, which called for the subjugation of non-Christian nations and peoples and "the propagation of the Christian empire." This is the root of the Doctrine of Christian Discovery that is still interwoven into laws and policies today that must be changed. The principles of subjugation contained in this and other such documents, and in the religious texts and documents of other religions, have been and continue to be destructive to our ways of life (religions), cultures, and the survival of our Indigenous nations and peoples. This oppressive tradition is what led to the boarding schools, the residential schools, and the Stolen Generations, resulting in the trauma of Indigenous Peoples being cut off from their languages and cultures, resulting in language death and loss of family integrity from the actions of churches and governments. *We call on those churches and governments to put as much time, effort, energy and money into assisting with the revitalization of our languages and cultures as they put into attempting to destroy them.* [emphasis added]

The message delivered has been largely heeded by the parliament. In meetings since the 2009 gathering, Indigenous Peoples have continued to play a central role in organizing the conference and the statements it produces. Indigenous values, therefore, are seen as the future of religion.

The Doctrine of Christian Discovery

At least since 1452, a succession of Catholic Popes gave Christian "discoverers" legal and moral dominion over non-Christians and obligated them to seize their people, goods, and lands. This sanction was first used on the West Coast of Africa, which led to the transatlantic slave trade. It was then used throughout the Americas, the Pacific Rim in New Zealand, the Philippines, and Australia. The "Age of Discovery," as it has been called, was fueled by a religious fervor to retake the Holy Land and establish the Christian empire (*imperii christiani*), or "Christendom."

This fifteenth-century shift to a Christian-centered worldview is still very much with us. In fact, for much of the corporate world, it is the modus operandi behind the modern laws used to take land and exploit its resources. The Church's efforts in the fifteenth century to classify Indigenous Peoples as antithetical to Christianity by utilizing the category of infidels—including pagans, barbarians, heathens, Sarcens, Satanist, witches, Jews, and Muslims—excluded them from those who were under Christian Ecclesiastical control. Up until this time, people throughout Asia, Africa, the Americas, Australia, and Polynesia practiced their own local traditions. There was no concept of being "Indigenous" in the land of their ancestors because, in large part, they were living in their traditional homes and living life just as they had always done. Once the Church determined that "Indigenous Peoples" (in today's parlance) were "enemies of Christ," they became the defined and targeted global community that stood in the way of establishing Christendom. The innovation of Indigenous Peoples since 1977 has been to transform this negative global category into something recognizably positive for Indigenous and non-Indigenous Peoples alike. As discussed earlier, the Haudenosaunee organize themselves around "condolence" and "peace" (Skä·noñh), like many other nations. Ironically, Christian discoverers characterized them as "primitive" or "savage," which is completely at odds with how they actually organized themselves.

The papal bull *Dum Diversas* of 1452 from Nicholas V to King Alfonso V of Portugal directed all Christians to "invade, capture, vanquish, and subdue all Saracens and pagans . . . to reduce their persons to perpetual slavery and to take away all their possessions and property."[11] In other words, if, during their adventures, Christians were to encounter non-Christians—even those found within their *own* homelands—it was their duty to take away all possessions and either kill or permanently enslave the inhabitants and assume dominion over their entire material lives.

Initially, there was little interest in converting non-Christians to Christianity. Christians took what had been intrinsic to an Indigenous worldview and determined the use value of the land—the resources and the people necessary to foster the kingdom of the Church. Essentially, this was a theological move toward the commodification of the world in order to realize Christian world domination. This accumulated wealth in riches, slaves, and land quickened the expansion of Christendom, all to finally realize the conquest of the Holy Land, which had been occupied by Muslims for nearly a millennium. Therefore, from an Indigenous perspective, the Age of Discovery issued forth from the aspiration of Christian world domination, overcoming the failure of the Crusades and finally occupying the site of the Christian hierophany.

Just after Columbus had returned to Spain and reported finding gold, Pope Alexander VI (the infamous Borgia Pope, who came from an all-powerful Spanish merchant family) issued the papal bull *Inter Caetera* on 4 May 1493, in which he called for "barbarous nations" to be "subjugated" and brought to the Catholic faith "for the propagation of the Christian empire (*imperii christiani*)." Many

---

11. *Dum Diversas*, Unam Sanctam Catholicam, 2011, https://doctrineofdiscovery.org/dum-diversas/ (accessed 3 February 2023).

believe that this language was adopted to justify the greed of European explorers and monarchs, but another concern of these fifteenth-century soldiers of fortune was for the perpetuation of the Church and the establishment of a single unified Christian empire.[12]

The inconceivable wealth obtained through the Church would propel enormous power and influence. Personal ambition drove the soldiers of fortune to implement the DoCD, for they too had much to gain as agents of the dream of Christendom. There was a link between personal ambition and the acquisition of wealth, power, and influence that connected and empowered the Church, monarchies, and explorers. The greed of explorers like Columbus is now seen as the "hook" in a cultural-religious strategic game that defined Europe throughout the Age of Discovery. Today, Columbus is the face of the DoCD.

In 1823, the US Supreme Court officially transformed what was a theology of conquest into a doctrine. In the *Johnson v. M'Intosh* decision, Chief Justice John Marshall outlined the history of the DoCD as a fundamental characteristic of US property law. The DoCD was the means by which "clean title" could be established throughout the "discovered" territory within the United States. In the decision, Marshall borrows directly from ideas of the fifteenth-century papal bulls, stating that, by law, the conquest of America created clear title because "Christian people" appeared on lands "inhabited by natives, who were heathens."[13] Although this association of John Marshall's was a complete fabrication, it was turned into US law. For the most

12. "Bulla del Papa Alexandro VI dada el año 1493, en que concede a los Reyes Cathólicos y sus sucesores todo lo que ganaren y conquistaren en las Indias no estando ocupado por otros" (1493-05-04, Roma, MP-BULAS_BREVES,4, Archivo General de Indias, Sevilla, Spain). A new translation of this bull is found at Indigenous Values Initiative, "Inter Caetera," translated by Sebastian Modrow and Melissa Smith, Doctrine of Discovery Project, 13 June 2022, https://doctrineofdiscovery.org/inter-caetera/.

13. *Johnson v. M'Intosh*, https://tile.loc.gov/storage-services/service/ll/usrep/usrep021/usrep021543/usrep021543.pdf (accessed 3 February 2023), 576–77.

part, "Christianity" had dropped out of Marshall's decision, to be replaced with "civilization" and the legal formulation of the "Doctrine of Christian Discovery."

The *Johnson v. M'Intosh* case is not a relic of the past, but is understood today to be fundamental to defining property law, as well as federal Indian law. It is among the primary documents studied in every first-year law school's property law class. Moreover, it has had a significant effect in defining international law.[14]

This case is monumental in that, in the early part of US history, this single decision transformed the Catholic principle of "discovery" into law and legitimated the Protestant project of "nation building." It pre-dated and justified, to give one example, the removal of native nations in 1830–36 from the southeastern United States with the infamous Trail of Tears. In spite of the fact that citizens of the United States were predominately Protestant and deeply suspicious of papal authority, when it came to the area of property law they would adopt the Catholic principle as set out in the fifteenth-century papal bulls and charters to justify land acquisition through the subversion of Indigenous Peoples as a way to effectively legitimize state control. While distinctive Christian groups could not agree on many aspects of ecclesiastical authority, they could come together around the issue of subduing Indigenous nations. The DoCD, therefore, unified the plurality of Christians in the United States. This decision has had an enormous impact around the world, particularly in countries with an Anglo-colonial legal tradition (Canada, Australia, New Zealand, and the United States).[15] This decision created a "secular" context

---

14. Lindsay Robertson's *Conquest by Law* delivers a basic understanding of *Johnson v. M'Intosh* and its consequences. In the five-volume work *The Life of George Washington*, Chief Justice John Marshall devotes the entire first volume to a timeline that begins with Columbus's discovery of the New World, leading to his developing a myth-history of America. See Robertson, "John Marshall as Colonial Historian"; and d'Errico, *Federal Anti-Indian Law*.

15. Miller et al., *Discovering Indigenous Lands*, looks at the effects of *Johnson v. M'Intosh* internationally.

where categories like "civilization of the continent" implied a Christian foundation.

The DoCD is active today in US law. For example, in the 2005 Supreme Court decision *Oneida Nation v. Sherrill*, Justice Ruth Bader Ginsburg—arguably the most liberal voice on the court—wrote the majority opinion against the Oneida Nation action to repurchase land that had been illegally taken by New York State throughout the nineteenth and twentieth centuries and return it to protected sovereign status. The first citation stated the DoCD as fundamental for the presumption of "clear title."[16]

In other words: this DoCD has remained the literal "law of the land" in US state and federal courts. It is the means by which US citizens and others have inherited a settler-colonial legacy to occupy the homeland of Indigenous Peoples. In effect, the DoCD is tantamount to a religious material transformation in the reappropriation and redefinition of land stolen from Indigenous Peoples and revalued by settler-colonial worldviews.

The DoCD is the primary obstacle prohibiting the world community from embracing fundamental rights for Indigenous Peoples' values and advocating for their religious freedom. The historic UN Declaration on the Rights of Indigenous Peoples (UNDRIP) of September 12, 2007, officially recognized their humanity. However, Canada, Australia, New Zealand, and the United States—the so-called CANZUS group of the former British colonies / now democracies that have historically opposed Indigenous Peoples' rights—voted against the UN declaration.[17] Because the DoCD is so closely tied to

---

16. *City of Sherrill v. Oneida Indian Nation*, 544 U.S. 197, 2005.

17. Tonya Gonnella Frichner, Onondaga Snipe Clan, director of the American Indian Law Alliance and North American Representative to the UN Permanent Forum on Indigenous Issues, was instrumental in forming the UN Declaration on the Rights of Indigenous Peoples. See "Impact on Indigenous Peoples of the International Legal Construct Known as the Doctrine of Discovery, Which Has Served as the Foundation of the Violation of their Human Rights," submitted by the secretariat of the UNPFII for the 9th Session, 19–30 April 2010, at the UN, New York City.

property and land title in these former British colonies, these states chose to uphold fifteenth-century anti-Indigenous Christian ideas in order to protect their unchecked access to natural resources.[18] Since 2007, the countries of CANZUS have reversed their positions and finally adopted the UNDRIP, but with conditions. The most recent of these was when President Obama announced his endorsement in December 2010 during a speech to representatives of the 574 federally recognized Tribal Nations meeting in Washington, DC. However, speculation remains throughout North America that these endorsements are all "with qualifications" and not the full endorsement of the entirety of the UNDRIP.

One of the primary qualifying issues is the degree to which sovereign Indigenous nations are allowed to control their own lands, designated as "free, prior, and informed consent" (FPIC) in the UNDRIP, on the use of their traditional territories. Today, according to the UN, Indigenous nations exist within the boundaries of modern-day nation-states and are held under their dominion. This has jeopardized the degree to which Indigenous Peoples can exercise their rights over the use of their lands. In other words, the question remains for those who have signed the UNDRIP (particularly CANZUS): Who will uphold the cultural and material integrity of the relationship of Indigenous Peoples with the land?

The adoption of the UNDRIP, even if it does not have the legal teeth that it could have, is an acknowledgment to modern international bodies that there is a fundamental flaw in our mythic narrative of colonial origins. Prime Minister Rudd's apology to the "Stolen Generation" in February 2008 for Australia's mistreatment of Aboriginal Peoples, and President Obama's remarks on the traumatic history of Native Americans in December 2010 are, in this sense, symbolic moves away from colonial forms of occupation, even if they

---

18. It has been estimated that approximately 80 percent of the remaining world's "natural resources" are currently in Indigenous Peoples lands. According to the United Nations study, Indigenous Peoples embody and nurture 80 percent of the world's cultural and biological diversity, and occupy 20 percent of the world's land surface.

are not material. These heads of state admitted that, although Indigenous Peoples' historical displacement, extermination, and genocide was seen in the past as a necessary precondition for the development of their nations, these policies are now perceived as detrimental to a viable future. These statements may be more about self-preservation, or possible hints at failure, but they are gestures toward embracing Indigenous values of habitation by attempting to bring the state into a more balanced relationship with the original Indigenous Peoples inhabiting this land. At this point, these are merely symbolic statements with sentimental value and therefore without substance, but the symbolism marks an important shift in the mythic structure (or myth-history) and master narratives of the modern nation-state, and perhaps something upon which to build new origin myths for the future. In this regard, the UNDRIP is also a document that could outline the future of religion—a blueprint for appropriate interactions between Indigenous and settler-colonial people.

For those religious organizations wishing to improve relationships with Indigenous Peoples, the UNDRIP has been an orienting document, but settler-colonial people can also embrace it as a move toward making peace with land that had been so violently colonized. Indigenous Peoples want to make Christians aware that the religious dimensions of the DoCD have served as the legal justification used to subjugate not only Indigenous Peoples but also Indigenous values. This has interfered with any consideration that Indigenous values could provide a viable future on how to heal the land, or to better understand material life. For example, according to UN press release HR/4950, in the Haudenosaunee statement delivered by Oren Lyons on 3 May 2008 to the UN, he said that "Papal bulls of 1493–1494, coupled with the First Letters Patent, issued by King Henry VIII to John Cabot and Sons in 1496, had established the process of colonization in the Western Hemisphere."[19] He stated that the introduction of the Christian doctrine of discovery into US federal caselaw had

---

19. United Nations, Permanent Forum on Indigenous Issues, 7th Sess., 29 April 2008, https://press.un.org/en/2008/hr4950.doc.htm.

opened American Indian lands for exploitation, which had quickly been seized by Christian settler states. Unraveling those events, which had set in motion the jurisprudential doctrines that sought to legitimize great injustices with regard to indigenous property, needed further investigation. Lyons went on to say that the Forum should initiate a study of the content and effects of the doctrine of discovery on the lands of indigenous peoples.

The Cabot Charter and the Episcopalians

The Cabot Charter (1496) mentioned in the Haudenosaunee quote above and issued by King Henry VII gave John Cabot the mission to "seek out, discover, and find, whatsoever isles, countries, and regions of the heathens and infidels that before this time have been unknown to all Christian people."[20] This charter, which was for exclusive rights of discovery, was Henry VII's attempt to expand the English empire similar to those of Spain and Portugal earlier in the fifteenth century. At that time England was a Catholic nation, but the Cabot Charter was issued by the English monarch, not the pope. This underscores the simmering conflicts between London and the Vatican. By the 1530s, and with the reign of Henry VIII, England had embraced the Protestant Revolution sweeping across northern Europe. In spite of the fact that the Cabot Charter pre-dated the establishment of the Church of England by thirty years or more, the US Episcopalians were the first Christian denomination to take up the issue and renounce the DoCD because Anglican and Protestantism was derived from the charter.

In July 2009, the US Episcopal Church unanimously adopted the resolution D035, "Repudiate the Doctrine of Discovery."[21] It reads in part:

---

20. "Patent Granted by Henry VII to John Cabot," Doctrine of Discovery Project, 23 July 2018, https://doctrineofdiscovery.org/patent-cabot-henry-vii/.

21. Thanks goes to John Dieffenbacher-Krall of Maine, who authored this document and pushed it through the General Convention for acceptance.

Resolved, That the 76th General Convention repudiates and renounces the Doctrine of Discovery as fundamentally opposed to the Gospel of Jesus Christ and our understanding of the inherent rights that individuals and people have received from God, and that this declaration be proclaimed among our churches and shared with the United Nations and all the nations and people located within the Episcopal Church's boundaries. This doctrine, which originated with Henry VII in 1496, held that Christian sovereigns and their representative explorers could assert dominion and title over non-Christian lands with the full blessing and sanction of the Church. It continues to be invoked, in only slightly modified form, in court cases and in the many destructive policies of governments and other institutions of the modern nation-states that lead to the colonizing dispossession of the lands of Indigenous Peoples and the disruption of their way of life; and be it further

Resolved, that The Episcopal Church review its policies and programs with a view to exposing the historical reality and impact of the Doctrine of Discovery and eliminating its presence in its contemporary policies, programs, and structures and, further, that this body directs the appropriate representatives of the House of Bishops and House of Deputies, to inform all relevant governmental bodies in The United States of its action and suggest similar and equivalent review of historical and contemporary policies that contribute to the continuing colonization of Indigenous Peoples and, further, to write to Queen Elizabeth II, the Supreme Governor of the Church of England, requesting that her Majesty disavow, and repudiate publicly, the claimed validity of the Christian Doctrine of Discovery.[22]

In spite of the fact that the Cabot Charter pre-dates the establishment of the Episcopal Church, this resolution points to something

---

22. Episcopal Church (USA), "The Episcopal Church USA Statements on the Doctrine of Discovery," Doctrine of Discovery Project, 27 July 2018, https://doctrineofdiscovery.org/the-episcopal-church-usa/.

fundamentally corrosive at the core of Christianity. In addressing the DoCD in this resolution, the US Episcopalian Church (excluding the Church of England as a whole) expressed concern for the continuing survival of Indigenous Peoples *and* for the future of Christianity and Episcopalianism. The key phrase here is that "the General Convention repudiates and renounces the Doctrine of Discovery as fundamentally opposed to the Gospel of Jesus Christ and our understanding of the inherent rights that individuals and people have received from God." The charter goes on to advocate for the archbishop of Canterbury to adopt a similar resolution as the UN Declaration on the Rights of Indigenous Peoples. The archbishop responded that because the Cabot Charter predated the establishment of the Anglican Church, there was no obligation to repudiate Henry VII's position; the US Episcopalians argued that the archbishop had missed the critical moral position.

From the point of view of Indigenous values, this recent statement of repudiation by US Episcopalians is a move to embracing Indigenous values. It will, then, be the future work of Episcopalians to *Indigenize* Christianity: to bring forward Indigenous values into Christianity so as not to follow the religious theology of colonization.

It is only in the last few generations that non-native people are beginning to question the real legacy and future viability of the DoCD and what has come to define our dominant colonial culture. Currently, grassroots movements are active among Catholics, Unitarian-Universalists, Methodists, Quakers, Presbyterians, Lutherans, Disciples of Christ, and many others that have resulted in similar resolutions to reject the DoCD. Currently, more than 350 Christian denominations and religious groups have repudiated the DoCD. Clearly, promoting social justice for Indigenous Peoples is of foremost importance among these Christian communities, but there is also the sense that these efforts to heal relationships with Indigenous Peoples will restore credibility to the Christian religion.

Both Indigenous Peoples and Christians understand that the human rights issues currently being addressed through the UN are fundamentally religious issues. In particular, they have to do with not only our interhuman/cross-cultural/international relationships, but also the fundamental human relationship with a living earth, which should also be understood as a religious issue. The current movement among religious groups to disown the DoCD unites the urgent global issues regarding the healing of society and the environment and defines what could be the future function of religion.

The Columbian Legacy

As addressed earlier, prior to 1492 it was inconceivable to categorize people who lived in the land of their ancestors as "Indigenous" because most everyone was living this way of life. After 1492, however, when European Christian empires set out to conquer the world for "Christ," they first needed to define the "enemy of Christ"; who better fit the bill than the Indigenous Peoples of Africa and the New World who were so fundamentally and radically "other" that they were unable to even conceive of Christ?

In effect, European processes of othering non-Christians as the enemies of Christ universalized what we now think of as "Indigenous." From the European vantage point, pushing into uncharted New Worlds created the need for new academic categories. As noted linguist Tzvetan Todorov has observed, the Christian missionization of the New World was characterized as bringing all of humanity into the "universal love of Christ," which would ultimately result in total destruction of all other peoples and traditions. In fact, missionizing activities were intended to destroy all human distinctions and differences, which are the intimate underpinnings of conquest and white supremacy.[23] European discovery, with its associated doctrines and cultural justifications, was a cultural invasion to take control of new lands and others whose values were purposely set in opposition to the Church.

By denigrating Indigenous Peoples and their proper relationship with an Earth with abundant resources, the "primitive" translated

---

23. See Todorov, *Conquest of America*.

as not only "stuck in the past," but literally standing in the way of "progress," and "civilization." Everything was rendered a natural resource, including human beings, who were mined to perpetuate the civilizing process through Christianization.

Today, the category of "Indigenous" works to undo the debilitating effects of the DoCD because "Indigenous" is the descriptive characteristic that defines how human beings can reengage with the Earth. Indigenous Peoples have used this terminology in their political efforts to gain recognition of their rights and the rights of the land but it can also provide insight into decolonization.[24]

At this point, we can consider it safely established that Europeans were motivated to spread Christianity throughout the globe and radically reshape the world. They articulated a particular understanding of a single monotheistic church that stood in sharp contrast to the Indigenous traditions they encountered. This has been expressed in values of human beings in a variety of ways as an understanding of the spiritual aspect of material life, which is most often the focus of ongoing ceremonial exchanges. From this vantage point, the category of "Indigenous values" has a specific history that is very different from the forces that moved aggressively around the world to develop a global economic system distinct from local, ceremonially based economies of exchange. As a consequence of globalization, religious understandings of the relationship between human beings and the sacred were radically transformed, or de-Indigenized. Specifically, the hierarchy of the Church completely removed the sacred from earthly and bodily existence. The material world was only a dim reflection of a deity who lived above and outside the phenomenal world.

---

24. See Huston Smith's film and accompanying book *Seat at the Table*. Smith admitted that his training in the academic study of religion did not originally allow for him to embrace the positive aspects of Native American Religions until he met people from the Onondaga Nation near Syracuse University, where he was teaching in the late 1970s. Since then, he dedicated himself to incorporating these traditions—which he called "primal" in a positive sense—as integral to understanding all the world's religions.

At the same time, theologians reasoned that God was immaterial, otiosus, understood to be all knowing and all powerful. This became the scope of European powers with their global imperial enterprises. The immediacy of the sacred, and the proximity of where the sacred resided, determined who was *primitive* or not, who was a *pagan* or not, who was *other* or not.

An important distinction: the institution of Christianity has been utilized to justify the *extermination* of Indigenous Peoples through the process of colonization. The degree to which Christianity has been used to legitimize the occupation of non-European lands is the same degree to which Indigenous Peoples were seen as an impediment to progress. Moreover, the colonial religious dimensions of occupying land were embodied by a particularly skewed relationship to land as private property. This has made it difficult to impossible for the modern world to understand or appreciate an Indigenous perspective of religion, or any concept thereof, as a living landscape.

1992, the five-hundredth anniversary of Columbus's discovery of the New World, saw an enormous amount of work being concentrated on the celebration of his legacy. Indigenous intellectuals seized the opportunity to expose the real history of Columbus, which the triumphal mythology tends to obscure. Numerous studies were published that portrayed him as a dubious and unsavory character, who at one point was returned to Spain in irons to face charges of crimes against humanity. It is not so much the man as the myth. Many Indigenous leaders referred to his legacy as akin to the rise of the Third Reich in Nazi Germany. In spite of Columbus's defeat in the cultural wars of 1992, devotion to and veneration of Columbus has persisted, particularly in the United States—a country that, by the way, he never visited.[25]

The symbolism and mythic history dedicated to Columbus is deeply engrained in US culture. By looking at the persistence of the Columbian legacy and the symbolism around Columbus, a clearer

---

25. One such publication is Barreiro, "View from the Shore."

picture emerges of the urgency of Indigenous values and the reason they were perceived the primary impediment to establishing the New World Order.

Until the fifteenth century, the Christian Church understood itself to be superior to Judaism and Islam and justified the conquest of many peoples and lands across the continent. Religious wars in Europe, the Mediterranean, the Near East, and North Africa were limited geographically, but the scale of conquest radically changed during the Age of Discovery. The enormity of wealth extracted from West Africa and the New World—especially gold and silver—provided the impetus for empires to establish Christ's Kingdom on Earth.

This also established the global perception of Indigeneity, which coincided with a radical shift within Christianity. Religion became more ideologically focused, to facilitate the process of bringing mankind into the spirituality of faith, thus enabling the rich and powerful full access to the abundant wealth of the Earth. These discovery expeditions garnered maximum profits for the sponsoring Catholic Church and its empires, thus inspiring British kings and Protestants to fund their own colonizing expeditions, so that they, too, could turn a profit, which was also one of the inspirations for the Protestant Reformation. During the sixteenth and seventeenth centuries, almost all ventures to the New World were backed by Christian merchants, whose profits directly benefited the great economic empires of Spain, Italy, England, Holland, and France. Christian conversion was directly linked with the development of global capitalism, although profits were now split between Protestant and Catholic empires. From colonialism and discovery sprang profound transformations in Christianity.

As a result of these invasive economies, some academics have suggested that Indigenous traditions are "religions of resistance." This is only half of the story. As we have seen, Indigenous values emanate from the art of building relationships, a gift economy of exchanges that is quite radically different from the theoretical hierarchical construct of Christendom. It is fundamentally an economic exchange of relationships that are local rather than global, where knowledge is exchanged between human and nonhuman beings that coincide within specific geographies. The care with which Indigenous Peoples nurtured this relationship with landscape was recorded by explorers in their personal journals, many of whom compared this New World with the Garden of Eden. Never before had they seen such a vibrant interactive world filled with strong, tall trees, birds, wild animals, plants, herbs (medicinal and otherwise), fish, and an abundance of topsoil. The water was so clean one could dip a cup into any stream and drink. This was unimaginable in Europe.

This land was far from a "wilderness," as we have been led to believe, but a collaborative engagement with the natural world so that humans could fully integrate with the regenerative Earth.[26] Europeans did not realize that it was these Indigenous values that created this vibrant New World; they could only see use value in turning the land for profit. From the Age of Discovery to the present, the continuing survival of Indigenous Peoples serves as evidence of the strength of these ancient traditions, especially in light of the fact that their very existence presents a potent critique in the development of what could now be perceived a failed experiment: the age of modernity.[27]

When the civilized world radically othered the uncivilized, this had profound consequences for the ways in which modern people would understand the phenomenon of religion. The idea that religion is separate from other aspects of life like politics, economics, or culture is often at odds with Indigenous values.

The consequences of the de-Indigenization and the globalization of religion were enormous. In its most radical formulation, religion has come to be understood as standing at direct odds with the

---

26. See Mann, *1491*.

27. For example, Bruce Lincoln's *Holy Terror* characterizes Native American religions as "religions of resistance." This view tends to misconstrue Native Americans who have held on to their ceremonial traditions in the face of the enormously destructive influences of US culture (e.g., boarding schools, missionization, ecological devastation, land theft).

material world, where Christianity has portrayed the phenomenal world as corrupt and where all human suffering originates. As I see it, the effects of this de-Indigenization of religion is all around us today in the environmental crisis, particularly in our inability to speak of that crisis in anything but apocalyptic terms. The overwhelming emphasis on monetary economic values is at the expense of Indigenous values. The problems we face today are material manifestations that emanated from the onslaught of global religious domination. In other words, the problems today originate from a settler-colonial religious worldview, the results of settler-colonial actions.

Religion and the Age of Discovery

The Age of Discovery did not simply appear in the fifteenth century. Its foundation originates in the fourth century, with the establishment of the Roman Church. Justifying and legitimizing discovery required an interpretation of Christianity that was directly associated with the imperial cults inherited from the Roman Empire. Roman Catholic Christianity had fused the Roman Empire with monotheism in the fourth century CE. It was in the New Testament, largely through the legacy of Paul and Saint Augustine, that this fusion was transformed into the dogma of Christianity. Without the imperial Roman legacy, it is likely that Christianity would have remained a local religious movement confined to the Near East. Rome needed monotheism, a cult of saints, and apocalypticism to unify the far-flung, demoralized empire. Romans elevated the importance of these Christian elements to amplify their usefulness in serving the empire.[28]

This makes for a very specific reading of the Bible. For example, there is tremendous uncertainty regarding who actually killed

---

28. James Carroll's *Constantine's Sword* focuses on the use of Christianity to unify the Roman Empire at the cost of distorting Jesus's message. His argument could extend into the fusion of the Roman Empire to Christianity in the fourth century, eventually becoming the impetus for the brutal excesses seen in the DoCD of the fifteenth century and beyond.

Jesus—the Romans or the Jews. While the Romans were actually the ones who carried out the sentence of execution, it is the Jews who are blamed. Why? It would be materially inconsistent to imagine that the Roman empire could co-opt the Christ story, proceed to bear the "message of Christ" to the world, while also being the villains of the Crucifixion. Instead, in light of the fact that Jesus was a Jew, and early Christianity was born of Judaic traditions, the Roman Church made the Jews the killers of Christ, a conviction that continued throughout the middle and modern ages. For these reasons, the European Jewry suffered enormous consequences because they challenged this Roman interpretation of Christianity.[29] For fifteenth-century European monarchs, "discovery" meant the forced appropriation of non-Christian lands, the enslavement of non-Christians, and the extraction of all valuable materials, including precious metals and spices.[30]

In other words, the whole of the non-Christian world was to be utilized for the propagation of the Church and the expansion of Christendom.[31] The entire world was to be *rendered* to serve Christendom, a violent process that involved martialing the material world and all of its value. By the tenth century, it was understood by Christendom that this wealth was to be dedicated to the retaking of the Holy Land, the site of the original Christian hierophany, which, prior

---

29. See Chidester, *Christianity*. Without the activities of St. Paul, it is likely that Christianity would have become a local religious movement that was indigenous to the Ancient Near East.

30. Technically there is no "Europe" during the time we are discussing; that designation came in later centuries. Nevertheless, I use this more recognizable term to indicate Christendom, Catholic and Protestant, in the geographical area of what is now known as "Europe."

31. Of particular concern was taking the Holy Land back from the Muslims—another complicated problem of religious dislocation and reconquest. From the eleventh century, European kingdoms had little permanent success in trying to instill Christianity in the Holy Land. By the fifteenth century, world domination became a more viable option for funding the expansion of Christianity than reconquering the Holy Land.

to the Crusades, had been held for centuries by Muslims. The Holy Land is where Jesus lived, was crucified, and rose from the dead. For Christians, Jesus was the hierophany in that he was the manifestation of God in human flesh. The Age of Discovery during the fifteenth and sixteenth centuries was fueled by the same desires that propelled the Crusades of the eleventh through thirteenth centuries: to unify the Christian empire and retake the Holy Land from the Muslims, who were deemed enemies of Christ.

While this violent process of conversion was profoundly devastating to Indigenous Peoples and their traditions, it was also traumatic for Europeans, who used religion to justify their actions. This European trauma is characterized here as a rejection of the Indigenous traditions of Europe and an acceptance of the utopian imperial fantasy of total world domination.

Europe becomes an important case for understanding the religious interplay between Indigenous and Imperial cultures. It was this inherited violence of Christianity that spread to the New World. As the noted historian of Native America Robert Venables argues, when developing the United States, European Americans decided to turn their backs on their European Indigenous past and choose instead to emulate their conquerors, the Romans.[32]

These radical anti-Indigenous values are now considered to be "normal" or "natural" religious attributes. These would include religious intolerance of other traditions and the religious justification for mechanized warfare, the point of which is the complete and utter destruction of one's opponent. Today, this is called "just war theory," which accompanies an unshakable confidence in a specific interpretation of God ("fundamentalisms" of all sorts) that is equally applicable to all human beings. Often, people assume that all religions have these extreme fundamentalist leanings, and therefore Indigenous religions must include these leanings as well. Yet, in spite of the reality of warfare among neighboring Indigenous groups, there was

32. Venables, "Founding Fathers."

rarely the idea that another group would have to be completely overthrown, destroyed, or occupied. We mistakenly understand Indigenous values through the lenses of European religions.

Acknowledging the imperial background of Christendom and the colonial projects of the DoCD, inconsistencies become apparent between the Indigenous characteristics we have covered and the ideological agenda behind European and European American recorded histories of contact. Inter-Indigenous community interactions were based on a different model of how human beings not only inhabit the land but also engage in reciprocal relationships with nonhuman beings. This quality alone distinctly contradicts the European model of Christendom. The idea that a singular manifestation of the sacred had appeared in human form, embodied as Jesus Christ, in a particular place and a specific time should be forced upon all groups, is antithetical to an Indigenous worldview. Instead, Indigenous Peoples understand that the sacred manifests itself in many different places at different times.

Imposing one hierophany over another would counter the Indigenous understanding about the need for an ongoing interaction between material and spiritual realities for the continuing vitality of the Earth. Even though it is often referred to as "tribalism," there is nothing natural or Indigenous about religious fundamentalism, nationalism, fanaticism, or intolerance. These religious innovations are part of the legacy of the DoCD.

Understanding these religious phenomena from the perspective of Indigenous values helps to clarify various strands of religious life that are most often characterized as "fundamentalism." People who care about the future of religion and the understanding that the sacred has been hijacked by the most extremist elements of civilization should find benefit from understanding Indigenous values.[33]

---

33. Vine Deloria Jr. points out much of this in *God Is Red*. In the chapter "Thinking in Time and Space," he suggests that Christianity's greatest mistake is its suggestion that a local hierophany in the life of Jesus Christ at Jerusalem in the Near East is universally valid for all people everywhere.

Reconquest: Indigenous Traditions in Europe

Previous to, and coterminous with, Christianizing the Indigenous Peoples of the world came the reconquest of non-Christian people of Europe. While this effort was underway from the eighth century, the Age of Discovery gave added enthusiasm to forced removal and conversion on the Iberian Peninsula. Jews, Moors (North African Muslims), women "witches," and others who had been residents for centuries were now subjected to the Inquisition, military invasion, and forced conversion/conformity with Christian monarchies and the Vatican. Throughout the fifteenth century, the Church became more specific in determining who was Christian and who was not.

For example, in 1484, Pope Innocent VIII issued the papal bull *Summis Desiderantes Affectibus* at the urging of the German Dominican inquisitor Heinrich Kramer, who later published the infamous book *Malleus Maleficarum*, usually translated as *The Hammer of Witches* (1486).[34] This text officially labeled millions of people, mostly women, as witches and friends of Satan, therefore categorizing them as heretics. This pamphlet gave rise to the infamous excesses of the Inquisition, leading to the witch trials that lasted into the seventeenth century.

Many of these women would now be categorized as Indigenous Peoples of Europe who were teachers, healers, and keepers of ancient ceremonial practices including midwifery, medicinal healing with herbs, and fertility rites.[35] Local leaders of these practices were likely seen as threats to the authority of men and the Church.

From a Haudenosaunee perspective, the predominant feature of this assault was the transference of power from the matrilineal, Earth-based gift economy, to the patriarchal, hierarchal, monetary economic authority of the Church. Diminishing women's authority became central to Church dogma and the process of Christianization,

---

34. Mackay, *Hammer of Witches*.
35. See Ginzburg, *Night Battles* and *Cheese and the Worms*, in which a much more ancient ceremonial process is revealed from Inquisition texts.

which was carried through to other parts of the world, including Africa, Asia and the Americas. As a result, gender identity became associated with the binary opposition between the patriarchy of the Christian Church and the matriarchy of the land, creating a culture that was out of balance with the natural world. This was an attempt by the Church to eliminate any threat to its religious authority, including any ancient tradition within its homelands. It was primarily the Church's assault on Indigenous traditions that resulted in an ongoing disparaging attitude toward women and nonbinary genders. Unfortunately, this attitude persists all over the world today.[36]

Columbus's World

During the fifteenth and sixteenth centuries, Inquisitors were busy in both the New and Old Worlds. In 1492, Columbus set sail in search of new lands for the glorification and extension of the Christian Church through the Spanish Crown. In that same year, Spain was undergoing a "reconquest" in which the central royal city of Madrid conquered the Spanish peninsula. Jews were being rounded up and either forcibly converted or forced to leave Spain. Also, Muslim communities, who were often of African descent, were forced into Northern Africa. From the point of view of the Spanish crown, the Jewish, Muslim, and Indigenous communities in Spain threatened the purity of the Christian Church and had to be either converted, removed, or destroyed.

Throughout Europe, Jews were viewed by Christians as the killers of Christ and demonized by all classes of the surrounding society from at least the tenth century. They were characterized as cults that were involved with blood sacrifices, called "blood libels," and depicted as greedy people who were only interested in money. They were also prohibited by law to own lands, so their survival depended

---

36. Marija Gimbutas's work on the matrilineal cultures of pre-Christian Europe has been experiencing renewed interest in recent years. See her most popular book, *Language of the Goddess*.

on their success as merchants and bankers. Jews were often the victims of scapegoating, in which violence was often leveled against them to alleviate the social pressure of their growing urban impoverished class. Jewish communities, therefore, kept isolated from the Christian population as much as possible, with their religious traditions based in rituals performed discreetly in the home and the synagogue. In sharp contrast with the Church, Jews were largely uninterested in converting outsiders—a religious trait that is much the same today.

Importantly, in 1453, Constantinople fell to Sultan Mehmed III of the Ottoman Empire. This was perceived by the Vatican and Christian monarchies as a direct threat to Christendom. Essentially, the Crusades that began four hundred years earlier failed in their objectives to exterminate Islam, so the Vatican looked elsewhere to prop up this enterprise. Papal bulls in 1452 and 1455 exhibited a keen desire that explorers conquer West Africa, where they could generate new sources of income from gold and slaves found along the coast. As a consequence of this raiding activity, slaves, lands, and great wealth fell into the coffers of Portugal and the Vatican.

Forty years later, the perceived threat of "Saracens" to Christendom had engulfed the Iberian Peninsula. After Columbus reported finding gold, silver, and other riches in the New World, the Vatican decreed that the conquest spread West to further expand Christendom. Muslims had been in Spain for nearly eight hundred years before the reconquest of 1492. In southern Spain, their architectural heritage was unmistakable in their awe-inspiring mosques, which dramatically enhanced Spanish culture. Several generations of Muslims lived in Spanish cities and participated in developing the unique character of places like Granada. In 1492 Muslims were forced to migrate into the areas of Northern Africa. The Church was perceived as purifying the Iberian Peninsula of heretics who were seen, again, as the enemies of Christ.

In 1492, another development took place during the reconquest that further threatened local non-Christian people: the publication of the first Spanish grammar by Antonio de Nebrija. Until 1492, several languages and multiple local dialects of Spanish were spoken throughout Spain. In 1492, Castilian Spanish, the Crown's Spanish in Madrid, was adopted as the official version of Spanish throughout the kingdom. This would expedite the process of reconquest by identifying and expelling foreign speakers to further establish the purification of the Christian Church.[37] In all of these elements of reconquest, the emphasis is clear: eliminate diversity in gender, religion, ethnicity, culture, and language. Conquest is utopian because it seeks to purify and eliminate the Indigenous elements that account for tremendous diversity throughout communities.

Displacement and the desire to retake the Holy Land and the Near East was the driving force behind the reconquest. Rome was a great distance away from the site of the crucifixion and resurrection of Christ; therefore, the authority of Rome was completely outside of its control. In turn, the authority of all European kingdoms was derived from Rome, establishing complete dependence on a foreign deity, a deity whose appearance in the world occurred elsewhere.

European Christianity, therefore, is a dislocated, disoriented religion where the Holy Land—the site of the hierophany and, therefore, the sacred authority of the Christian Empire—was controlled by non-Christians. Christianity, originally a breakaway sect of Judaism, had to be remade into a peripatetic (or mobile) religion. Colonization became globalized through the portability of Christianity. Christ was not just a religious figure of the Near East; his salvific influence on humanity became the colonizing force that extended throughout the known world. Discovery and reconquest undergirded this authority of domination and were no longer connected to the hierophany of place.

Physically, there was nothing new about Columbus. He was drawing on a dream of world unity under the legacy of the Roman Empire, the Crusades, and the Inquisition, all for the sole purpose

---

37. In *Conquest of America*, Todorov connects the Conquests in "New Spain" with reconquest of "Old Spain" that expelled Jews and Muslims and centralized language (120).

of retaking the Holy Land. By 1492, these ideas had been gripping European monarchies for more than one thousand years. The dramatic difference marked by Columbus's voyages, however, was the unrestricted aggression used by the Church against other cultures, peoples, and lands. Up until then, these religious conflicts had been confined to the greater Mediterranean area and Europe (geographically a cape of Asia). After 1492, however, European monarchs were bent on converting the entire world.

As discussed in chapter 4, colonialism is a process of occupying lands that belong to someone else by using military force. What followed was the formation of the modern state. Colonialism's relationship with land is one of "occupation," which starkly contrasts with an Indigenous relationship of "habitation." This colonial perspective of domination continues to influence our relationship with the land, which is utilized to serve and benefit human beings. The world is not autonomous but valued only when used for human consumption. This modern economic reality sees the natural world as a natural resource, where its use value is determined by human beings, and where it has no identity unto itself as a living being. This ideology is not logical; it is utopian—placeless.

Hermeneutics of the New World

The Americas had previously been visited by several people from around the world prior to Columbus's landing on the shores of present-day Haiti, including Norwegians, Britons, Africans, Asians, and Polynesians. Previous to the Age of Discovery, explorers would fish, trade, intermarry, and cohabitate with the people already in those places.

Why did the Age of Discovery, marked by Columbus's voyages, become such an important mythological moment in the creation of the Modern World? Indigenous Peoples reject the notion that their lands and peoples were "discovered" at all. How can Indigenous Peoples, who have existed in their lands since the beginning of time, be discovered? The answer is that the Age of Discovery represents a profound conceptual shift, originating in Christian European culture, that prioritizes the value of a human life above those of the Indigenous values that reciprocate with the living earth.

What Is the World For?

Christopher Columbus was sailing on behalf of the Spanish Crown and operating within a tightly confined set of criteria that methodically forged what became known as the New World. Unlike others who preceded him, he became the symbol of a new style of occupying land, which is articulated in his diaries.[38] Columbus, therefore, symbolically represents the religious dimensions of occupation that were to take hold and set a precedent. His story expands beyond the Americas and represents the conquering and colonizing powers that have spread all over the world. Columbus is the embodiment of the DoCD. The symbolism of Columbus as *occupier* is what disallows an Indigenous sense of *habitation*.

As we have seen in Columbus's hermeneutics, the meaning of the New World had already been predetermined. His overconfidence in the superiority of his relationship to and understanding of the sacred allowed him to envision a New World completely situated as a resource to be rendered in the service of the Church. Because the revelation of God was finalized and contained within a sealed Bible, no new religious revelations of the sacred were considered valid. Columbus (and the Christians that followed him) were not open to new notions of the sacred—neither to new religious understandings that

---

38. Columbus's diary of the First Voyage is saved only by the work of Bartolomé de Las Casas. For Las Casas, Columbus was a hero and a symbol of the coming of the Christian message into the New World. "Christopher," the name Columbus had chosen for himself, means "Christ bearer." In an ironic twist, Las Casas is also the author of the infamous "Black Legend" of the mistreatment of Indians by Spanish Catholic/Colonial forces. For many, he is regarded as the "friend of the Indian," and his legacy of this Christian style of love unfortunately lives on. See *Devastation of the Indies*.

Indigenous Peoples might have to teach, nor to new hierophanies that these "new" lands might reveal. Columbus is widely hailed as the first "discoverer" because he was the first to know the total significance of his experience *before he even encountered it.*

The New World—wherever it may be—is a pristine world that must be forcibly brought into the service of the Old World. Serving an omniscient God became the ambition for personal advancement, because colonists were increasing the fortunes of their home country and glorifying God through a unified Christian Church. Religious motivations, however, inform all of the individualistic and nationalistic drives toward discovery and conquest—not the other way around. Columbus symbolizes these bewildering motivations better than any of the early discoverers. His was a time when economic, political, and religious motivations necessarily commingled. Even though contemporary people want to separate these cultural forces, as is clear in the case of the DoCD, they are still interconnected.

Columbus has come to symbolize a hermeneutics, or the processes of interpretation, of the modern world. This accounts for the persistence of his presence in the mythic narrative of the United States. In spite of the fact that he had never been in what is now the continental United States, his statues grace most major cities. The DoCD, also symbolized by Columbus, holds that Indigenous values are in the way of materially transforming the "fallen" state of the Earth into a utopian heaven. This is in anticipation of Christ's return to the Earth at the end of time: the apocalypse. The defining characteristics of the United States have been its apocalypticism, as represented by his taken name "Christopher," the Christ-bearer.

In Anglo-colonial nations like the United States, a pervasive view of the natural inferiority of Indigenous Peoples has resulted in specific campaigns to strip from them their cultures, languages, ceremonies, and lifeways. Indian boarding schools, most often run by various Christian denominations and military and governmental agencies, are infamous for stealing young Indigenous children and radically transforming them into white people who would remain subjugated. In the United States, these boarding schools, which operated for about one hundred years, resulted in the loss of entire generations of native speakers and contributed to the deaths of tens of thousands of children. Although assimilation was their purported goal, these educational institutions were rife with abuse.

In 1978 the American Indian Religious Freedom Act became law. Prior to this, it was illegal for Indigenous Peoples in North America to perform or practice religious ceremonies. During the Termination Era of the 1950s, they were forcibly removed from their homelands and relocated to unwanted lands or urban centers. These attempted solutions to the "Indian problem" were most often heralded as a necessary step to assimilate or acculturate Indigenous Peoples and claimed to be for their own benefit. This justification follows the policy outlined in the DoCD: that Indigenous Peoples had to be either assimilated or exterminated because it was for the greater good of Christian civilization.

"Decolonization" has come to be a major thrust in academic circles. Connections between colonization and Christianity have left an enormous, ruinous swath across cultures and nonhuman species and have decimated land, air, and water. People are in search of a different mythic narrative and realizing the value in deconstructing a system that targeted Indigenous Peoples, those who understood that human survival depends on a harmonious and regenerative relationship with a living earth. This shift, which has been rapid and pronounced, indicates a deep dissatisfaction with the current ideas about where religion has brought us.

Conclusions: Ten Religious Dimensions of the Doctrine of Christian Discovery

With issuance of fifteenth-century papal bulls known as the Doctrine of Christian Discovery, religion has been used all over the world as a weapon against Indigenous Peoples and their lands. This globalized, aggressive, and destructive use of religion began here, with the Vatican's authorization for Portugal and Spain to raid West Africa and the Americas, resulting in the near-annihilation of traditions, ecosystems, and human life. Today, this religious framework has been codified into law and utilized by multinational corporations to seize Indigenous lands and extract resources for profit. Religion, therefore, is relevant today as foundational to social justice struggles and environmental devastation. To counteract this trajectory, we call for a turn away from religion to Indigenous values as a way of understanding and aligning ourselves with the Earth, which is the material and spiritual basis of all life and what constitutes our human survival. The opposition between religion and Indigenous values was initiated through the DoCD. The Indigenous Peoples of the Americas were often gracious in welcoming newcomers, until they realized that these newcomers had come to take possession of their bodies and lands.[39]

1. **Assumed superiority of Christianity (Christian hegemony).** Christian explorers who encountered non-Christians enslaved their bodies, seized their worldly goods and their lands (referred to as "terra nullius"), and deeded all possessions to the Vatican and sponsoring Monarchs. This Christian hegemony was developed in what is now known as Europe but expanded with explorers traveling to foreign lands. Christian hegemony was the driving force behind settler-colonization and is also foundational to the ideology of white supremacy.
   - **Indigenous values response: Human beings are not in charge of the world, but part of its regenerative life. The Earth provides everything we need; we are identified by the land and our traditions maintain that proper relationship.**
2. **Creation of Christian empire.** Christendom drives the need for material riches and fires the discoverer's imagination toward the insatiable acquisition of wealth and complete

---

39. Originally written by Philip P. Arnold and Sandra L. Bigtree for the Doctrine of Discovery site, September 2022, https://doctrineofdiscovery.org/10-religous-dimensions/ (accessed 3 January 2023).

domination of the non-Christian world, both human and nonhuman. Christianity joined with the militaristic Roman Empire in the fourth century with Constantine. The Crusades, which began in the eleventh century, were an attempt by the Vatican and Christian monarchs to remove Muslims from the Holy Land. Initiated in the fifteenth century and justified by the Vatican during the Age of Discovery, militarism was essentially a continuation of the Crusades, which resulted in the Inquisition, the war on witches, and the reconquest of the Iberian Peninsula.
- Indigenous values response: Material riches are meant to be shared, in the tradition of the potlatch and "One Bowl, One Spoon" wampum. Gifts of the Earth are intrinsically there for all beings and meant to be shared.
3. **Patriarchy and hierarchy.** Popes, kings, and aristocrats are at the top of the Great Chain of Being. Women, children, animals, and other nonhuman beings fall under their domination. White Christian Supremacy evolved into White Anglo-Saxon Protestants (WASPs) from the sixteenth century onward.
    - Indigenous values response: The Haudenosaunee follow matrilineal clans because women are responsible for life on this Earth, which is female. All beings have their respective responsibilities; there is no hierarchy.
4. **Apocalypticism.** Apocalyptical thinking eagerly anticipates the end of the world, the return of Jesus Christ, and the rapture, where the chosen people return to a heavenly paradise. This Christian message connects with millennialism and "end of the world" thinking, which drives the fanaticism of explorers, missionaries, and the like. Today, this paranoid thinking about how the world will end drives global capitalism and consumerism.
    - Indigenous values response: If there is to be an end of the world, it will not come with a promise of a new world. It is our responsibility to keep this Creation alive for seven generations into the future.

5. **"Original Sin."** This establishes the "natural" fallenness of human beings in the world, who are born in sin, and frames the need for salvation, whether alive or dead (in the case of conversion after death). The world is sinful without Christ's salvation, and only through human intervention is it made suitable for Christ's return. With God as otiosus, human beings are required to become the agents of fulfilling God's plan on Earth.
   - **Indigenous values response: We belong to the earth; therefore, all beings are constituted by the same fundamental spiritual and material reality that is regenerative and freely available to those who live without domination of others. If personal salvation is the only way out of the restraint of having been born in sin, how can anyone feel anything but dominated?**
6. **Reconquest of the Holy Land.** The drive to reattain direct relationship at the site of the hierophany (where the sacred manifested in the world) led to a violent Crusade against Muslims who inhabited the Holy Land. In Jerusalem, Christians could directly appeal to their God, who was removed from the world (Deus Otiosus), mediated by Jesus Christ's death and resurrection after arriving to save the world. European Christianity, therefore, is out of place (utopian) and outside immediate relationship with the sacred, but it is Christianity that gave religious authority to the pope and all Christian monarchies. Power is legitimated by removing Muslims and other non-Christians from the Holy Land. Complete Vatican and royal authority rests on the hierarchy of human relationships under a transcendent and displaced God.
   - **Indigenous values response: We live every day in close proximity to the hierophany—in the water, in the air we breathe, and in the regenerative lifeways of all living beings who constitute our very existence. To the earth and all living beings we say, *Nya weñha Skä·noñh* (Thank you for being well) because peace and wellness**

depend on living in proper relationship with the natural world.
7. **Biblical authority and literalism.** The Christian Bible, which was compiled in the fourth century, has been viewed as the ultimate religious authority. In Protestant Christianity, from the sixteenth century onward, it has often been understood to be the unfiltered word of God. The biblical text has been driven by a movement toward utopia (see Sir Thomas More's book by the same name). "No place," or the disengagement with the meaning of place, is what defines American Christian millennialism and its urgent determination to prepare for the end of the world, as with ideas like manifest destiny and the Great Awakenings.
    - Indigenous values response: "Oral traditions" have been reliable in maintaining our proper relationships with an everchanging natural world for hundreds of generations because we live our traditions every day through our wampum belts, ceremonies, language, music, dancing, clothing, foods, medicines, clans, and so on.
8. **Presence of ultimate evil in the world.** The Devil (Satan, Lucifer) is a divine being that is seen as directly opposing the good established from the salvation of Christ's sacrifice. There is a drama between the forces of Good and Evil being played out in the world. The terror of ultimate evil and hell motivates the drive toward personal salvation. The cosmic duality of good versus evil locked in an inexorable battle can only be resolved after the world has ended, and good triumphs over evil.
    - Indigenous values response: There are interactions of opposing forces in the world—life and death, sky and earth, light and dark—exchanges—that are necessary in creating and recreating the world and maintaining proper relationships. For the Haudenosaunee, the Earth was made through the interactions of the Creator Twins.

9. **Individual or personal salvation.** This is foundational to individualism and the understanding of the Self as a discrete being that is separate from the world. It is this Self that requires salvation by the grace of God through the sacrifice of Jesus Christ.
    - **Indigenous values response: The individual is an intersection of vital forces composed of all the beings of the world. Individuals exist as a web of material interactions, including the living and the dead.**
10. **Creation of the global monetary economy** (enacted by eleventh-century monastics). Acquisition of material goods through the slave trade and extractive industries is exemplified by the commodification of the world that has aligned and unified the Christian Empire. Wealth is proof that the individual has been blessed by God.
    - **Indigenous values response: Our ceremonies are based on a gift exchange economy that moves between different beings. Gratitude for these gifts of life orient all ceremonies. The circulation of gifts to and from those nonhuman beings makes all life possible.**

In this chapter, I have tried to articulate, in broad contours, an opposition between Indigenous and settler-colonial value systems. They have been described as uniquely focused on the places they inhabit and on their ceremonial exchanges with human, nonhuman, plant, animal, mineral and spiritual beings who share in their place. Conversely, Christians have understood Indigenous values as posing a threat to the European colonial understandings of religion, which have persistently tried to destroy Indigenous values. In this sense, they can be seen as a cultural critique of the direction contemporary, modern, and "civilized" worldviews have brought us. This highlights the intimate association of the urgent issues of the past, present, and future with Indigenous values and survival, and the ways in which we might rethink religion.

Epilogue
Value Change for Survival

We urgently need to adopt Indigenous values. Initially this urgency was discussed as a way that scholars of the academic study of religion could better understand the values of these traditions. How to represent another group's religious ideas and convictions is one of the greatest methodological issues in the academy, but a better sense of these traditions can emerge if ideas are exchanged regarding issues of *urgent mutual concern* between settler-colonial and Indigenous Peoples.

Most crucial is overcoming the oppressive legacy of colonialism so we can embrace the Indigenous values that can potentially direct us toward a more viably shared future. In my own work, for example, I have come to fully appreciate the more collaborative nature of writing and scholarship because it enlivens the classroom and makes teaching and doing research more relevant. Thus, the university becomes another site of collaboration between different constituencies of settler-colonial and Indigenous Peoples.

Likewise, there is an urgent need for understanding Indigenous values as foundational to the general phenomenon of religion the world over. Since academics have been attempting to understand the phenomenon of religion, Indigenous Peoples have been seen as a source of insight and inspiration. Indigenous values clarify the excesses of Western imperialism, which was largely driven by religion. If there is to be a future for religion, it will have to depend on value changes. The greatest urgency for human survival points toward a reorientation to the land—the heart of Indigenous values. It is the final issue with which we conclude this book.

I have found that students are drawn to the topic of Indigenous values because they are very concerned about our collective future. Environmental collapse has been looming larger and larger on our horizon as we move deeper into the twenty-first century. Of course, a variety of movements and technologies are being promoted to change the self-destructive course that we are on, but with too little effect. It is crucial that we find a more viable worldview to begin changing the processes that have brought enormous grief and destruction to the world's Indigenous Peoples and to the Earth. Only when that process begins can we recognize that the promotion of life is through the regenerative engagement with the Earth.

The academy has given much less attention to the question of how we can collaborate with Indigenous Peoples on this issue. As discussed in the preface, many of us in Onondaga Nation territory have been deeply committed to this challenge. In large part, this is the reason why I felt that this book needed to be written. As the leadership of the Haudenosaunee have said, and I will paraphrase, the environmental problems that human beings face today are not problems with the natural world per se, but with our relationship with the Earth. The Earth will be fine, with or without us. The problems that we face are in the way we relate to the natural world. In order to make the shift, we need to change our values, which have been developed from the Doctrine of Christian Discovery and settler-colonialism. I find this an encouraging statement in that the shift required is not so much in adopting new technologies but a new (and, in this case, ancient) worldview that prioritizes the needs of the Earth—Mother Earth—over the needs of human beings.

Basic Call to Consciousness

I want to return to the beginning and put forth "Indigeneity" as a way of suggesting future work. *Basic Call to Consciousness* was originally delivered to the UN in Geneva, Switzerland, in 1977.[1] A delegation of Indigenous representatives from all over Turtle Island carried this message. I have quoted extensively from the book that records this historic journey. Many of these passages bring together essential elements that have been discussed and serve to underscore the urgency of making a categorical shift for religion. In a chapter titled "Spiritualism, the Highest Form of Political Consciousness: A Haudenosaunee Message to the Western World," the authors distinguish between "spiritualism" and "religion" from an Indigenous perspective. In spite of the fact that *Basic Call to Consciousness* is given from the Haudenosaunee perspective, the values they discuss are shared by all Indigenous Peoples. It reads:

> In the beginning, we were told that the human beings who walk about the Earth have been provided with all the things necessary for life. We were instructed to carry a love for one another, and to show a great respect for all the beings of this Earth. We are shown that our life exists with the tree of life, that our well-being depends on the well-being of the vegetable life, that we are close relatives of the four-legged beings. In our ways, spiritual consciousness is the highest form of politics.
>
> Ours is a Way of Life. We believe that all living things are spiritual beings. Spirits can be expressed as energy forms manifested in matter. A blade of grass is an energy form manifested into matter—grass matter. The spirit of the grass is that unseen force that produces the species of grass, and it is manifest to us in the form of real grass.[2]

This communicates a fundamental element of religious life that is similar to our previous discussion of the hierophany, or manifestation

---

1. *Basic Call to Consciousness* (Native Voices, 2005). The authorship of this important book is anonymous, so as to make it a statement by the entire delegation in 1977, but most of the words have been attributed to the late John Mohawk, a Seneca traditionalist, scholar, teacher, activist, and friend.

2. *Basic Call to Consciousness*, 85.

of the sacred. The distinction here is that the hierophany for Indigenous Peoples is an ongoing, everyday attribute of material life and revealed in the cycles of the natural world, not a discrete event that happened in another particular place and time. To relegate this ongoing process of material life to a specific human activity of "religion" would be a violation of these Indigenous realities.

They continue:

> All things of the world are real, material things. The Creation is a true, material phenomenon, and the Creation manifests itself to us through reality. The spiritual universe then is manifest to man as the Creation, the Creation that supports life. We believe that man is real, a part of the Creation, and that his duty is to support life in conjunction with the other beings. That is why we call ourselves Onkweho'n:we—The Real People.[3]

Creation is not understood as something only of the past but as the essential knowledge of a spiritual world that is continuously manifesting itself in to material form. All material life is fundamentally spiritual in that it is continually coming in to being.

A great deal hinges on the word "manifestation" in this passage. In contemporary society, "spiritualism," or "spirituality," has a different meaning. Generally, spirituality today tends to be understood as taking possession of a human being. That is to say, "I am working on *my* spirituality," or "*My* spirits are down today," or "They're in good spirits." In a consumerist society, spirituality gives one license to pick and choose from different religious traditions for their own individual benefit. In other words, spirituality in modern society, when wedded with consumer culture, maintains that there is a "Self" at the center of this spirituality, rather than an animating spirit that is all of life.

From an Indigenous perspective, spirituality is quite the opposite, for human beings are completely dependent on the harmoniously

3. *Basic Call to Consciousness*, 85–86.

reciprocal relationship between spirit and matter. There is no Self that arbitrates between worlds. Being attentive to Creation is being attentive to how spirit manifests in the world, inclusive of one's own life. The human being's spiritual self is no more or less important or significant than any other spiritual self. Indigenous ceremonies and traditions arise to facilitate this process of manifestation. This process creates a home place, a habitation. In Mircea Eliade's language, it "founds" the world and continues to do so again and again into history and into the future. As they say in *Basic Call to Consciousness*,

> Our roots are deep in the lands where we live. We have a great love for our country, for our birthplace is there. The soil is rich from the bones of thousands of our generations. Each of us was created in those lands, and it is our duty to take great care of them, because from these lands will spring the future generations of the Onkweho'n:we. We walk about with a great respect, for the Earth is a very sacred place.[4]

In this process of inhabiting a place of one's ancestors and one's future generations, these ceremonial exchange practices occur. This means they are the real and responsible people. As they say,

> We are not a people who demand or ask anything of the Creators of Life, instead, we give greetings and thanksgiving that all the forces of life are still at work. We deeply understand our relationship to all living things. To this day, the territories we still hold are filled with trees, animals, and the other gifts of Creation. In these places we still receive our nourishment from our Mother Earth.[5]

Human beings are always in exchanges with a world that is a manifestation of spirit. Breathing, eating, drinking are ways that human beings engage in regular ongoing exchanges with the world.

---

4. *Basic Call to Consciousness*, 86.
5. *Basic Call to Consciousness*, 86.

This all abruptly changed when European powers landed on these shores with the incursion of a religion whose written dogma was justified by the DoCD, as they set out to traumatize this Indigenous understanding of Creation and the world. In the words of *Basic Call to Consciousness*: "The forests were leveled, the waters polluted, the Native people subjected to genocide. Western technology and the people who have employed it have been the most amazingly destructive forces in all of human history. No natural disaster has ever destroyed as much. Not even the Ice Ages counted as many victims."[6] The question raised here is, when do the destructive elements of religion cease, or do they?

For historians of religions, the hierophanies that are described here are the basis of religion. Yet the destructive forces brought from Europe are also described as religion. Is religion both simultaneously life-promoting *and* life-destroying? Is religion an inherent attribute to being human, an Indigenous or an intruding/conquering reality? This begs the question: Which of these is more desirable and essential to human survival? To be able to answer these questions, we need to interject Indigenous values into this conversation. The authors of the *Basic Call to Consciousness* also suggest a new form of liberation theology:

> The people who are living on this planet need to break with the narrow concept of human liberation and begin to see liberation as something that needs to be extended to the whole of the Natural World. What is needed is the liberation of all the things that support life; the air, the waters, the trees—all things that support the sacred Web of life.[7]

They go on to suggest that Indigenous Peoples, who carry this worldview, have something to contribute to deliberations within governmental bodies like the UN; their values can articulate a way

---

6. *Basic Call to Consciousness*, 89.
7. *Basic Call to Consciousness*, 91.

forward. In the past, scholars understood Indigenous values to be detrimental to progress, but they neglected to appreciate that this ancient wisdom had maintained a healthy coexistence for tens of thousands of years. Indigenous values can contribute to developing more regenerative technologies and strategies for our shared future. Their voices are needed now more than ever.

In the section "Policies of Oppression in the Name of 'Democracy,' Economic History of the Haudenosaunee," the authors identify the fundamental nature of oppression in the concept of "private property." Contrary to a stereotypical understanding of "chiefs" as the biggest, baddest men in the community, they are actually the poorest and most humble people. Their title, "Hoyane," is not hierarchical, but instead translates to "Men of the Good Mind." This is in sharp contrast to leadership in contemporary society.

> In accordance with our ways, we are required to hold many kinds of feasts and ceremonies that can best be described as "giveaways." It is said that among our people, our leaders, those whom the Anglo people insist on calling "chiefs," are the poorest of us. By the laws of our culture, our leaders are both political and spiritual leaders. They are leaders of many ceremonies that require the distribution of great wealth. As spiritual and political leaders, they provide a kind of economic conduit. To become a political leader, a person is required to be a spiritual leader; and to become a spiritual leader, a person must be extraordinarily generous in terms of material goods.[8]

Private property would fundamentally violate the economic process by which Indigenous Peoples live. It would destroy their culture. Using Indigenous values, everything in Creation is alive with a spirit. It follows that the idea of private property is holding the land in bondage: the enslavement of living beings for the sole purpose of elevating human life above all else.

8. *Basic Call to Consciousness*, 104.

Since the Age of Discovery, overwhelming destructive forces have inflicted harm on the regenerative activities of Creation and Indigenous Peoples, their traditions, and their lands. Addressing this genocidal state of affairs, the Indigenous Peoples who delivered this text in Geneva in 1977 decided that the solution was to cling to their ceremonial traditions. Specifically, they expanded Indigenous practices to develop "liberation technologies" among their people that more effectively relate human beings to the material world. Revitalizing Indigenous values is not done solely for their communities, however, but on behalf of communities of people and other living beings throughout the world. It is said that the natural world recognizes these ancient languages and songs. The Onondaga Nation has never stopped performing their cyclical ceremonies of gratitude to the natural world on behalf of us all.

Value Change for Survival

Celebrating its fortieth year, in 1985 the UN established the Global Forum of Spiritual and Parliamentary Leaders on Human Survival.[9] This forum was charged to promote dialogue between religious and political leaders in order to turn the tide on the current growing environmental crisis. Forum conversations and deliberations were dedicated to the survival of future generations and the Earth. This international group of religious and political leaders included the Dalai Lama, Mother Theresa, the archbishop of Canterbury, US senator Al Gore, and Russian president Mikhail Gorbachev. Between 1985 and 1991, they met in New York, Moscow, Oxford, and Tokyo. Representing Native America was Oren Lyons, Joaguisho, Turtle Clan Faithkeeper of the Onondaga Nation, which is located just a

---

9. Global Forum of Spiritual and Parliamentary Leaders on Human Survival, UN Archives and Records Management Section, Folder S-1032-0059-0010, https://search.archives.un.org/global-forum-of-spiritual-and-parliamentary-leaders-on-human-survival (accessed 4 January 2023).

few miles south of Syracuse, New York. Since he went to Geneva in 1977, Oren has been active at the UN in securing rights for Indigenous Peoples and advocating for environmental healing of the Earth. At the global forum's final meeting in Tokyo, the group was called upon to summarize their work for the executive coordinator, Akio Matsumura. All agreed that it could be distilled to four words: *value change for survival*.[10]

From an Indigenous perspective, this charge takes on particular importance. Value change, for Indigenous Peoples, would mean returning to their "original instructions," as Melissa Nelson has put it: to those orientations received from Creation that were interrupted by an invading, colonizing religion. Original instructions arose in human communities all over the world that had an intimate relationship with the living spiritual beings within their territories for over centuries. Nelson refers to this being epitomized by the "Law of the Seed," where regeneration is the primary orientation of human activity.[11]

Winona LaDuke notes something similar when discussing how non-native people tend to react to the resurgence of Indigenous traditions as "going back."[12] She says that it is not about going back, but it is about being on your path. Because Indigenous Peoples' paths have been interrupted by the religious invasion of the West, it does not mean that Indigenous Peoples have to go back; rather, it is about getting back to the path given them by the Creator. This is not just a going-back path, but the integration of a going-forward path that is oriented and guided by the ancient wisdom received. Indigenous Peoples understand that this is their responsibility to themselves, their community, the environment, and the entire cosmos at large.

10. Chief Oren Lyons, "Four Words, Value Change for Survival," YouTube video, 1:37, 2011, https://www.youtube.com/watch?v=CCJMwHwdDBE (accessed 4 January 2022).
11. Nelson, *Original Instructions*.
12. Smith and Cousineau, *Seat at the Table*, 39–57.

Universal Declaration on the Rights of Mother Earth

Many people refer to Evo Morales as the first democratically elected Indigenous president. He was elected president of Bolivia in a special election in 2005 and was reelected in 2009. He began his rise by organizing coca farmers to push back against the US-led drug wars that were trying to stop cocaine production. For the Indigenous Peoples of Bolivia, the coca leaf is a sacred plant that people use ceremoniously to communicate with the sacred world. For the United States, however, the coca plant is the necessary ingredient for its refined production of cocaine; therefore, the US government instituted a policy to entirely eradicate it.[13] In the case of coca, the war on drugs meant that, because the United States was involved in internal Bolivian matters, those Indigenous Peoples held it accountable. Morales came into his presidency extremely critical of US involvement in Bolivia, as well as of global capitalism and the consequences of these economic practices for his people and land.

On April 22, 2010, the Bolivian government passed the Universal Declaration of the Rights of Mother Earth—a unique document in the world of international law, in that it assumes that the Earth is a living being with rights of its own that need to be protected and maintained. The declaration reflects Indigenous values in its understanding of the world as alive and active and in need of protection by human beings. The preamble reads:

---

13. We could add that, likewise, tobacco has been used ceremonially throughout the Americas as a way of connecting human beings with a host of other spiritual beings. Yet the plant was refined into an addictive vice that required deep inhalation and is now considered a poison. Many other indigenous plants have inspired the pharmaceutical industry. However, through their molecular refinement and commodification of these indigenous plants, which were originally used in ceremonial healing processes, they, too, have been altered and often rendered harmful. From an Indigenous religious perspective, as reflected in the statements above, commodifying plants kills their spirits, and we all must suffer the side effects.

We, the peoples and nations of Earth:

- considering that we are all part of Mother Earth, an indivisible, living community of interrelated and interdependent beings with a common destiny;
- gratefully acknowledging that Mother Earth is the source of life, nourishment and learning and provides everything we need to live well;
- recognizing that the capitalist system and all forms of depredation, exploitation, abuse and contamination have caused great destruction, degradation and disruption of Mother Earth, putting life as we know it today at risk through phenomena such as climate change;
- convinced that in an interdependent living community it is not possible to recognize the rights of only human beings without causing an imbalance within Mother Earth;
- affirming that to guarantee human rights it is necessary to recognize and defend the rights of Mother Earth and all beings in her and that there are existing cultures, practices and laws that do so; conscious of the urgency of taking decisive, collective action to transform structures and systems that cause climate change and other threats to Mother Earth;
- proclaim this Universal Declaration of the Rights of Mother Earth, and call on the General Assembly of the United Nations to adopt it, as a common standard of achievement for all peoples and all nations of the world, and to the end that every individual and institution takes responsibility for promoting through teaching, education, and consciousness raising, respect for the rights recognized in this Declaration and ensure through prompt and progressive measures and mechanisms, national and international, their universal and effective recognition and observance among all peoples and States in the world.

This echoes many of the Indigenous values expressed in *Basic Call to Consciousness*. Both documents are strong critiques of what global capitalism has done with respect to Mother Earth that emphasize the unsustainability of the current state of affairs. There is no denying that the Bolivian statement is empirically true. In many ways, it is responding to the rise of environmentalist agendas around the world but in a way that is aligned with what, in 1977, the delegation to Geneva referred to as "liberation technologies": ways of directing us to the future with respect to Indigenous values. Others have been working on ways to include the rights of nature in our legal structure beyond Indigenous nations.[14] It is perhaps unsurprising that political forces backed by extractive industries removed Morales from Bolivian leadership.

Winona LaDuke reminds us of the urgency of "recovering the sacred" in her book of the same name. Taking back the meaning and significance of the world heals both Indigenous Peoples and their land, but it is also incumbent on settler-colonial people to change our relationship to the world to an Indigenous one. Michael McNally also reminds us of what is at stake in these legal battles that go far beyond the return of property.[15]

Our survival depends on recovering a relationship with the Earth. When the world is reduced to a commodity, its only significance is as a natural resource for human beings, and, to use Eliade's oppositions, its only meaning is profane or chaotic.[16] Recovering the sacred at Onondaga Lake in the middle of Syracuse, New York, is the purpose of the Skä·noñh—Great Law of Peace Center. In spite of the fact that Onondaga Lake was used as a dump for over one hundred years and is the most chemically polluted lake in the country, it is still sacred. It is still the place where the Peacemaker arrived in his white stone canoe to bring five warring nations together establishing the Great Law of Peace of the Haudenosaunee. The place still locates

---

14. Boyd, *Rights of Nature*.
15. LaDuke, *Recovering the Sacred*; McNally, *Defend the Sacred*.
16. In *The Sacred and the Profane*, Mircea Eliade demonstrates how the dichotomy of opposition forms the character of religion. As we have discussed, however, his view does not take into account an Indigenous perspective, or how the material world can alternate meanings because oppositions are ever changing. The sacred is not stagnant. This implies that the meaning of the world can shift. This offers hope.

the Indigenous roots of Western democracy and the women's rights movement in the United States. Doesn't the sacred and profane—or the cosmos and chaos—that is exhibited in the history of Onondaga Lake act as a moral inducement for embracing Indigeneity and our future survival? The Skä·noñh Center is an example of changing the mythic narrative of the United States from a settler-colonial to an Indigenous one.

Decolonizing the Narrative of the "French Fort"

In Haudenosaunee heartlands, we have been involved in this decolonizing effort by renarrating the history of the "French Fort," which had stood for a fictitious account of history at Onondaga Lake since 1933. As discussed in chapter 1, it took a combined effort with educational and cultural institutions, and the Onondaga Nation to finally communicate what the missionary fort meant to the Haudenosaunee and Onondaga.[17] We wanted visitors to understand this shift from the triumphal colonial story of the seventeenth-century Jesuits' incursions into Onondaga Nation territory to an Onondaga account of having survived European forced colonization and resisting religious missionization. The new message of the French Fort represents, therefore, a radical break from the Indigenous values presented in the Skä·noñh Center. In this context, it can also be thought to represent both the urgency of Indigenous values and the future of religion.

Next Stage in Repurposing the Skä·noñh Center: Decolonizing the French Fortified Mission

We will begin with decolonizing the French Fort narrative by giving voice to the Haudenosaunee, who had enjoyed peace through values they had nurtured for over one thousand years at Onondaga Lake.

17. This is draft language that is now being considered by the academic collaborative. It was written by me and Sandy Bigtree in March 2021 to indicate the trajectory of the new messaging of the French Fort.

A fortified mission is established to expand land holdings of a colonial empire through the use of conversion to a religion by either persuasion or by force. Ste. Marie among the Iroquois was established in 1656 by the French colonial government in Montreal to convert the Onondaga people to the Catholic faith. Jesuit priests, working with the French state, were tasked with converting the Onondaga to Christianity.

Converting the Onondaga people to Catholicism meant that they would be subjects of the French crown and to the Vatican. The lands, goods, and bodies of the Onondaga would be used in the service of France and the Catholic Church to further extend the colonial and Christian empires. Both of these institutions were ruled by a king or pope at the top of the hierarchy, with peasants and laymen at the bottom. People subject to colonial governments were not citizens at this time, but considered indentured servants, or slaves of the noble classes.

A fort implies an opposition between different human groups. Ste. Marie among the Iroquois implies an opposition and a collision of worldviews. The fort is a building that implies that Christians are opposed to non-Christians (referred to as "enemies of Christ"). Other oppositions were implied, including civilized vs. primitive; Christian vs. savage; and male vs. female.

Collision of Values

Perhaps the most glaring distinction between Indigenous Peoples of the Americas, like the Onondaga Nation, and Europeans, like the French Jesuits, is in their respective understandings of the land. The Jesuits arrived in 1656 at Onondaga Lake with a deed to about six hundred square miles (ten leagues). This "land grant" was issued to the Jesuit Society by the authority of King Louis XIV (or the "Sun King") through his governor, Jean de Lauson, chevalier, in Montreal, the seat of the settler-colonial government of "New France." Land, for European monarchs, was something to be owned and controlled by divine human beings, like the king or pope.

This was the first time that this idea of land as property had been conceived in Onondaga Nation territory. Indigenous Peoples never had a concept that human beings could own land, or that land could be bought and sold. Rather, it was understood to be a living being—Mother Earth in English—and it had to be regarded and thanked in ceremonies of gratitude.

The relationship to land marks a stark difference between Indigenous and settler-colonial worldviews. For the Onondaga Nation and the Haudenosaunee, human beings belong to the land; for the colonists, land belongs to people. Moreover, the Haudenosaunee had elaborate exchange systems between themselves and other human and nonhuman beings. This has been called a "gift economy." Colonists brought with them a monetary economy that prioritized the use value of things for human consumption.

This collision of worldviews is essentially the same today as it was in the seventeenth century. The Missionary Fort is an example of these continuing conflicts between Indigenous and settler-colonial values.

Following this introduction to the French Fort, we discuss invasions by Samuel de Champlain in 1615, the Beaver Wars and the commodification of animal skins, the arrival of the Jesuits with a deed to six hundred square miles of land (an obvious example of the DoCD), and the failed mission itself. At different stations we discuss regenerative agricultural practices and the distinctive ways the woods were regarded among the Haudenosaunee, and, conversely, how the colonists coveted gold and silver, while forcibly converting the "Iroquois" (whom they had already renamed) to Catholicism.

We conclude with the Onondaga Remembrance Wampum Belt that tells this story from a Haudenosaunee perspective, which contrasts sharply with that of the Jesuit accounts. But be reminded that the significance of weaving these ritual belts with wampum beads exemplifies that the truth of our words have direct effect on maintaining the fragile line between peace and grief.

An Onondaga Account of the Jesuits: The Remembrance Wampum Belt

> A French priest who was stationed at Onondaga [Lake] told a French boy captive of the Onondagas that a French army was to invade the Iroquois Country, starting with the Onondagas. The priest was secretly storing gun powder and other military supplies in a small house in back of the mission that he received from time to time from French traders who visited Onondaga. The boy, who had lived with the Onondagas and was adopted by them, and who liked their ways and considered himself an Onondaga, told the chiefs. The Onondaga then demanded to see the inside of the little building behind the mission. The priest refused, saying that the log building was a holy place that only he could enter. The Onondaga forced their way in and found that the boy's story was true. They cut off the little finger of black robe, which the Haudenosaunee called the Jesuits, and renounced Catholicism. The belt was made as a record of the event so that they would not be taken in again and fooled by words. The cross at the top of the belt represents French Canada. The long line to the figure of the man is the trail of the priest from Canada. The human figure is the priest and the single purple bead represents his black heart. The diamond-shaped design at the bottom represents Onondaga.[18]

With this language, we are simultaneously decolonizing the Jesuit narrative at Onondaga Lake and advocating for a shift from settler-colonial values to Indigenous values. The French Fort has been an iconic presence in the Syracuse area, and, because of its longevity, Haudenosaunee contributions to Western democracy, the women's rights movement, regenerative agriculture, and lacrosse have been completely overshadowed, challenging the possibility of change.

---

18. This account of the Jesuit failed mission at Onondaga Lake is taken from personal communications of Oren Lyons and from *Wampum Belts of the Iroquois*, Tehanetorens (Ray Fadden), 1999.

6. Remembrance Belt reproduction by Tony Gonyea. Gift to the Center from Sandy Bigtree and Philip P. Arnold.

However, being aware that stories and mythic histories continue to inform human beings, we must now decide whether these stories are guiding us toward a path of destruction or regeneration.

Decolonization and the Future

> Christians today need to put the same amount of money, devotion and energy into the restoration and healing of Indigenous Peoples and our lands as they have put into our destruction.
> —Jake Haiwhagai'i Edwards (Onondaga Nation), Taking on the Doctrine of Discovery conference, August 2018

Decolonization is a focal point of Native American and Indigenous studies.[19] Adoption of Indigenous values requires a decolonization process. This book is dedicated to concerns for the ongoing survival of Indigenous Peoples and their traditions and languages. The survival of human beings depends on our defense of Indigenous Peoples survival. As Jake Haiwhagai'i Edwards tells us, settler-colonial people like myself need to focus on putting as much treasure, time, effort, and energy into supporting Indigenous Peoples as we have into destroying them over the last several centuries.

Decolonization is sometimes equated with doing good, or working toward social justice. These are worthwhile aims, but, as Eve Tuck and K. Wayne Yang have expressed, decolonization is not a metaphor.[20] It is an urgent and necessary process and reality that connect with the land.

Just choosing from the North American context, this includes materially supporting the return of Indigenous Lands (the #LandBack movement), advocating for the Missing and Murdered Indigenous Women movement (the #MMIW movement), the protection of water as an embodiment of the sacred (#WaterIsSacred movement), recovering the remains from the hidden graves of lost children who

---

19. Linda Tuhiwai Smith's *Decolonizing Methodologies* is one of the groundbreaking works in this area.
20. Tuck and Yang, "Decolonization Is Not a Metaphor."

were in Christian-run Indian residential schools and Indian boarding schools (#EveryChildMatters movement), and other more regional issues that need attention.

Decolonization includes an examination of the material value structures that have been created antagonistic to Indigenous values. For example, this book is being published on the two-hundredth anniversary of the famed *Johnson v. M'Intosh* Supreme Court decision, which we discussed in chapter 2.[21] By interrogating the roots of setter-colonialism as a religious/theological framework of value, couldn't we reprioritize the cosmology of property as something akin to the Bolivian statement in defense of Mother Earth? Would a shift in the language around our way of inhabiting the land be a change worth making as we look to the future?

Our future will depend on bringing gift and monetary economies into better alignment with one another. Our economic realities will need to be supportive of a vital, regenerative Earth. Sometimes referred to as the "triple bottom line," our economic lives will have to include the health of the natural world and the nonhuman beings upon which we all rely.[22] Even more than that, however, our economy will need to be based on putting priority on the flourishing of nonhuman beings above our own.

Indigenous values systems have been developed over millennia and can align with a monetary system in ways that radically change

---

21. The author is the principal investigator of the grant project titled "200 Years of Johnson v. M'Intosh: Indigenous Responses to the Religious Foundations of Racism" (Henry Luce Foundation, 2022–24) with Indigenous Values Initiative and Syracuse University. The focus of this project is the conference "Religious Origins of White Supremacy," which brings together the past, present, and future challenges in addressing the DoCD. https://doctrineofdiscovery.org/blog/religious-origins-white-supremacy/.

22. The Triple Bottom Line is a "business concept that posits firms should commit to measuring their social and environmental impact—in addition to their financial performance—rather than solely focusing on generating profit, or the standard 'bottom line.'" https://en.wikipedia.org/wiki/Triple_bottom_line (accessed 6 February 2023).

priorities. Repudiations of the DoCD by Christian and religious groups around the world are a symbolic beginning toward decolonizing our systems of values, but symbolic beginnings must lead to revoking and rescinding these racist religious structures to result in a material shift.

Collaboration around issues of "mutual urgent concern" is where we began this book, and where we end. Urgent issues abound in our world today, and, wherever we are, Indigenous Peoples flourished where we now make our homes. We don't have to go far to do the work of changing values, and this work cannot wait any longer.

The Future of the University

As in other colleges and universities, Syracuse University has adopted a "land acknowledgment." It states: "Syracuse University would like to acknowledge with respect the Onondaga Nation, firekeepers of the Haudenosaunee, the Indigenous Peoples on whose ancestral lands Syracuse University now stands."[23] This statement has been perceived by some as a symbolic gesture; however, along with flying the Haudenosaunee flag and, more importantly, initiating a Haudenosaunee Promise Scholarship for Haudenosaunee students across their territories in Canada and the United States, the effort has made a huge impact on the culture of Syracuse University, which has taken a step beyond the symbolic and given the gesture substance.

These measures are transformative. They make Syracuse University a place where value change can happen. Decolonizing education happens slowly, but it has taken hold here in the heartland of the Haudenosaunee because of courageous leadership on both sides.

I'd like to conclude this book with the most recent commissioned art installation at Syracuse University that celebrates the effect that Indigenous values of the Haudenosaunee have had on all our lives. Recently created by the Onondaga artist and educator Brandon

---

23. "Land Acknowledgment," Syracuse University, https://thecollege.syr.edu/land-acknowledgment (accessed 6 February 2023).

7. *Gayaneñhsä·ʔgo·nah, The Great Law of Peace.* Painting by Brandon Lazore. University purchase. Syracuse University Art Museum.

8. "Religious Origins of White Supremacy" conference at Syracuse University. Sponsored by the "200 years of Johnson v. M'Intosh: Indigenous Responses to the Religious Foundations of Racism" (Henry Luce Foundation). Image photo by author taken at the Skä·noñh—Great Law of Peace Center.

Lazore, this work is a complicated assemblage of traditional Haudenosaunee stories of Creation, the Founding of the Great Law of Peace at Onondaga Lake, the role of woman in leadership, and other more subtle references. It also captures the role that the Haudenosaunee played in the founding of Western democracy, the women's rights movement, and lacrosse. This is a remarkable illustration of the message of the Onondaga Nation, and what we tried to encompass in the narrative of the Skä·noñh—Great Law of Peace Center.

In all, it serves as a summation of how Indigenous values have continually influenced our world. While these stories have been hidden, bringing them to light has a decolonizing impact on all of our students. As a work of art, Lazore's painting continually works on our community in subtle ways, shifting our values and influencing our shared future. To me, it sums up perfectly what this book has been trying to say. It is a picture of the past and of a hopeful future, worth far more than one thousand words.

Bibliography

Index

Bibliography

Arnold, Philip P. "'And Now Our Minds Are One': The Thanksgiving Address and Attaining Consensus among the Haudenosaunee." In *Native American Rhetoric*, edited by Larry Gross and dedicated to Inés Talamantez, 17–46. Albuquerque: Univ. of New Mexico Press, 2021.

———. "Eating and Giving Food: The Material Necessity of Interpretation in Thai Buddhism." *Journal of Ritual Studies: The Religious Dimensions of Food* 14, no. 1 (2000): 4–22.

———. *Eating Landscape: Aztec and European Occupation of Tlalocan*. Boulder: Univ. of Colorado Press, 1999.

———. *The Gift of Sports: Indigenous Ceremonial Dimensions of the Games We Love*. San Diego, CA: Cognella, 2013.

———. "Haudenosaunee History: Replace the Colonial Conquest Story to Begin Healing." *Syracuse Post-Standard*, March 16, 2012, A-13. https://www.syracuse.com/opinion/2012/03/replace_colonial_conquest_stor.html.

———. "Indigeneity: The Work of History of Religions and Charles H. Long." In *With This Root about My Person: Charles H. Long and New Directions in the Study of Religion*, edited by Davíd Carrasco and Jennifer Reid, 24–38. Albuquerque: Univ. of New Mexico Press, 2020.

———. "Indigenous 'Texts' of Inhabiting the Land: George Washington's Wampum Belt and the Canandaigua Treaty." In *Iconic Books and Texts, Part 5: Power and Scholarship*, edited by James Watts, 361–72. Sheffield: Equinox, 2013.

Asad, Talal. *Genealogies of Religion, Discipline, and Reasons for Power in Christianity and Islam*. Baltimore: Johns Hopkins Univ. Press, 1993.

Astor-Aguilera, Miguel, and Graham Harvey, eds. *Rethinking Relations and Animism: Personhood and Materiality*. New York: Routledge, 2018.

Barreiro, José, ed. "View from the Shore: American Indian Perspectives on the Quincentenary." Columbus Quincentenary Edition, special issue, *Northeast Indian Quarterly* 7, no. 3 (Fall 1990).

Bastien, Joseph W. *Mountain of the Condor: Metaphor and Ritual in an Andean Ayllu.* Long Grove, IL: Waveland, 1978.

Basso, Keith H. *Wisdom Sits in Places: Landscape and Language among the Western Apache.* Albuquerque: Univ. of New Mexico Press, 1996.

Bigtree, Sandra, and Philip P. Arnold. "Forming a 'More Perfect Union' through Indigenous Values." *Orion Magazine*, 17 September 2020. https://orionmagazine.org/2020/09/forming-a-more-perfect-union-through-indigenous-values/.

———. "Why Removing Columbus Matters: From Foundational Narratives of Domination to Inclusivity." Commons, March 2021. https://www.aprilonline.org/why-removing-columbus-matters/ (accessed 23 December 2022).

Bourdieu, Pierre. *Outline of a Theory of Practice.* Translated by Richard Nice. Cambridge: Cambridge Univ. Press, 1977.

Boyd, David R. *The Rights of Nature: A Legal Revolution That Could Save the World.* Toronto: ECW, 2017.

Brown, Joseph Epes. *The Sacred Pipe: Black Elk's Account of the Seven Rites of the Oglala Sioux.* Norman: Univ. of Oklahoma Press, [1953] 1989.

Burris, John P. *Exhibiting Religion: Colonialism and Spectacle at International Expositions, 1851–1893.* Charlottesville: Univ. of Virginia, 2001.

Carrasco, Davíd, ed. *The History of the Conquest of New Spain* Albuquerque: Univ. of New Mexico Press, 2009.

———. *The Imagination of Matter.* British Archaeological Reports, 31 December 1989.

———. "Imagination of Matter: Mesoamerican Trees, Cities, Human Sacrifice." In *The Wiley Blackwell Companion to Religion and Materiality*, edited by Vasudha Narayanan, 258–73. Hoboken, NJ: John Wiley & Sons, 2020.

———. *Quetzalcoatl and the Irony of Empire: Myths and Prophecies in the Aztec Tradition.* Chicago: Univ. of Chicago Press, 1982.

———. *Religions of Mesoamerica: Cosmovision and Ceremonial Centers.* New York: Harper & Row, 1990.

Carroll, James. *Constantine's Sword: The Church and the Jews, a History.* Boston: Mariner, 2002.

Cave, Alfred A. *The Pequot War: Native Americans of the Northeast.* Amherst: Univ. of Massachusetts Press, 1996.

Cervantes, Fernando, *The Devil in the New World: The Impact of Diabolism in New Spain.* New Haven, CT: Yale Univ. Press, 1994.

Chidester, David. *Christianity: A Global History.* New York: HarperOne, 2001.

———. *Religion: Material Dynamics.* Berkeley: Univ. of California Press, 2018.

———. *Savage Systems: Colonialism and Comparative Religion in Southern Africa.* Charlottesville: Univ. of Virginia Press, 1996.

Columbus, Christopher, and Bartolomé de Las Casas. *The Log of Christopher Columbus' First Voyage to America in the Year 1492.* Mansfield Centre, CT: Martino Fine Books, [1892] 2011.

Cousineau, Phil. *The Olympic Odyssey: Rekindling the True Spirit of the Great Games.* Wheaton, IL: Quest, 2003.

Cowie, Robert H., Philippe Bouchet, and Benoît Fontaine. "The Sixth Mass Extinction: Fact, Fiction, or Speculation?" *Biological Reviews* 97 (2022): 640–63.

Cronon, William. *Changes in the Land: Indians, Colonists, and the Ecology of New England.* New York: Hill & Wang, 1983.

Crosby, Alfred W. *The Columbian Exchange: Biological and Cultural Consequences of 1492.* Westport, CT: Praeger, [1972] 2003.

Deloria Jr., Vine. *For This Land: Writings on Religion in America.* New York: Routledge, 1999.

———. *God Is Red: A Native View of Religion.* 2nd ed. Wheat Ridge, CO: Fulcrum, [1973] 1994.

———. "Sacred Lands and Religious Freedom." *Native American Rights Fund Legal Review* 16, no. 2 (Summer 1991): 1–6. https://sacredland.org/wp-content/PDFs/SacredLandReligiousFreedom.pdf (accessed 4 February 2023).

Democracy Now! with Amy Goodman, https://www.democracynow.org/2013/8/9/onondaga_leader_oren_lyons_pete_seeger.

Denevan, William. *The Native Population of the Americas, 1492.* Madison: Univ. of Wisconsin Press, 1994.

d'Errico, Peter P. *Federal Anti-Indian Law: The Legal Entrapment of Indigenous Peoples*. Westport, CT: Praeger, 2022.

Derrida, Jacques. *Specters of Marx; The State of Debt, the Work of Mourning, and the New International*. New York: Routledge, 1993.

Eliade, Mircea. *The Forge and the Crucible: The Origins and Structure of Alchemy*. 2nd ed. Chicago: Univ. of Chicago Press, [1956] 1979.

———. *The Myth of the Eternal Return, or, Cosmos and History*. Translated by Willard R. Trask. Princeton, NJ: Princeton Univ. Press, 1954.

———. *Patterns in Comparative Religion*. Translated by Rosemary Sheed. New York: Meridian, 1958.

———. *The Sacred and the Profane: The Nature of Religion*. New York: Harcourt Brace Jovanovich, [1957] 1987.

———. *Shamanism: Archaic Techniques of Ecstasy*. Princeton, NJ: Princeton Univ. Press, [1951] 2004.

Eliade, Mircea, Joseph Kitagawa, and Charles H. Long. "A New Humanism." *History of Religions* 1 (1961): 1–8.

Fabian, Johannes. *Time and the Other: How Anthropology Makes Its Object*. New York: Columbia Univ. Press, 1983.

Frazer, Sir James George. *The Golden Bough*. Abridged ed. New York: Dover, [1890] 2002).

Gadamer, Hans-Georg. *Truth and Method*. 2nd rev. ed. Translated by Joel Weinsheimer and Donald G. Marshall. New York: Crossroad, 1989.

Galanda, Gabriel. "Tribal Nationhood Requires Citizen Civil Rights Protection: The ACLU Called Disenrollment 'one of the most compelling defects in Indian law.'" *Indian Country Today*, 7 March 2022, https://ictnews.org/opinion/tribal-nationhood-requires-citizen-civil-rights-protection.

Gill, Sam. *Native American Religions: An Introduction*. Boston: Cengage Learning, [1982] 2004.

Gimbutas, Marija. *The Language of the Goddess: Unearthing the Hidden Symbols of Western Civilization*. New York: Harper & Row, 1989.

Ginzburg, Carlo. *The Cheese and the Worms: The Cosmos of a Sixteenth Century Miller*. Translated by John and Anne Tedeschi. London: Routledge & Kegan Paul, [1976] 1980.

———. *The Night Battles: Witchcraft and Agrarian Cults in the Sixteenth and Seventeenth Centuries*. Translated by John and Anne Tedeschi. Baltimore, MD: Johns Hopkins Univ. Press, [1966] 1983.

Goldman, Irving. *The Mouth of Heaven: An Introduction to Kwakiutl Religious Thought.* New York: John Wiley & Sons, 1975.

Goodman, Ronald. *Lakota Star Knowledge: Studies in Lakota Stellar Theology.* Rose Bud Reservation: Sinte Gleska Univ., 1992.

Harvey, Graham. *Animism: Respecting the Living World.* New York: Columbia Univ. Press, 2005.

Haviland, John B. "Guugu Yimithirr Cardinal Directions." *Ethos* 26, no. 1 (March 1998): 25–47.

Higgs, Robert J. *God in the Stadium: Sports and Religion in America.* Lexington: Univ. Press of Kentucky, 1995.

Jackson, Michael. *The Politics of Storytelling: Violence, Transgression, and Intersubjectivity.* Copenhagen: Museum Tusculanum, 2002.

James, William. *Varieties of Religious Experience: A Study of Human Nature.* CreateSpace, [1902] 2009.

Jemison, G. Peter, and Anne M. Schein, eds. *Treaty of Canandaigua, 1794.* Santa Fe, NM: Clear Light, 2000.

Jennings, Francis. *The Invasion of America: Indians, Colonialism, and the Cant of Conquest.* Chapel Hill: Univ. of North Carolina Press, 1975.

Johnson, Greg. *Sacred Claims: Repatriation and Living Tradition.* Charlottesville: Univ. of Virginia Press, 2007.

Jonaitis, Aldona, ed. *Chiefly Feasts: The Enduring Kwakiutl Potlatch.* Seattle: Univ. of Washington Press, 1991.

Jones, Lindsay. *Twin City Tales: A Hermeneutical Reassessment of Tula and Chichén Itzá.* Photographs by Lawrence G. Desmond. Boulder: Univ. Press of Colorado, 1995.

Jones, Ryan Tucker. "When Environmentalists Crossed the Strait: Subsistence Whalers, Hippies, and the Soviets." *RCC Perspectives*, no. 5 (2019): 81–88.

Kimmerer, Robin. *Braiding Sweetgrass: Indigenous Wisdom, Scientific Knowledge, and the Teachings of Plants.* Minneapolis: Milkweed, 2013.

Kitagawa, Joseph M. *The History of Religions: Understanding Human Experience.* Ann Arbor, MI: Scholars, 1987.

La Duke, Winona. *Recovering the Sacred: The Power of Naming and Claiming.* Boston: South End, 2005.

Las Casas, Bartolomé de. *A Short Account of the Destruction of the Indies.* New York: Penguin Classics, [1552] 1999.

Lévi-Strauss, Claude. *Mythologiques Series: The Raw and the Cooked (Vol. 1); From Honey to Ashes (Vol. 2); The Origin of Table Manners (Vol. 3)*. Translated by John and Doreen Weightman. Chicago: Univ. of Chicago Press, [1971] 1983.

———. *The Savage Mind*. Translated by George Weidenfeld. Chicago: Univ. of Chicago Press, 1966.

Lincoln, Bruce. *Holy Terrors: Thinking about Religion after September 11*. Chicago: Univ. of Chicago Press, [2003] 2006.

Little, Lester. *Religious Poverty and the Profit Economy in Medieval Europe*. Ithaca, NY: Cornell Univ. Press, 1983.

Long, Charles H. *Alpha: Myths of Creation*. New York: George Braziller, 1963.

———. *Ellipsis: The Collected Writings of Charles H. Long*. New York: Bloomsbury, 2018.

———. "Matter and Spirit: A Reorientation." *Local Knowledge and Ancient Wisdom: Challenges in Contemporary Spirituality*, edited by Steven Friesen, 12–16. Honolulu: Institute of Culture and Communication, East–West Center, 1991.

———. "Mircea Eliade and the Imagination of Matter." *Journal for Cultural and Religious Theory* 1, no. 2 (Spring 2000). https://jcrt.org/archives/01.2/long.shtml (accessed 4 February 2023).

———. *Significations: Signs, Symbols, and Images in the Interpretation of Religion*. Philadelphia: Fortress, 1986.

Lyons, Oren, and John C. Mohawk, eds. *Exiled in the Land of the Free: Democracy, Indian Nations, and the US Constitution*. Santa Fe, NM: Clear Light, 1998.

Machiavelli, Niccolò. *The Prince*. London: Reader's Library Classics, [1532] 2021.

Mackay, Christopher S. *The Hammer of Witches: A Complete Translation of the* Malleus Maleficarum. Cambridge: Cambridge Univ. Press, 2009.

Malinowski, Bronislaw. *Coral Gardens and Their Magic, Vol. 2: The Language of Magic and Gardening*. Bloomington: Indiana Univ. Press, [1935] 1965.

Mann, Barbara, and Jerry L. Field. "A Sign in the Sky: Dating the League of the Haudenosaunee." *American Indian Culture and Research Journal* 21, no. 2 (August 1997): 105–63.

Mann, Charles C. *1491: New Revelations of the Americas before Columbus.* New York: Vintage, 2006.
"Marvin and Tappan Head Lysander-Van Buren Park at Lake Parade Yesterday: Nine Floats from Two Townships Are Features of Mile-Long Cavalcade Showing Early History in All Sections of Onondaga County." *Gazette and Farmer's Journal*, 17 August 1933, 1.
Marx, Karl. *Capital: A Critique of Political Economy.* Translated by Ben Fowkes. New York: Penguin, [1867] 1974.
Masuzawa, Tomoko. *The Invention of World Religions: Or, How European Universalism Was Preserved in the Language of Pluralism.* Chicago: Univ. of Chicago Press, 2005.
Mauss, Marcel. *The Gift: The Form and Reason for Exchange in Archaic Societies.* New York: W. W. Norton, [1925] 2000.
McNally, Michael. *Defend the Sacred: Native American Religious Freedom beyond the First Amendment.* Princeton, NJ: Princeton Univ. Press, 2020.
Melville, Herman. *The Confidence-Man: His Masquerade.* London: Penguin, [1857] 1990.
Menchú, Rigoberta. *I, Rigoberta Menchú: An Indian Woman in Guatemala.* Edited and introduced by Elisabeth Burgos-Debray. Translated by Ann Wright. Brooklyn, NY: Verso, 1984.
Merleau-Ponty, Maurice. *Phenomenology of Perception.* Translated by Colin Smith. London: Routledge & Kegan Paul, [1945] 1962.
Metcalf, Peter, and Richard Huntington, *Celebrations of Death: The Anthropology of Mortuary Ritual.* Cambridge: Cambridge Univ. Press, 1991.
Miller, David. *Gods and Games: Toward a Theology of Play.* New York: World, 1970.
Miller, Robert J., Jacinta Ruru, Larissa Behrendt, and Tracey Linderg. *Discovering Indigenous Lands. The Doctrine of Discovery in the English Colonies.* Oxford: Oxford Univ. Press, 2010.
Modrow, Sebastian, and Melissa Smith, trans. "Inter Caetera." Indigenous Values Initiative, Doctrine of Discovery Project, 13 June 2022, https://doctrineofdiscovery.org/inter-caetera/.
Mohawk, John C. *Basic Call to Consciousness.* Summertown, TN: Native Voices, [1978] 2005.
———. *Iroquois Creation Story, John Arthur Gibson, and J. N. B. Hewitt's Myth of the Earth Grasper.* Self-published, 2005.

———. *Utopian Legacies: A History of Conquest and Oppression in the Western World*. Santa Fe, NM: Clear Light, 2000.

Munn, Nancy. *The Fame of Gawa: A Symbolic Study of Value Transformation in a Massim Society*. Durham, NC: Duke Univ. Press, 1991.

Nandy, Ashis. *The Intimate Enemy: The Loss and Recovery of the Self under Colonialism*. Oxford: Oxford Univ. Press, 1983.

Neihardt, John G. *Black Elk Speaks: Being the Life Story of a Holy Man of the Oglala Sioux*. New York: Washington Square, [1932] 1972.

Nelson, Melissa, ed. *Original Instructions: Indigenous Teachings for a Sustainable Future*. Rochester, VT: Bear, 2008.

Newcomb, Steven T. *Pagans in the Promised Land: Decoding the Doctrine of Christian Discovery*. Wheat Ridge, CO: Fulcrum, 2008.

Obeyesekere, Gananath. *The Apotheosis of Captain Cook: European Mythmaking in the Pacific*. Princeton, NJ: Princeton Univ. Press, 1992.

Olupona, Jacob K. *Beyond Primitivism: Indigenous Religious Traditions and Modernity*. New York: Routledge, 2004.

Onondaga Nation Land Rights Case (2005). https://www.onondaganation.org/land-rights/ (accessed 23 December 2022).

Otto, Rudolf. *The Idea of the Holy: An Inquiry into the Non-rational Factor in the Idea of the Divine and Its Relation to the Rational*. Translated by John W. Harvey. London: Oxford Univ. Press, [1923] 1950.

Porter, Tom. *And Grandma Said...Iroquois Teachings as Passed Down through the Oral Tradition*. Xlibris, 2008.

Powless, Irving, Jr. *Who Are These People Anyway? The Iroquois and Their Neighbors*. Edited by Lesley Forrester. Syracuse, NY: Syracuse Univ. Press, 2016.

Raheja, Gloria Goodwin, and Ann Gold. *Listen to the Heron's Words: Reimagining Gender and Kinship in North India*. Philadelphia: Univ. of Pennsylvania Press, 1994.

Robertson, Lindsay. *Conquest by Law: How the Discovery of America Dispossessed Indigenous Peoples of Their Lands*. Oxford: Oxford Univ. Press, 2005.

———. "John Marshall as Colonial Historian: Reconsidering the Origins of the Discovery Doctrine." *Journal of Law & Politics* 13, no. 4 (Fall 1997): 759–78.

Roessel, Monty. *Kinaaldá: A Navajo Girl Grows Up*. Minneapolis: First Avenue Editions, 1993.

Rosen, Jack. *Corey Village and the Cayuga World, Implications from Archaeology and Beyond*. Albany: State Univ. of New York Press, 2014.

Ryan, Debora. "A French Fort in the Salt City: Revisioning Sainte Marie Among the Iroquois." (PhD diss., Syracuse University, 2017).

——— and Emily Stokes-Rees. "A Tale of Two Missions: Common Pasts/Divergent Futures at Transnational Historic Sites." *The Public Historian* 39, no. 3 (2017): 10–39.

Rydell, Robert W. *All the World's a Fair: Visions of Empire at American International Expositions, 1876–1916*. Chicago: Univ. of Chicago Press, 1987.

Sahlins, Marshall. *How "Natives" Think: About Captain Cook, for Example*. Chicago: Univ. of Chicago Press, 1995.

———. *Islands of History*. Chicago: Univ. of Chicago Press, 1987.

Said, Edward. *Orientalism*. New York: Pantheon, 1978.

Salisbury, Neal. *Manitou and Providence: Indians, Europeans, and the Making of New England, 1500–1643*. Oxford: Oxford Univ. Press, 1982.

Simmel, Georg. *The Philosophy of Money*. Edited by David Frisby. Translated by Tom Bottomore and David Frisby. New York: Routledge, [1900] 1978.

Smith, Huston, and Phil Cousineau. *A Seat at the Table: Huston Smith in Conversation with Native Americans on Religious Freedom*. Berkeley: Univ. of California Press, 2005.

Smith, Jonathan Z. *Imagining Religion: From Babylon to Jonestown*. Chicago: Univ. of Chicago Press, 1982.

———. *Map Is Not Territory: Studies in the History of Religions*. Leiden: Brill, 1978.

———. *To Take Place: Toward a Theory of Ritual*. Chicago: Univ. of Chicago Press, 1992.

Smith, Linda Tuhiwai. *Decolonizing Methodologies: Research and Indigenous Peoples*. London: Zed, [1999] 2012.

Smith, Robertson W. *Lectures on the Religion of the Semites*. Brookline, MA: Adamant Media Corporation, [1889] 2005.

Stannard, David E. *American Holocaust: The Conquest of the New World*. Oxford: Oxford Univ. Press, 1993.

Sullivan, Lawrence E. *Icanchu's Drum: An Orientation to Meaning in South American Religions*. New York: Macmillan, 1988.

Tehanetorens, (Ray Fadden). *Wampum Belts of the Iroquois.* Summertown, TN: Native Voices, 1999).

Todorov, Tzvetan. *The Conquest of America.* Translated by Richard Howard. New York: Harper & Row, [1982] 1984.

Tuck, Eve, and K. Wayne Yang. "Decolonization Is Not a Metaphor." *Decolonization: Indigeneity, Education & Society* 1, no. 1 (2012): 1–40.

Tylor, Sir Edward Burnett. *Religion in Primitive Culture: Part 2 of "Primitive Culture."* New York: Harper Torch, [1871] 1958.

United Nations Declaration on the Rights of Indigenous Peoples. 13 September 2007. https://www.un.org/development/desa/indigenouspeoples/declaration-on-the-rights-of-indigenous-peoples.html.

Van der Leeuw, Gerardu. *Religion in Essence and Manifestation.* Princeton, NJ: Princeton Univ. Press, [1938] 2014.

Venables, Robert. "The Founding Fathers: Choosing to be the Romans." In *Indian Roots of American Democracy*, edited by José Barreiro, 67–106. Ithaca, NY: Akwe:kon Press, Cornell Univ., 1992.

Vennum, Thomas. *American Indian Lacrosse: Little Brother of War.* Baltimore, MD: Johns Hopkins Univ. Press, 2008.

Wach, Joachim. *Sociology of Religion.* New York: Routledge, 1947.

Wall, Steve. *To Become a Human Being: The Message of Tadodaho Chief Leon Shenandoah.* Charlottesville, VA: Hampton Roads, 2002.

Wheatley, Paul. *Pivot of the Four Quarters: A Preliminary Enquiry into the Origins and Character of the Ancient Chinese City.* London: Aldine, 1971.

Zogry, Michael J. *Anetso, the Cherokee Ball Game: At the Center of Ceremony and Identity.* Chapel Hill: Univ. of North Carolina Press, 2010.

Index

Africa, 100, 139, 184, 189, 202, 209, 210
Age of Discovery: environmental collapse and, 144; harms from, 228; influence of, 89, 101; modern age rise within, 186; overview of, 6, 189; religion and, 204–7; significance of, 212–13; utopian religion and, 138–39
agriculture, 99–100
Alexander VI (pope), 190–91
Alfonso V (king), 190
Alpha: Myths of Creation (Long), 121
American buffalo, 182
American Indian Law Alliance (AILA), 45, 183
American Indian Religious Freedom Act, 215
American religion, 130n18, 137–38. *See also* religion
Americas, discovery of, 212–15
ancestors, 130, 151, 152–56
animals, 23, 129–30
animism, 88, 92
apocalypticism, 217
archaic concept, 93n15
archetypal meanings, 93n15
ash borer insect, 86
assimilation, 100, 214–15
axis mundi, 134

Aymara bodies, 150–51
Aztec people, 89–91, 135

Basic Call to Consciousness, 52, 222–23, 225–27
bias, 85
Biblical authority, 219
Bigtree, Sandy, 12
birth, significance of, 74–75
Black Elk, 126
Black Hills, South Dakota, 124, 126
blood libels, 209
boarding schools, 214–15
Bolivia, 230
British Empire, centrality of, 89
Broken Treaties, 47–48
Brown, Esmeralda, 186n9
Buddhists, 158
Bureau of Indian Affairs (BIA), 17, 18n6, 175–76
bury the hatchet, 42
Bush, George W., 173

Cabot, John, 195, 196
Cabot Charter, 196–99
Canandaigua Treaty, 18
CANZUS group, 193–94
capitalism, 145, 202

257

Carrasco, Davíd, 4
casinos, 175–76
Castilian Spanish, 211
Catholicism, 58–60, 190–91, 234
Cayuga Nation, 15, 16, 45n23
ceremonies, Indigenous: ancestors and, 154; birth, 75; clothing for, 73; collaboration within, 165; condolence wampum, 40; directors of, 165; as economic activities, 168; emphasis of, 164; events and, 73–76; exchanges of, 160–61; extended family and, 65; food and, 67, 69; funeral, 77–78; gift economies within, 165–70, 220; gratitude within, 160, 161, 177, 220; for health, 65; human body existence and, 151; living landscape, 135; mythic paradigms to, 161–65; at Onondaga Lake, 95–96; orientation, 132; place of, 64; practice of, 219; purpose of, 55, 161; sacred place and, 131–32, 131–32n19; sacrifice, 63, 71; by the sky, 124; as taking place, 75, 75n14; technology in, 68; as thanksgivings, 177; transaction within, 163–64
Champlain, Samuel de, 235
Chicago's World's Fair, 187
chiefs, elective, 17–18
cholesterol, 152–53
Christendom (Kingdom of Christianity): characteristics of, 202; contradictions of, 207; establishment of, 189; expansion of, 190, 205–6, 210; influence of, 92; overview of, 6, 216–17; theology of conquest of, 187–89; threats to, 210

Christianity: Bible of, 219; colonization and, 176; domination of, 99–100; fasting and, 158; God within, 55–56; Indigenous values into, 198; infidel categories by, 189; justification of, 43, 184, 186–87, 201; missionization of, 199–200; motivations of, 200; as religion of the book, 180; sacred places of, 134; spread of, 90; superiority of (Christian hegemony), 186–87, 202, 216; as utopian belief, 98–99
Christian merchants, 202
City of Sherrill v. Oneida Indian Nation, 185
city space, hierophanies and, 134
civilization, mythologies of, 11
civilizational foundations, 11
Clan Hoyane, 39, 119
Clan Mother, 18, 39, 119
clan system, 17, 119
Cleveland, Grover, 187
clothing, culture regarding, 72–73
coevalness, 111n30
cohabitation, 21–24
collaboration: within academic study, 14; around issues of urgent mutual concern, 240; attentiveness within, 116; in ceremonies, 165; from description to, 24–31; effectiveness of, 85, 115–16; within Indigenous Peoples, 29; knowing through, 25; with the land, 147–48; of locative and utopian people, 146–48; methodologies for, 111–12; of natives and non-natives, 20; with Onondaga Nation leadership, 34; reciprocal, 118, 119; in

scholarship, 29, 149; significance of, 147–48; as talking with, 112; through Indigenous Values Initiative (IVI), 48–49; within university setting, 109, 112; writing within, 30–31
colonialism, 145, 212
colonization: Christianity role within, 176; dominion viewpoint of, 23; effects of, 226; of Haudenosaunee People, 42–43; justification for, 104, 184, 201; learning within, 99–100; materiality of, 99; overview of, 103–5; religion's role within, 9, 98–99; utopian value of, 104
Columbus, Christopher, 190, 191, 201–2, 209–12, 213–15
commodities, competition and, 172
competition, 80, 172
condolence wampum ceremony, 40
Confederacy Belt ("Hiawatha [Hayenhwátha'] Belt"), 15–16
consciousness, call to, 222–28
Constantinople, 210
consumerism, 174–75
conversation approach, 27, 28
conversion, violent process of, 205–6
Cortés, Hernán, 89–91
cosmos, forces within, 80
Cousineau, Phil, 183
Covenant Chain analogy, 110
creation, 13, 37–38, 69, 162–65, 224
Creator Twins, 13, 37–38
Crusades, 210, 217
cultural contact, 9
cultural identity, of Indigenous People, 138
currency, 172, 173

Dalai Lama, 228
death, 76–78, 92, 130
debt, 71, 167
Declaration on the Rights of Indigenous Peoples (United Nations), 5n5
decolonization, 215, 238–40
Deloria, Vine, Jr., 131–32n19, 163
Deskaheh (Cayuga Chief), 185
Deyhontsigwa'ehs ("They Bump Hips") (lacrosse), 13, 37–38, 41–42, 47
Díaz del Castillo, Bernal, 89–90
disenrollment epidemic, 18n6
disintegration, 76–77
displacement, 123
diversity, History of Religions and, 108–10
Doctrine of Christian Discovery (DoCD): conferences for, 47; overview of, 184–87, 189–96, 214; religious dimensions of, 215–20; renouncing of, 196–98; theology of conquest and, 187–89
Dum Diversas, 190
Dutch, cohabitation agreement with, 23

"The Eagle's View," 46
Earth/land: axis mundi of, 134; care from, 118; centrality of, 120; close, personal relationship with, 129–30; collaboration with, 147–48, 203; communication with, 70, 121, 131–32; as dead, for land ownership, 142; dominion over, 184; ecological collapse of, 144–46; as foundational

Earth/land (*cont.*)
  reality, 70; historical hierophany of, 128; interactive oppositions within, 127; as living being, 120, 125, 143; in the modern world, 140–41; names for, 120; recovering relationship with, 232; religious value of, 123–25; value significance of, 122. *See also* natural world
eating, killing as linked with, 71. *See also* food
Economic and Social Council (ECOSOC), 45n22
economy, 220
Edwards, Jake Haiwhagai'i, 238
Eliade, Mircea: quote of, 60, 170, 225; viewpoint of, 69n10, 93, 93n15, 94, 101–2, 107, 114n31, 116–17, 134; work of, 98
empirical other, 94–95, 96, 97, 102
Enlightenment, 98
environmentalism, 135–37
Episcopalians, 196–99
ethnography, 25–26, 27
Europe/Europeans: breeding by, 100; Christianity of, 9, 211; contact and genocide of, 42–43; cultural forces of, 21; expansionist cultures of, 89; famine in, 99; freedom of movement by, 103–5; Indigenous traditions in, 208–9; Jews within, 209–10; religion spread within, 206; religious imagination of, 6. *See also* colonialism
events, significance of, 73–76
#EveryChildMatters movement, 239
evil, 28, 219
exchange practices, 150, 158, 164, 165–70, 174, 225–26
experiences, significance of, 73–76
extended family, in Indigenous values, 64–66

Fabian, Johannes, 111n30
faculty, demographics of, 6
Fadden, Ray (Tehanetorens), 21
faith, of immigrant religions, 130–31. *See also* religion
Faithkeeper, 119
faith tradition, defined, 138
food: acceptance of, 159; acquisition techniques of, 67; creation and, 69; culture, 66–72; diversity in, 157; exchange and, 158; as gift, 159; human body and, 151, 156–60; materiality of, 71; sovereignty, 101n23; as spiritual, 69, 157
Founding Fathers, 18, 32, 41, 44, 110
Frazier, James George, 93
free, prior, and informed consent (FPIC), 194
freedom of movement, 103–5
French Fort, 32, 33, 233–35
Frichner, Tonya Gonnella, 44–45
fundamentalism, 179, 207
funerals, 77–78

"Gaiwiyo" ("Good Message"), 86
Gayaneñbsä·ʔgo·nah, 241
gender identity, 209
genetic conditions, 152–53
Geneva Convention, 103, 103n25
genocide, 42–43, 104
George Washington Treaty, 18
gifting: ceremonial, 165–70; economy of, 175–81; exchange of, 164; medium of, 168–69; significance

of, 220; traditional practice of, 165–66
Ginsburg, Ruth Bader, 185, 193
Global Forum of Spiritual and Parliamentary Leaders on Human Survival (UN), 228–29
globalization, 200, 203–4
God, 55–56, 112–13, 143, 163, 174
Gonella Frischner, Tonya, 186n9, 188
Gorbachev, Mikhail, 228
Gore, Al, 228
Grand Council, 41
gratitude, 36–37, 160, 161, 177, 220
Great Law of Peace, 15, 16, 19–20n11, 38–42, 44, 95, 232–33
Great Sea Turtle, 37
Great Tree of Peace (Skaęhetsi?kona), 41–42
greed, 191
grief, 78

habitation, 120, 122, 148, 212
Handsome Lake prophecies, 86
Harvey, Graham, 88
Haudenosaunee People: Christian characterization of, 190; clan relationship to land by, 119–20; clan systems of, 17, 119; cohabitation agreement with, 23; colonization of, 42–43; condolence organization by, 189–90; engagement by, 110; European contact with, 42–43; flag of, 16–17, 17n4; freedom concept to, 104; genocide of, 42–43, 104; governance system of, 18; Hiawatha Belt and, 15; influence of, 44; land claims of, 19; map of influence of, 16; narrative of, 34–35; origin of, 36; overview of, 2; peace organization by, 189–90; societal organization of, 97; statement of, 195–96; territory of, 12; values, amplifying and extending of, 15–17. *See also* Onondaga Nation
Haudenosaunee Wooden Stick Festivals, 47, 48
health, 78
Henry VII (king), 184, 196
Henry VIII (king), 195, 196
hermeneutics, of the New World, 212–15
Hiawatha ("Hayenwátha'"), 15n2, 32–33, 32–33n20, 39–40, 41
hierarchy, 217
hierophany: of city space, 134; defined, 60; as descriptive sense, 95; disruption from, 144; founding point of origin and, 61; function of, 94; historical, 128; for immigrant tradition, 133; Indigenous value response to, 218–19; "in my backyard," 143–44; material world and, 60–61; nature of, 61; religious origins within, 121
Hill, Tadodaho Sid, 36
Hindus, 158
History of Religions: challenges of modernity and, 98–103; as crypto-theological, 116; diversity and, 108–10; interpretive strategies within, 106–7; materiality and, 105–10; methodological commitment within, 147; methodological issues regarding, 24; methodologies of, 108; nature of religion and, 91–92; overview of, 5; perspectives within, 106n28; primary task of, 114;

History of Religions (*cont.*)
sacred places within, 134–35; sacred reality within, 133; scholarly training within, 27–28; self-consciousness within, 116; as values understanding pathway, 7–9, 10–11
Holy Land, 190, 205–6, 205n31, 211–12, 218–19
Holy Other, 94–95, 96, 102–3
homeland, 122–23, 128, 138–39n26
homo faber, 69n10
homo-religiosus, 170
Hoyane title, 39, 43
human body: ancestor reflection on, 151; care for, 73; death of, 76–78; food significance to, 151, 156–60; genetic conditions of, 152–53; health within, 153; Indigenous reflection on exchange and, 150–51; materiality of, 73–76, 151, 152, 170; sickness of, 78–79; transgressions and, 154–55
human rights, 198–99
humble environmentalism, 137
hunter-gatherer communities, 67

Iberian Peninsula, 208, 210
immigrant religion, 130–31, 133, 138–39n26. *See also* religion
Indigeneity: defined, 53, 62, 146; differences within, 97; global perception of, 202; material and spiritual sensibilities of, 119; requirements of, 62, 105; sacred and profane within, 125–31; understanding of, 186
Indigenous, definition and significance of, 62, 81–82, 131

Indigenousness, 62, 66
Indigenous Peoples: academic interest in, 62–63; breeding with, 100; campaigns against, 214–15; categories of, 2–3, 51, 61; classification of, 189; clothing culture of, 72–73; as collaborators, 29; cultural contact of, 9; death statistics of, 182; denigration of, 199–200; European interactions with, 207; exclusion of, 97; food culture of, 66–72; harms to, 228; as "heathens," 5; issues of mutual concern of, 30; knowledge transfer from, 99–100; limitations to knowing about, 26–27; modern world development and, 111–12; names for, 2–3, 120, 120n3; natural world relationship by, 1, 3; objectification of, 111; oppression to, 7; personal expression by, 113–14; population of, 54; as research resources, 107; scholarship regarding, 25–27; sensitivities of, 30; as signified, 97; spirituality of, 55; term use for, 52; traditions of, 52–53; tribal recognition of, 17; unifying characteristics of, 53–54. *See also specific nations*
Indigenous spirituality, 51, 174n24, 224–25
Indigenous Values Initiative (IVI), 44–49, 183
infant, as unbroken chain of life, 152
Innocent VIII (pope), 208
Inter Caetera, 190–91
intercultural conversation, 27–28, 112, 113–14

Iroquoianists, 15
Islam, 134, 158, 180, 205–6, 205n31, 209, 210
issues of urgent mutual concern, 25, 30, 114–17, 137, 146–48, 240

Jacques, Freida, 36
James, William, 93
Japan, 130n17
Jesuits, 31–32, 33, 43, 234
Jesus Christ, 205, 211, 214, 217
Jews/Judaism, 158, 180, 209–10
Jikonsaseh, 39, 41
Joaguisho, 228
Johnson v. M'Intosh (JvM), 191–92
just war theory, 206

killing, eating as linked with, 71
Kills Straight, Birgil, 186n9
Kimmerer, Robin, 37
Kitagawa, Joseph, 98
knowledge, 70, 85, 89, 125–26, 148
Kramer, Heinrich, 208

lacrosse (Deyhontsigwa'ehs ["They Bump Hips"]), 13, 37–38, 41–42, 47
LaDuke, Winona, 229, 232
Lakota, 65, 124, 132
Lakota Star Knowledge, 124–25
land: acquisition, 192; claims, 19; ownership, 42–43, 140, 141–44, 227. *See also* Earth/land; natural world
Land Rights action, 18–19, 19–20n11, 20
Lauson, Jean de, 234

Lazore, Brandon, 47–48, 241, 242–43
League of Nations, 185
Le Moyne, Father, 32, 33
Lévi-Strauss, Claude, 80n19
liberation technologies, 228, 232
liberation theology, 226
literalism, 219
location, significance of, 70–71, 75
locative religion, 137–40, 146–48. *See also* religion
Long, Charles H., 4–5, 28, 71n13, 87, 98, 121, 162
Longhouse, 15, 16, 18, 18n7, 36–37, 95
Louis XIV (king), 234
Lyons, Betty, 45
Lyons, Oren, 149, 161, 182, 183–84, 186n9, 188, 195–96, 228–29

Machiavelli, Niccolò, 91
Malinowski, Bronislaw, 69
Malleus Maleficarum (Kramer), 208
manifestation, 224
maple trees, 86
Marion apparitions, 58–60
marriage, 75–76
Marshall, John, 191–92
mass extinction, 182–83
materiality: attributes of, 114n31; of death, 77–78; God's removal from, 174; History of Religions and, 105–10; of the human body, 73–76, 151, 152, 170; of Indigenous People, 120; of modernity, 98; money and, 173; as mythic historical construction of the past, 110; overview of, 103–5; of religion, 60–61, 71n13, 107, 120; Western ideology and, 101

material world, 60–61, 66
Mauss, Marcel, 168
Mayan people, 135
McNally, Michael, 232
Medicine Game ("Creator's Game"), 13
Mehmed III, 210
Menchú, Rigoberta, 123, 140
militarism, 217
Missing and Murdered Indigenous Women movement (#MMIW movement), 238
missionization, 179, 199–200
Mixtec people, 121
Moctezuma, 91
modernity: as ambiguous, 102; beginnings of, 96n20; challenges of, 98–103; development of, 11, 98; ecological collapse and, 145; freedom of movement and, 103, 104; function of, 170; materiality of, 98; opposing values within, 178; overview of, 96–97; religion and, 96–97
Mohawk, John, 138–39n26
Mohawk Nation, 15, 16, 45n23, 176n26
moments, significance of, 73–76
money, 170–73, 174, 175–81
Morales, Eva, 230
Mother Earth, 41, 120, 143. *See also* Earth/land
Mother Earth's Pandemic, 49
movement, 103–5
Muslims, 134, 158, 180, 205–6, 205n31, 209, 210
myth, function of, 161–62
mythical paradigms, to ceremonial processes, 161–65

nationalism, 179
nation building, 192
Native American and Indigenous studies, 6
Native American students, 29
natural resources, 194n18
natural world, 1, 3, 118–19, 122, 123–24
Nebrija, Antonio de, 210–11
Neighbors of the Onondaga Nation (NOON), 20
Nelson, Melissa, 229
new animism, 88
Newcomb, Steven, 184, 186n9, 188
New World paradigm, 186, 212–15
Nicholas V (king), 190
nonhuman beings, human exchanges with, 68

Obama, Barack, 173, 194
occupation, 212
Olympics, 79–80
Oneida Nation, 15, 16, 45n23
Oneida Nation v. Sherrill, 193
Onondaga Historical Association (OHA), 32, 33, 34
Onondaga Lake: ceremonies at, 95–96; ecological changes at, 95–96; French Fort at, 32, 33, 233–35; Great Law of Peace at, 38–42; Haudenosaunee Wooden Stick Festivals at, 47, 48; historical site near, 32–33, 32–33n20; land claim of, 19, 19n10; as place of healing, 95; significance of, 95. *See also* Skä·noñh—Great Law of Peace Center
Onondaga Lake Park, 34

Onondaga Nation: ceremonial practices of, 228; challenges regarding, 13–14; clans of, 14; collaboration with, 34; in Confederacy Belt, 15, 16; continuance and contributions of, 43–44; flag of, 16; Iroquoianists and, 15; issues of mutual concern of, 25; Land Rights action by, 18–19, 19–20n11; White Pine and, 45n23; working in territory of, 17–21. *See also* Haudenosaunee People
opposition, significance of, 80
oral tradition, 129, 164–65, 219
orientation, 131–35
original sin, 218
Otto, Rudolf, 93, 94
Oxford University, 87

Parliament of World Religions, 187–89
patriarchy, 217
paying attention, 83–84, 86–87, 108, 111
peace, 36, 41–42
Peacemaker, 38–42
Pequot Massacre, 146
pharmaceutical industry, 230n13
Pickering Treaty, 18
place, significance of, 70–71, 102
place of birth, 65–66
plants, 230n13
primitive category, 87, 97
primitive religion, 63, 93–94
private property, 140, 141–44, 227
profane space, 125–31, 133
Promise Scholarship (Syracuse University), 240
property law, 184–85, 191–92

Quetzalcoatl, 90–91
Quiché Maya people, 123–24

real estate religion, 141–44
regeneration, 74, 80
religion: as academy construct, 51; Age of Discovery and, 204–7; as ambiguous, 57–58, 60, 98, 102; American, 130n18; anthropocentric approach to, 122; authorities within, 156; categories of, 7; centrality of, 62; challenges regarding, 7; cipher of, 101–2; collaborative methodologies and, 111–12; in colonization, 9, 98–99; conversations regarding, 113; death phenomenon and, 92; deemphasizing the sacred within, 128; defined, 137; disagreements regarding, 57; diversity of, 91–92; ecological collapse and, 144–46; exclusivity of, 99; experience of the sacred and, 129, 161; faith tradition and, 138; fervor within, 179; founding point of origin of, 61; future of, 111–12, 175–81; globalization of, 203–4; habitation and, 120, 122, 148; as hierarchical, 99; hierophany of, 60–61; human rights and, 198–99; immigrant, 130–31, 138–39n26; Indigenous Peoples' viewpoint regarding, 3, 55; influence of, 106n28; justification through, 55, 99, 206; locative, 137–40, 146–48; manifestation of the sacred and, 59; Marion apparitions and, 58–60; materiality of, 60–61, 71n13, 107, 120;

266   Index

religion (*cont.*)
  modernity and, 96–97; nature of, 91–92; as orientation, 131–33; origins search regarding, 96–97; personal empowerment through, 161; phenomenon of, 58, 60; possibilities of, 56–62; postmodern method for studying, 116; problem with, 55–56; real estate, 141–44; self-consciousness and, 51; relevancy of, 216; sacred objects of, 87–88; sacrifice within, 63; as social evolutionary phenomenon, 92; talking about God within, 160; technologies and, 68–69; theology and, 28; as tool, 98–99; uniformity and, 53; utopian, 137–40, 146–48; values and, 56; wealth transfer through, 100; as weapon, 215–16; in the world, 51–52; world domination and, 87–91
Religion and Sports course, 12–13
Religion in Primitive Culture (Tylor), 92n14
religious orientation, to the natural world, 118–19
Remembrance Wampum Belt, 235–38
rites of passage, 73–76
rivalry, as exchange of gifts, 166n15
Robertson Smith, W., 63
Roman Catholic Christianity, 204–5
Rome, 211

sacred/sacred places: features of, 70; in History of Religions, 134–35; human presence within, 127; within immigrant religion, 130, 133; lack of connection with, 128; nostalgia for, 131–32; orientation to, 132–33; profane category *versus*, 125–31; proximity of, 129; within religious ceremonies, 178–79; religious conviction depth and, 180; significance of, 126; text, 129, 179–80
sacrifice, 63, 71, 177
Sainte Marie among the Iroquois, 31–32, 33
salvation, 220
Satan, 219
scholarship, 25–26, 29, 30, 149
Self, as closed system, 175
Semites, 63
Seneca Nation, 15, 16, 45n23
shamans, 154–56, 154n2
Sherpa bodies, 150–51
sickness, 78–79
Six Nations Grand Council, 17
Skä·noñh, 35–36
Skä·noñh—Great Law of Peace Center: creation story and, 37–38; Great Law of Peace, 38–42; narrative of, 34–35; overview of, 2, 31–34, 49–50; purpose of, 232–33; repurposing, 233–35; Thanksgiving Address and, 36–37
sky, 124, 127
Sky Woman, 37–38
slavery, transatlantic, 99
sleep, 68
Smith, Jonathan Z., 51, 104n26, 114, 138–39
social place, clothing and, 72
Spain, 209, 210–11
spiritual beings, 68, 70, 174
spiritual home, 183–87
spiritualism, 93, 224. *See also* religion

spirituality, 55, 224–25. *See also* religion
sports: connection through, 80; Deyhontsigwa'ehs ("They Bump Hips") (lacrosse), 13, 37–38, 41–42, 47; Indigenous values through, 13; rivalry within, 166n15; significance of, 79–81
structuralism, 80n19
sub-Hoyane, 119
subjugation, 188
Summis Desiderantes Affectibus, 208
Syracuse, New York, 12
Syracuse University, 12–13, 14, 240

Tadodaho, 38, 40, 41
tattoos, 73
technology, 68–69
Tehanetorens (Ray Fadden), 21
Tenochtitlan, 89–91
Teresa of Calcutta, Mother, 228
Termination Era, 215
Tewa peoples, 121
Thanksgiving Address (Ganonhanyonh or Words That Come Before All Else), 36–37, 166
theodicy problem, 28
theology, 28
theology of conquest, 187–89
thunderstorm, 158n4
time, as Terror of History, 163
tobacco, 230n13
Todorov, Tzvetan, 199
Tonawanda Seneca Nation, 17
To Take Place (Smith), 104n26
traditions, Indigenous, 52–53, 60, 82. *See also* ceremonies, Indigenous

Trail of Tears, 192
transatlantic chattel slavery, 99
transgressions, 154–55
trauma, 98
tribalism, 207
triple bottom line, 239, 239n22
Tsha'Hoñ'noñyeñ'dakwa', 79n17
Tuck, Eve, 238
Turtle Clan Faithkeeper (Onondaga Nation), 228–29
Turtle Island, 38
Tuscarora Nation, 15n3, 17
Two Row Wampum (Guswentha), 21, 22, 23–24, 110
Tylor, E. B., 63, 87, 89, 92–93, 92n13, 92n14

ultimate evil, 219
United Nations, Indigenous People's concerns to, 185
United Nations Declaration on the Rights of Indigenous Peoples (UNDRIP), 5n5, 185, 193–95
universal, knowledge of, 89
Universal Declaration of the Rights of Mother Earth, 230–33
university/university culture: collaboration within, 109; future of, 108–10, 240–42; intellectual values of, 108; interpretive strategies within, 148–49; knowledge creation within, 148; objectification within, 112
UN Permanent Forum on Indigenous Issues, 186n9
utopian concept, 104
utopian religion, 137–40, 146–48. *See also* religion

values/values, Indigenous: anthropocentric approach to, 122; category of, 3; changes for survival, 228–29; characteristics of, 202–3; into Christianity, 198; of cohabitation, 21–24; collision of, 234–35; defined, 56; as Earth-oriented, 52–53; as ethical, 125; European religious lens regarding, 207; extended family and, 64–66; in gift relationship, 177–78; history of, 200; History of Religions approach to understanding, 7–9, 10–11; in modernity, 178; nexus of, 1; overview of, 7, 185; rejection of, 186; relationships within, 202–3; religion and, 56; response to Doctrine of Christian Discovery (DoCD), 215–20; significance of, 221–22, 223; sports and, 13; urgency regarding, 221
van der Leeuw, Gerardus, 93
Vatican, 184, 210
vegetarianism, 158
Venables, Robert, 206

Wach, Joachim, 93
wampum shells, 40
Washington, George, 18
#WaterIsSacred movement, 238–39
Western civilization, 88
Western ideology, 101
Wheatley, Paul, 124
White Pine, 42, 45n23
White Plume, Alex, 186n9
white supremacy, 6
witches, 208
women, 18, 39, 119, 208–9
Women's Rights Movement, 18
wool, 72
world domination, 87–91
worldview, 83, 115
writing, in collaboration, 30–31

Xocoyotzin, Moctezuma, 89–90

Yang, K. Wayne, 238

Zulu (South Africa), 92n13

Philip P. Arnold is Associate Professor in the Religion Department and core faculty in Native American and Indigenous Studies at Syracuse University. He is Founding Director of the Skä·noñh—Great Law of Peace Center. His books are *Eating Landscape: Aztec and European Occupation of Tlalocan* (1999); *Sacred Landscapes and Cultural Politics: Planting a Tree* (edited with Ann Gold, 2001); and *The Gift of Sports: Indigenous Ceremonial Dimensions of the Games We Love* (2012). The *Urgency of Indigenous Values* (2023) is part of the Syracuse University Press series Haudenosaunee and Indigenous Worlds, for which he is coeditor. He established the Doctrine of Discovery Study Group (2005) and Indigenous Values Initiative (2014). He is the Principal Investigator for "200 Years of Johnson v. McIntosh: Indigenous Responses to the Religious Foundations of Racism," a three-year (2022–24) grant from the Henry Luce Foundation.